THE BREACH IN
THE WALL

THE BREACH IN
THE WALL

A Memoir of the Old China

ENID SAUNDERS CANDLIN

Macmillan Publishing Co., Inc.
NEW YORK

Collier Macmillan Publishers
LONDON

*To all my friends
of the old days in China
and especially in memory of
Nansi and Isabel*

Macmillan Publishing Co., Inc.
866 Third Avenue, New York, N.Y. 10022
Collier-Macmillan Canada Ltd., Toronto, Ontario

Library of Congress Catalog Card Number: 72–11952

First Printing 1973

Printed in the United States of America

Acknowledgments

A number of people have been most kind in helping me with this book, either by refreshing my memory on certain points, by suggesting sources, or simply by encouraging me. Among these are my sister, Pocetta Saunders, Mrs. Margaret Jamieson, formerly of Kansu, Mr. Peter Chang, Mrs. Jean Kale, and Mrs. Pat Allen Rae. Pocetta sent me her notes on the two great monasteries of the Western Hills—Chieh T'ai Ssu and T'an Cheh Ssu, which were very useful. My thanks are also due to Mr. Duncan Leach, now of Malaysia, who was one of the children aboard the *Tungchow* when she was pirated, and who took the trouble to write to me of the affair.

I am very grateful to my husband, Stanton Candlin, and to our two daughters, Rosalind and Celia, as well as Dinah Goodes, who read the manuscript either wholly or in part, and made useful suggestions. Stanton and Celia, in particular, went to great trouble on my behalf, and were wonderfully helpful, carefully reading the whole typescript and making notes of what they thought might be changed, in which they were generally right.

Writing is solitary work, and no one values an outstretched hand more than the author.

Translations of Chinese poetry not otherwise accounted for are by the writer.

Contents

Contents

Part I

THE MIDDLE KINGDOM

The Great Wall

THE GREAT WALL was built near the end of the third century B.C. as a barrier against the nomadic Tatar tribes to the north, in an effort to stop their raids into China. In this it was only partially successful. What wall, however strongly manned and bastioned, however long, high, and wide, could keep out a Genghiz Khan?

Sometimes, for a season, the Tatars were successful in conquering parts—even the whole—of China, but after a time, which might be centuries, they were always rejected. Ultimately, however, the fatal breach of the wall came from an unexpected quarter—the West. By this time it was less a physical barrier than a mental symbol of exclusion, invulnerability, superiority. The Western nations made a mockery of these claims, either directly by their own dealings with the country, or indirectly through the devious passage of the doctrines of Karl Marx.

Before it was constructed there had been many lesser walls built at passes and in regions where the way to China was dangerously open and inviting, but these were piecemeal affairs. The Great Wall incorporated some of them into itself—extending for three thousand and more miles (taking into account its loops and winding sections), it was a conception on an entirely new scale—a unique scale. Probably no other people could ever have carried it through so rapidly to completion, so immense was the task, and so terrible its cost in suffering and human lives.

The workmen were the peasants, the politically suspect, the disgraced noblemen. They called it, with loathing, the Ten Thousand Li* Long Cemetery. Shih Huang Ti, the tyrant of Ch'in who forced it through, did not long survive its building, and his dynasty soon collapsed.

It stretches from Shan Hai Kuan (the Gateway at the Mountains and the Sea) on the Gulf of Peichili, to the Yü-men, or Jade Gate in Kansu, in the far west of China. Between these two points it climbs sometimes as high as 4,000 feet; following the border between Inner Mongolia and China it passes south of the Gobi, pressing on, on, on, westward to Central Asia. At a distance of every two hundred yards watchtowers were built on it, nine sentries patroling between them for the whole of its length. The workmanship was so honest and perfect that it was not seriously overhauled till some sixteen centuries later.

Strategically it proved to be a deterrent rather than a true barrier. Even the most formidable wall in the world is not a match for the determined spirit—somehow people will get round it, batter it down, scale it, or buy off the sentries. It was not only of no importance to a man like Genghiz Khan, but it could not check lesser invasions. In spite of it the Toba Wei found their way down into China, where they looted, despoiled, and finally conquered certain minor Chinese kingdoms which flourished between the Han and the T'ang. Again, early in the twelfth century the Golden Tatars, the Kitans, swept down on the Northern Sung, forcing them south of the river, occupying half the country. Militarily the Tatars were often more than a match for the people within the wall, but the barbarian so coveted and envied that civilization, so wanted to emulate it, and become a part of it, that he was a ready prey to absorption. The Chinese came to feel that they always had the final word.

This splendid structure, noble in design, inspiring and grand, became, as time passed, interwoven with the very soul of the nation. The songs, legends, poems written about it tended to blind the vision of the people as it was made a symbol of their national consciousness, contributing to their xenophobia, their pride. Those within the wall and those without came to represent respectively the civilized and the barbarian, while in an irrational manner it gave the Chinese a false sense of security. They felt as

* A *li* is a third of an English mile.

4

though the wall embraced the whole country—not only the northern flank—so that a Japanese, for instance, being a man from without the wall, was a barbarian just as much as though he had been a Tatar. The north being the compass point from which danger arose, and that being sealed off, they felt an easier contempt for the lesser breeds which lived in a world outside the Middle Kingdom.

There was something of a parallel here with the attitude the British came to have in India. They assumed that the subcontinent was in danger of invasion only from the northwest, and therefore were always on their guard on that frontier, accepting the myth that the jungle was impenetrable, and that their navy held the sea (which was not nearly so fanciful an idea). Malaya, Burma, the oceans, and the Japanese were to show them how mistaken they were. The Japanese lost the war, but they brought down the British Empire with it, nonetheless.

When the Great Wall was breached, finally, the blow came from the distant, despised, unknown West. Many a westerner who never saw the wall played his part in knocking holes in it, in disproving the fantasies which had so long paralyzed the minds of the world's most populous, perhaps most artistic, people.

I saw the Great Wall one summer, when I was staying at Peitaiho, a resort with fine beaches, on the Gulf of Peichili, not far to the south of Shan Hai Kuan. I was particularly eager to have a look at it, as I had tried to visit it outside Peking not long before, but the trains were in such confusion that we had never reached Nan K'o. Here the excursion was much easier: a friend and I left Peitaiho early one fine morning, so that we would avoid the great heat of the day, for Shan Hai Kuan, where the wall comes down to meet the sea. When we left the train we engaged donkeys, and rode off into the hills.

It was a still day, with a cloudless blue sky, in which a few hawks circled high above. The hills were covered with low brown grasses, in which crickets sang; otherwise there was not a sound, apart from the jangling of our donkeys' bells. Soon we could see our objective, winding away over the hills—and were caught up in a great sense of anticipation. There was no one in sight—we had all this wonder to ourselves. At the foot of the wall we dismounted, gave our reins to the donkey boys, and walked up the ramp which led to the top.

From here, in that clear sharp air of North China, we could see far away on all sides. Behind us the wall mounted up on the summits of the low hills. Before us, and below, was the bay and its littoral—a stretch of calm blue waters, with a few fishing boats lying far out, and on one side was the little town. Immediately below us, perhaps forty feet down, the donkeys were cropping grass, their attendants lying prone, taking their ease.

Peggy and I walked up and down, marveling and rejoicing, and then sat down, leaning our backs against the crenellations, and examining the grey bricks whose tone had become soft and beautiful with the dull green and ochre colored lichen which has, during these many centuries, grown upon them. They are some twenty inches long by eight thick, and as hard and durable as stone itself.

Here at Shan Hai Kuan there were few of those rigors which went into the making of most of the wall; here the laborers were still in the world of men, where grass would grow, where there was water. As the work progressed, and they went westward, they had continually to set up camps and establish brick kilns. They tried to raise crops, but the soil became always worse—thin and sandy, and the climate was too harsh, too windy and dry. There were frequent dust storms, as the desert was almost upon them, and the winters were long and bitter. Even when land was given the garrisons, or the workmen, as an inducement to longer service, it was found such a gift was worthless, however eager these men were to own their own ground—nothing would grow, no one could live there. Even in their desperation these Chinese never thought of turning into nomads.

In an attempt to conciliate the Tatars, when the Chinese were weak, Chinese princesses were sometimes sent as brides to the khans. These poor maidens, exiled usually for life from their own people and the luxuries of the court, made to live in felt tents and drink mares' milk, are the subject of many piteous tales and ballads. One such princess, who died and was buried near the wall, has a special place in Chinese poetry and legends—here, so it was believed, was the only place where grass would grow. It was known as "the green grave," and a symbol for exile, loneliness, suffering, and danger.

But on that sunny, smiling summer's day at Shan Hai Kuan, the wall seemed only a marvelous monument—strong, vital. Yet, for all that, it was breached, it was even then succumbing to fatal blows. Innocents that we were, pulling grasses from between the bricks and whistling through them, we foresaw nothing of the years ahead.

A wall like this startles you at first; it seems a tremendous barrier; but in the end you look back at it, and think, "Could *that* have stopped me?"

The horn, the horn of Roland, the hunting horn, is one of those words which is compounded of overtones.

> J'aime le son du cor, le soir, au fond des bois, . . .
> Dieu! que le son du cor est triste au fond des bois.

In China this image occurs in relation to the Great Wall:

> The sound of the horn breaks the clear autumn air
> And sentries lean back in their watchtowers.
> Here, where the winds of spring blow on the green grave,
> Where the white sun drops down below Liangchou,
> No one threatens the troops of the Great Han,
> Men may pass freely all along the frontier.
> But—the barbarians are like this stream
> Which must flow to the south.
>
> CHANG CH'IAO, On the Border

The China Coast

You cannot speak of the ocean to a well-frog,—the creature of a narrower sphere. You cannot speak of ice to a summer insect,—the creature of a season. You cannot speak of *Tao* to a pedagogue: his scope is too restricted. But now that you have emerged from your narrow sphere and have seen the great ocean, you know your own significance, and I can speak to you of great principles.

CHUANG TZU

THE BROAD DESIGN of history admits of such infinite variations that not one hamlet on a dusty plain has ever been quite like its fellow, nor ever will be. Between races, nations, and situations the contrasts have always been extreme; yet, among them a few developments stand out as markedly strange. One of these was the condition of the Holy Land during the centuries of the Crusades; another the China Coast in those decades of Western dominance. Surprisingly enough, with so great a diversity of cause and background, the effects had a certain amount in common.

The weary and disillusioned Crusaders, who discovered that their long and arduous journey was ending in disaster, with nothing accomplished, were sometimes faced with a choice of what to do. Should they go back, back to the cold and dark, the narrow social constrictions, the problems they had been glad to leave behind them, and take it all up again, provided they survived the march? Or would they stay on in this beautiful, warm, southern region? Their views on the religious issue had altered with experience, and they realized that they could, in point of fact, live quite reasonably in a society which included Jews and Moslems as well as Christians. They were nearly always short of money; here were many opportunities for profitable trade. The standard of life they could command was superior to that which the ordinary person could have at home: cleaner, more comfortable, more pleasant. In Outre-Mer they could be relatively independent of the dominance of the church, and of their liege lord. It was stimulating to be in contact with many of the peoples of the Levant, to gain a new outlook. It was agreeable to wear silk, to have so many fruits and warm-weather delicacies at hand, to be out of the old rut.

Life was often dangerous and turbulent, but so it was at home. Evidently to those who stayed the advantages of life on that coast outweighed those of North Europe.

There is obviously no real parallel between the life of the Europeans along the eastern border of the Mediterranean, in the Kingdom of Jerusalem and the other principalities, and that of the merchants and missionaries who went out to China in the nineteenth century, but there is an affinity between them beyond that of mere factual comparison.

The newcomer on the China Coast was somewhat adventurous, or he would never have come. He was, very often, a religious man. He stayed, once he was there, generally for most of his life, his trips home being infrequent. He endured unsettled conditions, some physical danger, many limitations, receiving instead a much wider horizon, a more international point of view, than he could have had anywhere else, perhaps. Because servants were so good and so cheap, he had a better standard of living than he could have had at home, nine times out of ten.

The position of the Westerner on the China Coast proved ephemeral, but something of that tenure remains, both with the Chinese and ourselves—the roots went down too deep, really to have been eradicated. Certain influences, stirring the minds of everyone involved, are still at work. That must have been true, too, of the Holy Land, with those bold kingdoms set down in the midst of an alien culture, to flower for their season in the sun.

The Christians who settled in the counties of Edessa and Tripoli, in the principality of Antioch, and the rest, were of a feudal and martial spirit; they must also have been, in the main, philistines. Yet they could not resist the riches of the bazaars, they must

9

have learned in spite of themselves a good deal of geography, and they came to some extent in contact with a way of life which was infinitely more graceful than that of the harsher tempo of Europe in the Dark Ages. The gentle manners of the Syrian ladies, the elegance of their cuisine, the romantic elements of their literature, the importance the Arabs gave to medicine, chemistry, arithmetic, astronomy, could not have escaped the attention of at least some of the northerners, though there seem to have been few intellectuals among them. The ex-Crusaders did not discover the *Rubaiyat*, nor did they delve into the great civilizations which had flourished in this corner of the globe—they seem to have been in the main hearty, superficial, pleasure-loving, outgoing.

When the Westerners lived on the coast of China, and to a lesser extent in the interior, few had much comprehension of the great cultural wealth of the country, though there were always among us a few outstanding sinologues. Many of us loved the arts of China, but few books had been published about them in Western languages, and Chinese (after the early stages) is difficult to learn.

People worked hard at their jobs, in their firms or missions, administering the various enclaves—the luxury of study was not available to many, even if the taste for it had been there. Those who were not philistines did see through a bright portal, even if they were never able to pass the threshold.

The Westerners did give, richly, of what they had to offer. Perhaps if they had not been so intent in passing to the Chinese in their sore need, new ideas of government, medicine, education, religion, philanthropy, military and scientific knowledge, technical skills, they would have had more time and inclination to find out what this secretive country had done itself in these fields. But time was so short—there were only a few decades in which to attempt so much.

Some will answer that many Westerners had no wish to give China anything at all, caring only to bleed her. That sort of leech exists everywhere, sadly enough. Business may allow philanthropy to attend its footsteps, but it is not philanthropic itself in any way. But in spite of this, taking it all together, there was a high proportion of Westerners in China who were wonderfully charitable, generous, and tolerant.

China with a Broad Brush

G EOGRAPHICALLY China was set apart from the rest of the world on every point of the compass: on the north by deserts and by the vast frozen plains, by mountain ranges stretching up to the Arctic Circle; on the east by the Pacific, on the west by the desert lands and tremendous, almost impassable mountains of the "Roof of the World"; southward by the jungles and the sea.

Through this isolation, and because of the enormous extent of the country, which contained within its own borders everything its people seemed to need, it became mentally extremely self-contained. Its philosophies and way of life developed in quite a different manner than those evolving in the West, the national temperament becoming more unified than was ever the case in Europe. The Chinese within the wall did not experience that ceaseless action and reaction of mind and custom, of religion and aims, which so altered and molded those countries which constantly came up against each other's ideas. Though they came in contact very often with the nomadic Tatars who lived on their perimeter, and were sometimes conquered by them, the victors were always so charmed with China's superior civilization that they adopted Chinese ways and became sinicized themselves.

China is extremely beautiful, and her people, very early developing a highly sophisticated culture and innately gifted in the arts, did not feel the impulsion to look outward, as most of the West has done. They had so much within, they were not curious as to what lay beyond their horizons. The original Chinese came from a point far inland, within the great bend of the Yellow River. From the first they were an agricultural people, the sea playing a very small part in their history and imagination. Occasionally, notably during the Ming dynasty, they might, had they so wished, have become a great sea power, but they turned away from such schemes. Had they continued then to build fleets and go out on the oceans, encountering other peoples, for good or ill their isolation would have been broken, and the course of history might have been very different.

Their earliest records indicate their dominant traits: patience, industry, intelligence, artistic genius, humor, and a penchant for ceremony and good manners. They have had, on the whole, little understanding of personal liberty, and little competence in government, in spite of having been able to set up a remarkable civil service, chosen by selective examination, as long ago as the Han.* This bureaucracy, in some ways very effective, persisted century after century, outlasting the rise and fall of dynasties, giving the country a type of continuity; the Chinese were content to leave the regulation of their affairs to these officials, provided they did not become too corrupt or too inefficient. As in the nature of things these faults frequently became obvious, and as there was no system of checks and surveillance from the people themselves, Chinese history abounds in rebellions and uprisings of every scale, most of which were unsuccessful. The central authority tended to concentrate power in its own hands.

As a people, they have shown little ardor for religion, though they have had their enthusiasms in this direction. At one time Buddhism was a popular faith; Confucianism exerted a strong ethical influence, and the Taoists have always had their followers. But none of these, in China, exerted a comparable sway to that which Christianity has had in the West; except for the monks, relatively few individuals have been ardently and exclusively devoted to understanding their mysteries.

Their civilization is so ancient, and developed so fast, producing so widespread a culture, that they have thought of themselves as a superior race. They were, naturally, proud of their achievements: their beautiful calligraphy and painting, their bronzes, porcelains, and silk, their poetry, their monuments, their elaborate cere-

*Han 206 B.C.–A.D. 219 (Western Han 206 B.C.–A.D. 24; Eastern Han A.D. 25–219).

monies, their endurance as a nation. For most of their history they have been conservative, instinctively averse to change, though in the nineteenth century as they came into contact with the West, they began to see that they must change in order to survive as a nation. No one then foresaw how great these changes would ultimately be.

That rigidity which marked their administrations in the past, and which occasionally called forth periods of desperate rebellion —sometimes on a vast scale, resulting in millions of dead—led to experiments in other forms of government, but these were generally short-lived. The most notable was the dictatorship which the Ch'in dynasty imposed on the country, a wholly totalitarian form of control, reducing the individual to nothing but the slave of the state. It was this dynasty which built the Great Wall, and which, as well, was remarkable for road building and effective administration—effective within the context of dictatorship. It did not endure, for the people could not stand its repression, and it was followed by the Han, a dynasty of extraordinary inventiveness and success, of great art and expansiveness. After the repression of the Ch'in, the relative liberality of the Han set in train a flowering of the native genius.

China's acceptance of communism came after a century of stress. The arrival of the West in a country which had long been closed, the stimulus, often unwelcome, provided both by missionaries and merchants of all nations, was highly unsettling to the Chinese, controlled, as they then were, by an alien dynasty, the Manchu. Having overturned this house, they were not able to establish, in the forty years of the new republic, a government sufficiently strong to resist the penetration of communist propaganda and action. These doctrines were promulgated in a period when the country was weak, unsure of its values, and torn by war.

Standing before a globe, let us turn it so that we have the widespreading contours of China before us. Down from the Pole an enormous stretch of country extends southward to the boundaries of China; on the east, till very lately the only large coastal city was Vladivostok, ice-bound for most of the year. Westward the plains extend for thousands of miles, till they come up against the Urals.

South from Siberia are those regions which over the centuries have sometimes lain within, sometimes without, the sphere of

Chinese dominance: Mongolia, Manchuria, Korea. Till the middle of the seventeenth century it was from the north that invasion most often came—it was then, in 1644, that the last of these conquerors, the Manchus, came down and took the country which the Ming were not able to defend. They were the last, in the sense, that is, of a bodily presence. In modern times invasion from the north has come in the form of ideas rather than people.

On the southern frontiers of Mongolia we pass the Great Wall, the long monument of many interpretations, perhaps the most obvious being that it exemplifies that theory of government that the end justifies the means; a thesis perennially proved wrong, yet continually attempted anew.

Going on toward the south on our globe, we now arrive at the eighteen provinces of China proper, the "Middle Country," which has a favorable climate and a long coastline, though no good natural harbors. Within the heartland of the country the scene is dominated by two great rivers, the Yellow and the Yangtze. The first, "China's Sorrow," was never, in the past, effectively diked, and changed its course many times, drowning millions while enriching the soil for the patient, stricken survivors. The Yangtze, hundreds of miles to the south, also has a record of destructive floods, but none really comparable to the appalling devastation of which the Huang Ho was capable—the Yangtze floods, but does not change its course. Its spectacular feature is its spring rise in the Gorges, when the water will sometimes rise ninety feet in a day.

In the west is Szechwan, the province of the Four Rivers, with its rich plain, one of the granaries of the country. Beyond lies arid, once impoverished Kansu, that long province running out to Central Asia and the high plateaus of Sinkiang and Tibet. These, like the regions of the north, were sometimes wholly independent of China, sometimes obliged to submit and pay tribute. Tibet, in fact, once turned the tables on her great neighbor, and occupied part of China for over a century.

Sinkiang and Tibet were in the past—even the recent past—so remote, so difficult of access, that they were generally virtually independent. The Chinese have accentuated the periods in which Tibet appeared to be dependent, because of the "special relationship" between the Dalai Lamas and the Manchu emperors, the former acting as chaplain or primate to the latter. This is the origin of the term "suzerainty," which was twisted in later years by the Chinese communists to mean actual sovereignty.

In ancient times the fabled Silk Route ran through Sinkiang. This old territory had closer ties with China than Tibet; even in the Han it was sometimes under Chinese governors. It was important that the caravans be protected, as they went westward with their cargoes of silk, jade, tea. There were then no true roads.

No railway lines joined China and the West till in our century the Trans-Siberian was inaugurated, which, starting from Moscow and going due east, passed down Lake Baikal and went on to Vladivostok. At Manchouli, a small frontier town in western Manchuria, passengers en route for China might detrain, and take there the old Chinese Eastern Railway to Mukden or Dairen.

And there was, once the West became interested in China, an immense amount of foreign shipping calling at the ports, going up rivers. But, before the age of the airplane this still amounted to isolation, in great part, for the vast interior of China. The hinterland remained much as it had been for centuries until the comparatively recent past.

Then, down in the south, is Indo-China, the northern part of which, Annam, was under Chinese rule from the Han through the T'ang dynasties—a thousand years; afterward, it came sometimes again loosely and briefly into that orbit. The Chinese were accustomed to link this region with the southern provinces of their own country—they thought of it, too, as remote, barbarous, too hot, too brilliant, too highly scented—suspect, in fact. Yet the area was of vital importance in maintaining Chinese trade round the sea routes, as far as Arabia. All this southern part of their empire the Chinese called then "Nam-Viet"; a place no official wanted to administer, yet, as they came at last to realize, seductive through its soft beauty, its strangeness.

Historically, the Chinese have not really liked the strange—they were too enamored of their own ways and patterns, persuaded that these were inevitably the best. This conviction was part of the cement which bound the enormous tract of country together. It might fall apart into warring kingdoms—it often did—but the unifying element was stronger than the disruptive. Their common language, even though greatly diversified by dialects, was another bond. It was reinforced by their calligraphy, which no divergence in accent could affect. Another cohesive factor lay within their philosophies, chiefly Confucianism.

Confucianism degenerated, soon after the death of its sage, into a system he would have been the first to deplore. He himself had laid no stress on ceremonies, tradition, ironclad rules, and yet this is what it came to, the servant of the Prophet taking over in China as elsewhere, and reducing inspiration to organization.

Confucius was a reformer. Born in the fifth century B.C., he grew up in troubled times, when China was divided into bitterly antagonistic states. The lot of the poor and of the intellectuals was intolerable, everything being in the power of the feudal lords, nearly all of whom were lawless, ferocious, predatory beings. A natural and gifted teacher, who had evolved in his own mind the importance of certain fundamental principles, he tried to teach these to the disciples who gathered round him, and to find some ruler who would give him the chance to put his ideas into effect.

His goal was the common good: the end of strife and selfish aims. He did not believe that mankind needed to live in perpetual discord. Virtue and intelligence were to him the cardinal points which should be expressed in government, and he ardently wished that the rulers (of whom he did not expect these qualities) would appoint officials of goodwill to administer their kingdoms with equity. He believed that people were teachable, provided they were willing to work and would use their intelligence. No one ever allowed him to take charge of a state, and all he could do was to propagate his ideas, trying to persuade his hearers of the beauty of merit. He was eager to reform society, and it was as difficult then as now. It was much easier just to change what he had said, and twist his teachings into a system of ceremonies.

This philosophy became therefore sterile, but safe. It was used to maintain social stability and reduce the daily friction of people who live too closely together. Yet, in spite of everything, some of his ideas took root. He was, for instance, convinced that birth should not be a factor in the choice of officials, and in fact, due to this teaching, the hereditary aristocracy which had in general proved a scourge to the country, was superseded in time by administrators chosen on the basis of open examinations. It was a long and costly process to prepare for these examinations, but they were open to anyone who had the intelligence to cope with them. Only the imperial families were permitted to continue on the hereditary principle.

Confucius thought it extremely important that people should be happy, and he believed that this should be borne in mind by the state. Surveying the tragic records of Chinese history, it is hard to feel that many people took this goal seriously. As it worked out, the Confucian "code" came to provide a detailed pattern of the relationship of one person to another: the emperor to his subjects, the son to the father, the wife to her husband, and so on. The family unit was given the over-riding importance it held up to present times. There were no displaced persons in this plan, though many people might find themselves very unhappily situated, and women, in particular, were placed in a wholly subordinate role. Ancestor worship was included in the Confucian ceremonies, though in reality it was more a question of veneration than worship. The scholar was given those disproportionate honors which resulted in the creation of the scholar-gentry caste. The system exerted an orderly, sober influence, on the one hand; on the other the repression it inevitably included made it at last perfectly unbearable.

Then there was Taoism, which was either highly metaphysical and led to a great sense of personal freedom and individual expression (as a partial reaction from the Confucian rigidity), or else a system of magical superstitions. To the flexible Chinese mind, it was possible to embrace both Taoism and Confucianism at once; they did not feel one necessarily excluded the other. This was true, too, of many of the Buddhists. Buddhism was brought to China from India in the first century by Indian monks who made their way, with incredible hardships, over the Pamirs. Their gentle, compassionate teaching, with so much beauty and poetry bound up with it, had a strong appeal for many Chinese, in their times of stress and difficulty. Millions of converts were made.

Buddhism also, rather surprisingly, attracted the allegiance of many of the Tatar invaders, notably the Toba Weis. They wanted to identify themselves with the country they had conquered, but Confucianism, with its scholastic, austere demands, was too class-ridden, too exclusive, for them. Buddhism welcomed everyone.

Buddhism was responsible for much of the great art of China, inspiring its followers to hew caves out of the cliffs and fill them with splendid statuary, to build temples, monasteries, stupas. The message of that founder was more easily translated into this channel than into true spirituality. Between the third and the ninth centuries there was a flowering of religious art, promoting and popularizing the religion, but in the end aiding its downfall. The outward show, the obvious wealth, the materialism of the organization degraded its teachings and also aroused envy. For the chauvinistic, it was easy to deride it as a "foreign religion." But it was never quite rooted out, continuing to experience moments of revival, and its visible effect on the country remained strong in the beautiful temples and monasteries, in Buddhistic paintings, in the symbols of the religion.

There were also, much later in time, great numbers of Islamic converts, particularly in the northwest. At one time there were in the country tens of millions of Chinese Mohammedans. There have been a few Chinese Jews, and both the Zoroastrians and the Manichaeans came as missioners to the country. Under the tolerant early period of the T'ang, the Nestorian Christians entered the country and preached freely. Most of these people were obliged to leave when the great Buddhistic persecutions began in the latter part of the T'ang. It must be admitted that the Chinese have been tossed about by many winds of doctrine for a very long time.

Finally, in modern times, came the great missionary effort of the Christian churches.

Throughout all this long period of conflicting philosophical and religious persuasion the average Chinese remained a Confucian, as much as he was anything. He was interested in many ideas, but seldom convinced that one was of exclusive importance. The Chinese willingness to accord credence to, to harbor simultaneously conflicting beliefs, was repellent to the Christian missioners, with their burning zeal. A few, like the early Jesuits, compromised, allowing their converts to continue with ancestor worship, till this practice was forbidden by Rome, in a sequence of events which led to the Jesuits being expelled from the country. The Christians confused their flocks, as they came in increasing numbers, by presenting so many different aspects of Christianity, so many churches and creeds, often inimical one to another, in spite of their protestations of brotherly love.

At first many of these Christians had high hopes of converting the whole country, aware that nothing had ever wholly captured the Chinese mind and affections in this direction. But they also were unable to capture it. Though their converts ran into millions, still, after more than a hundred years, the great mass of the people were indifferent to their teaching, though they were generally willing to avail themselves of the mission schools, bursaries, hospitals, and poor relief.

Now at last it would appear that the mind of a great part of this people has been captured by a sort of faith, if you could call communism that. But the conversion came with immense coercion, allows of no apostates, and has not endured long enough to be called final.

It is frequently asserted today that China was satisfied with her own philosophies and system of government, that it was arrogant and harmful for the missionaries, many of whom were ignorant and bigoted, to come crowding in, forcing strange doctrines upon them while their governments were nibbling away at the sovereignty of the country, selling opium, gun in hand.

However, in point of fact, for most of their history, the Chinese were both dissatisfied and unhappy with their systems of thought and their government, as anyone knows who has informed himself of their past. Though no nation has been torn with more internal strife, nor suffered more Draconian measures of repression, somehow the world has accepted the image of a calm and smiling people, happy in their rustic simplicities, their government in the hands of a wise and benevolent officialdom of scholars. In the long and weary cycles of Chinese records this has been true only for rare, short intervals—if ever.

The Christian missionaries were Belgians, British, Danes, Germans, Swedes, Norwegians, Americans, French—from practically every Christian nation, in fact, and they came as the Buddhists and other religious persons had come in the past, primarily to succor a people who appeared to be in terrible need. Even in peacetime the Chinese lost millions to famine, disease, and poverty, and their helplessness—for all their innate intelligence—made these would-be helpers feel that the country was benighted. If some of the missionaries were limited in their capacities, others were of high caliber, and many became noted sinologues, from Morrison and Legge onward.

In certain respects some of the missionaries enjoyed in China a higher material standard of living than they could have had at home. They had servants—not as many as the business people, but still they were free of drudgery. They had reasonably comfortable, spacious houses, and could go away to the hills or the sea during the summer's heat, often for several months. That was a respite few in the business fraternity could allow themselves. There were long journeys across the world when their furloughs fell due.

On the other hand, not all missionaries went away in the summer—in the beginning none did. The furloughs came seldom, sometimes only once every seven or nine years, entailing painful family separations. The missionaries often lived in deep isolation in inland towns and villages, where they had to create their whole environment while striving to lift and enlighten those about them. They needed holidays to restore themselves. Mails were slow. The Roman Catholics, who were celibate, often never returned home, and seldom had any summer vacations; they were always at their posts. Their converts far outnumbered those of the Protestants, and they were ceaselessly busy. All of these persons faced real danger during uprisings, anti-foreign attacks, and local wars.

Why did they do it? Coming from a thousand different backgrounds, they had one common tie. They had felt within them that impulsion, that necessity, which was named "a call," to go forth and spread the Word of the Gospel. To those who do not understand its spiritual implication, this unseen influence is inexplicable, yet it was this basic motive, expressed in many forms, always very strong in the individual, which took these people to China. There was more sympathy and understanding for their stand in a time when Christianity was less under attack than today.

In China they sometimes were obliged to endure a certain amount of ridicule from the business community, and were unpopular with many Chinese, some of whom regarded their teachings with real aversion. A Chinese schoolboy in England, writing an essay on the subject of missionaries, said of them, "These sometimes become troublesome and it is found necessary to kill them," an outlook he had certainly learned at home. The missionaries had to ride this tide of misunderstanding, and with grace. It is easy to laugh at them, but such an attitude doesn't bear much scrutiny.

Roughly speaking, there have been over the last three thousand years of recorded history in China about ten major changes of dynasty, aside from many minor ones. A dynasty fell through its own weakness and corruption, or when it was conquered by foreigners like the Mongols, under Genghiz and Kublai Khan, or by the Manchus. In this case, when the Manchus took the country, the Ming dynasty which they supplanted was falling of its own decay; the advent of the newcomers only hastened the process. Whenever a foreign power was victorious, the usurpers invariably came to adopt the superior culture of the Chinese, taking over their administrative machine, ceremonies, dress, and using their language, leading the Chinese to believe that whatever happened, ultimately they were always the winners. From the days of the Han the scholar-gentry kept the reins of actual administration in their hands, so that the day-to-day business of the country usually could proceed without long-enduring interruptions. In theory this civil service was open to everyone by competitive examinations— a marvelously democratic conception to date back so long ago— but only really feasible if education is free. In a country like China, where most of the people were very poor, only a relative few had the leisure and means to study. Seldom could a poor boy rise to eminence.

In the eighteenth century there was an enormous increase in the population of the country. The land was already under intensive cultivation; now there came to be increased pressure on existing arable acreages—rents went up, a new group of profiteering landlords arose, and the misery of the peasants was heightened. In the next century the advent of the West, with traders who had completely different products and ways of doing business flocking in, further dislocated the economic pattern of the country. The ancient procedures of the merchants were thrown into confusion; the guilds could not function properly in this new climate of thought. Economic troubles steadily increased, contributing to the political collapse which came about early in the twentieth century.

The first Europeans to visit China were the Polos from Venice, who went there when Kublai Khan was reigning (in the thirteenth century). They immensely admired the monarch and the country, not seeming to realize that the Chinese were groaning under an enemy occupation. Then, early in the seventeenth century the astute, adroit Jesuits managed to establish themselves in the capital as mathematicians and astronomers, and finally as priests. At the same time the Dutch and Portuguese mariners discovered the southern ports, but not till the advent of the industrial age did the real assault of the West begin. Our merchants needed new, wider markets, and, having made a foothold in India, quite naturally went on to China. The East India Company sponsored the first voyages, which were, disgracefully, devoted to the opium trade. There was nothing else of comparable profit to take to China, which was satisfied with what it could supply to its own home market. There was already opium in the country, but not very much. The local merchants could always sell more. The government, however, knew it was an evil, and attempted to forbid its entry.

The story of those early years reflects much odium upon us. After 1842 the West forced open the ports of China, and insisted upon reasonable terms of trade. That first war had taught the astonished Chinese that they were helpless before us, living in a world of illusion. Their discomfiture was very great, but they were not wholly convinced of the military potential of the Western world and its determination till after 1860 and another war. Then one country after another moved in upon the scene, obtaining concessions and trade rights, building railways, imposing a quasi-colonial status upon much of the country. It is this that the nation now so bitterly resents, and with some justice. Yet there is another side to this coin. The Manchu government was primarily to blame for the conditions which had resulted in the Chinese being unable to fend for themselves. The shock produced by the advent of the West helped to precipitate their downfall. In the long period of anarchy and disunion which followed, when the Chinese were torn between opposing ideas, they received a great deal of help from the strangers who had come to live there.

The Chinese were exploited commercially, but many of them also made great fortunes. They had from us schools, universities, libraries, hospitals, technical aid and teaching, generous help in times of flood and famine, and the individual ministrations of thousands of missionaries and social workers. This should not be belittled.

In the long and often tormented era which lay between the First Opium War and the Japanese attack at Lu Ko Chiao, the awakening element among the Chinese had a great wish to change their institutions, their government, their educational system, themselves—they were intensely interested in reform. The T'ai-p'ing Rebellion was a symptom of this feeling, as were scores of other movements. Sun Yat-sen's reforms, the "New Life" movement of the Kuomintang, and today, the Thoughts of Mao Tze-tung indicate how seriously the Chinese took this issue. Slogans writ large on prominent walls are no new thing.

At the time of the T'ai-p'ing Rebellion, and during the siege of the city of Anch'ing, General Hu Lin-yi rode one day to the summit of Dragon Mountain to study the lie of the land. He came to the bank of the Yangtze, where he caught sight of two foreign steamships, sailing westward as fast as a galloping horse and as light as the wind. Hu changed color, and for a long time was unable to utter a word. Then he gathered up his reins and made for his barracks.

He died soon afterward.*

The effort these people put out in their struggle for reform makes a piteous chapter. So many tried so hard, so much enthusiasm, so many meetings and speeches were lavished in this cause—and yet in the end it all seemed a failure. Hence the last great experiment—Marxism. But a hundred years and more ago in China, that was an undreamed-of solution—socialistic schemes were not unknown in the West, long before Marx was born—but they had no real counterpart in China.

After the middle of the nineteenth century the youth of China, and some of their elders who were not too timorous to air their views, began to form themselves into societies to debate the question of their national destiny, education, and direction. These groups were often obliged to go underground, and some went to Japan, where they could speak openly. As the years passed they published hundreds of reviews and journals.

Serious books began to appear, discussing the problems the West was creating, scholarly books attempting to explain the phenomenon which had appeared in their midst. One of the most important of these early studies came out in 1844, written by one Wei Yüan, and called *Hsi-kuo t'u-chih*, or *An Illustrated Gazetteer of the Maritime Countries*. This discussed Western nations, in some detail, attempting to summarize their history, geography, politics, armaments, shipbuilding, and mining. The book was written with a distinct purpose in mind, as the author frankly stated, when he recommended "using barbarians to attack barbarians, using barbarians to negotiate with barbarians, and *learning the superior techniques of the barbarians to control the barbarians.*" Wei Yüan had evidently taken the First Opium War very much to heart, which was not universally the case. The first modern world geography written by a Chinese also appeared about this time: the *Ying-huan chih-lüeh*, or *A Brief Survey of the Maritime Circuit*. Up to this time most Chinese, and this emphatically included the scholars, were both ignorant of and indifferent to the outer world.

As China's danger became more and more apparent, a move-

* Hsiao Ch'ien, *The Dragon Beards versus the Blueprints*, London: Pilot Press, 1944, p. 10.

ment called Self-strengthening was started; it recognized that the nation must learn from her enemies how to regain her own stature. Famous men took up the issue, important books were written, and the country did undoubtedly stir in its sleep. There was endless criticism, argument, and planning among the students. People went abroad to plot the downfall of the Manchu dynasty. A few names indicate the trend: the Revive China Society, the Society in Expectation of a Parliament, the Political Learning Society, the Root out Tyrants Society—and there were hundreds of others. Among the periodicals were *New Life*, *New Thought Tide*, *Republican Daily*, and the *Science Weekly*.

Around 1870 a remarkable experiment was launched, when it was decided to turn away from the educational system which had been in force for some two thousand years. To do this it was concluded that the first step would have to be the dispatch of carefully selected young men abroad, where they would study. They were to discover how foreign countries conducted their affairs, so that when they returned these techniques could be adopted at home. While they were away they were to keep up their Chinese studies, and wherever they were sent they were to be constantly watched, and reports sent back on each one's conduct.

It was felt that the studies which were of first importance pertained to military and naval subjects, as well as technology in general. The boys who were chosen were certainly to be pitied, as they were the objects of an impossible scheme, and were almost wholly unprepared for the venture. Intelligent and gifted they undoubtedly were, but they did not know the languages of the countries to which they were sent, they knew nothing of science, and they could not manage their new assignments as well as going on with Chinese. Few, at the beginning, were able to learn a language quickly enough really to assimilate anything of their proposed curricula.

In over eighty years about a hundred thousand young men were sent to Japan, France, England, Germany, and the United States. They came from every part of China, and meticulous records were kept of each individual, while the government tried to control them by regulations, inspectors, and committees. Huge sums were spent on this, and the primary and secondary schools within the country neglected, so that their grants could swell the total going abroad. Then, when these students, after a long and usually unhappy spell in the West, returned to China, they found themselves strangers. There had, naturally enough, always been a gap between the scholar and the peasants (who comprised most of the population)—now there was an impassable breach between the educated and the illiterate.

What would be the condition of any of the major powers today, if for nearly a century the flower of their scholastic youth had been sent off to another land for five years and more, to undergo a wholly different system of education, to be subjected to entirely new and alien ways of thought, with the expectation that on their return they would rapidly transform their own country into a place which would be immensely strong, formidable, and of another century?

Yet this actually was the plan, drawn up in cold blood. Of course it was impossible, though as the years passed it became less chimerical. As the students began to absorb other ideas and feel easier in their new surroundings, they came to the point where they would not endure the surveillance they were expected to take for granted. The government, finding its rules could not be enforced, was obliged to relax them. Technology, which at first was held to be of over-riding importance, was admitted to be only one of many goals. The young men were urged to study the question of political leadership. Western ideas became better known in China, and the interchange of peoples was more accepted. More and more schools were started up in China itself which were patterned after Western models. Students began to go abroad sponsored by missions, or by their own families, and were consequently much freer. They went for themselves, not for their government.

Also, in time, there was no longer any pretense made that these youths could study successfully abroad, and at the same time continue with Chinese subjects. They dropped the old disciplines, but they could not really supplant these with Western knowledge—there were for many decades extraordinary lacunae in their knowledge. They became men who really did not fit in either in the West or in the East. When they went back to China they were more than ever disgusted with Manchu rule, but they were still in its clasp. Then came the rise of an aggressive policy in Japan and the Great War. Chinese nationalism grew apace in these years.

The later groups of students profited from the sorrows of the earlier contingents. They knew a greater or lesser extent the languages of the countries where they were sent, before they left home. But a man who had spent years at Oxford, Heidelberg, the Sorbonne, or Yale, really enjoying himself, could not afterwards endure the narrow life of some rustic town in the interior of China. The philosophical question was also serious: they no longer felt deeply about the Confucian way of life, and many had no wish to become Christians. What ethical principles were to guide them? Very often the answer was: None. They would settle down in the Treaty Ports, living in a partly Western style, but without sufficient ties in either the Chinese or the Western community. At that time few of their wives had had any educational advantages, or had been abroad.

There were many exceptions to this. Some of the students were convinced of the truth of Christianity, some were philanthropic, some had a talent for adjustment. Among the Chinese who studied abroad are great names like Hu Shih, V. K. Ting, and Lin Yutang.

The Chinese who went abroad did not, as the Japanese had done before them, go into the shipyards and factories of the West and learn to use their hands, mastering the actual techniques of these places; they nearly always remained apart, as scholars. But the impact of science upon them was very great. The ideas which were then making such inroads into the thought of the West affected them to such a degree that a high proportion of them became convinced that everything could be explained and known through scientific methods. The world of Newton, Comte, Darwin, opened before them so abruptly that they were at once bewildered and captivated; it was clearly not possible for them to balance these concepts with the Chinese wisdom which they had traditionally accepted. This intellectual ferment came to a head about 1930, after the students and intellectuals in the country had argued for many years as to the relative values of science, religion, and the old Chinese philosophies. They emerged from their intellectual wrestling in a state of mind which was ready to be captured by dialectical materialism.

This struggle, which can only be suggested here, had of course the most enormous and deep-rooted effect on the development of the country. It had lasted long enough to involve three generations, and is not easy to summarize or assess. Thousands of persons were preoccupied with it, innumerable influences and points of view entered into it. But, whatever one thinks of the final outcome, it must at least be admitted that the evolution of Chinese society was not taken lightly—that it cost its protagonists dear, in thought, suffering, hesitations, and resolves.

The ordinary Chinese, the uneducated man, as one encountered him at that time, was generally amiable, gentle, clever with his hands, patient, pitiful, and defenseless. His capacity for work and his endurance were both monumental. This was one side of his nature. There was another, not so often evident, which would break out when some strain had become at last unendurable; then the cruelty latent in him would break out like devouring flames. And there was another characteristic which revealed itself in relation to this trait, when a cruel act did not even seem important to the perpetrator. On such occasions it was terribly disconcerting to us to find that many of these people seemed callous as to the value of human life—while mindful of the importance of property.

Some friends of ours had gone up country on a houseboat trip, and through a series of accidents, their houseboat had turned over. Everyone got out in time, it was thought, and they were about to move away and arrange for the ship to be righted, when they heard a knocking on the hull. The foreigner in charge of the party seized an ax and rushed to a place where he thought he could quickly make effective opening, only to be immediately resisted by his boy, who cried out, "Oh no, Master! *Maskee!* Only belong number two cook!" ("*Maskee*"—never mind, in the Shanghai dialect.)

My father, as a young man newly come to China early in the century, was once down in the port of Amoy pursuing some project connected with tea. One Sunday afternoon, being at a loose end, a Chinese colleague suggested to him that to wile away the time perhaps he would like to witness an execution. These were normally not carried out on a Sunday, his acquaintance told him, but for, say, ten *taels*, one could be put forward so that he could watch it when he had leisure.

Everyone could produce similar instances. My father, trying to explain this attitude, would remark, "Le monde, où le coeur se bronze ou se brise."

The Flowery Land

SPRING BEGAN EARLY in the Yangtze Valley, after a raw, sharp, unpleasant winter. In February we would have our first intimations of the heavenly season which was approaching, when the *mei hua* opened on the low, twisted, grey branches of their parent tree. These resembled the flower of the plum, but were of a clear, pale yellow, with the sweetest fragrance of any flower. Then came the prunus and the peach, as the season advanced. We had no apple blossoms; apples in our part of the world were looked upon as a special fruit, peculiar to Korea. It was too hot for them in our summers, and the winters were neither cold nor long enough. These conditions also militated against snowdrops, crocuses, and tulips, but the narcissus, native to the country, throve.

We grew narcissi indoors, the bulbs placed on heaps of smooth, rounded pebbles, each one a pleasure to look upon in itself, arranged in beautiful ceramic bowls (then, every bowl in China seemed to be beautiful, unless its maker had tried to make it look foreign). The Chinese are deeply attached to the narcissus, the *shui hsien hua*, or "immortals of the water," and will take infinite pains in its cultivation.

Flower sellers went about the streets, coming to your door, with two huge baskets balanced on their carrying poles, baskets which were cornucopias of daffodils, narcissi, pussy willows, violets, tulips, hyacinths. Soon these gave way to roses, daisies, larkspur, wallflowers, cornflowers, all the familiar plants of Western gardens. Wisteria grew everywhere in that region, crowning the houses, drooping over doorways, sweetening fences, making moon doorways even more beautiful. And willows were everywhere too, spreading their green mist over the creeks. They were reflected in the temple pools and graced the moats under town walls. Bamboo was ubiquitous; clumps rose in the corners of gardens and down alleys, with their high, smooth, noble stems, their feathery growth. There are great numbers of species, tall and short, thick and sparse, and we loved them all. We also delighted in their shoots, one of the most common vegetables, and the most delicious.

Four flowers were traditionally held preeminent: the plum blossom, the peony, so luscious and pure, the lotus, which was a sacred flower, and the chrysanthemum. The orchid was also particularly beloved. The Chinese were not exaggerating when they called their country the "flowery land." The south is rich with hibiscus, poinsettia, bougainvillea. China is the native heath of the azalea and the rhododendron. Everywhere you go, from the coast even far inland to Tibet, whether you go north or south, there is an abundance of flowers.

This was true also of the birds of the country. There was birdsong everywhere you went. Orioles skimmed across the fields, swallows flew swiftly down from the eaves, scarlet cardinals flashed over the lawns. The thrush, the woodpecker, the dove, were as well-known here as in any Western country. There were jays, rooks, hawks, gulls, egrets, and game birds—duck and snipe, pheasants—and in great numbers. Kingfishers haunted the streams, and there were many rare birds, as befitted a country which held the phoenix so much in honor that one almost believed in it, accepting as fact that it had been dancing by moonlight on high terraces.

Perhaps the enthusiast for the visual Chinese scene always speaks too much in hyperbole, but it is difficult for me not to think that Chinese mountains are more entrancing, more fantastic, than any others. There is so often a sameness, a repetitiveness, about hills in other countries. The presence on so many of China's heights of beautiful ancient temples, guarded by gnarled cypresses, enhanced the hills, too, fitting harmoniously into the background, complementing and perfecting the whole. Not that the temple was necessary to accentuate what you saw—in the Lushan, for instance, the grandeur of the mountains was so great that they wholly absorbed the artists—nature and its creator making mankind seem insignificant, as the Taoists thought.

There are few places in China where you can catch glimpses of the eternal snows; but in compensation the mountains have this great fascination of themselves. For instance those amazing hills near Kweilin, in Kweichow, are the very mountains of the scrolls. The heights which the Chinese artists have given us in their long scrolls, of peaks encircled by mist, of precipices with a narrow path winding upwards beside them, of deep gorges, are really what the mountains of China are like. The feeling of the immensity of space, with our dusty ochre ground disappearing in an opalescent mist far below a peak, which the pictures convey, is not visionary, it is fact.

The same masters of the brush have depicted the humble aspect of the genial countryside, the thatched cottages by the creeks, where the mandarin ducks are swimming, the fields yellow with rape, or jade green with the young rice, the fisherman's net poised over a lake, the little boats launching forth. They have shown us how, as evening fell, the threads of blue smoke went slowly upward, creating scenes of rural quiet and calm, which seemed wholly harmonious. These artists, and the poets, have faithfully reproduced the outward aspect of old China. Their greatest painters have seldom been equaled and never surpassed anywhere in the world, and what they drew with their swift brushes was this amazingly beautiful country. Those Sung scrolls are not figments of the imagination, they are really the way China struck the discerning eye.

The genre scrolls, giving pictures of historical scenes or village life, showed with equal fidelity the walled towns and camel-backed bridges, the open shops lining the narrow streets, their signs, with their bold, handsome calligraphy, hanging down into the wind. They have shown us how the donkeys went down the lanes, their paniers brimming with scarlet peppers, they have shown the junks coming up to an anchorage outside a wall, their brown sails slanting, attended by cockleshell ferries.

Watching the clouds in China was a recognized pleasure. It was a luxury even the very poor could sometimes enjoy, and no one missed its poetic happiness. The moon too came more fully into her own in that country, perhaps, than in many of ours. The long warm summers, when people would find their only rest and respite outside, when there was relatively little electric light, and not even many oil lamps, meant that moonlight could be really savored. The soft glow of a candle might come through the paper that covered a wooden grill, casting strange shadows on the court-yard outside; but the moon held her own with that. Moon shadows emphasized the tilt of the black-tiled roofs, the windows cut in the shape of peaches and quinces. It was hard if you wanted to read; but most people couldn't, and they could luxuriate in the quiet and the tender light, the soft benediction of that familiar satellite they called *yüeh liang*.

On the bright autumnal days, when the sun shone so beautifully, the days of the pheasant and the crisp wind, when the harvests were being winnowed, and you could ride your pony far into the hills, the beauty of China seemed unutterable, there was no end to it.

Part II
SHANGHAI

Shanghai Generally

The ships of Tarshih did sing of thee in thy market:
and thou wast replenished, and made very glorious in
the midst of the seas. . . .
And in their wailing they shall take up a lamentation
for thee, and lament over thee, saying, What city is like
Tyrus, like the destroyed in the midst of the sea?

EZEKIEL

M Y SHANGHAI would not be yours. We all had our own kaleido-
scopes in the years when it was a Treaty Port, some of them
similar in range, most, in a glassy, hard-colored manner, at least
arresting. Anyway, they're all gone now; people threw them away
in 1926 and 1932, in 1937 and 1939, and finally in 1950. All we can
do is to remember. That brings another sort of kaleidoscope into
play, one with a long, wavering handle. But the designs are clear
enough.

For instance, everyone, it seems, speaks of that famous bar of
the old Shanghai Club on the Bund. One is told, often, that it was
the longest in the world, a hundred and fifty yards long! Was it? I
wonder. No doubt there was a bar. But in *my* Shanghai the Shanghai Club was the place where my father played chess, with deep
satisfaction and refreshment, every day after tiffin. He did this so
regularly, before going back to his office, that there was once a
cartoon of him in the *North China Daily News*, his pipe in his

mouth, his hand poised over the board. When he came home in the afternoon he would bring back armfuls of books from the Club's splendid library, the best on the Coast. It was the source of our incessant reading. That's my Shanghai Club.

That was during the years when the Shanghai skyline was known the world over—the Bund and the River, the dome of the Hong Kong and Shanghai Bank, the bronze angel of the War Memorial, looking down Avenue Edward VII where the French Concession began. This was the handsome part of the city. You may not have liked Shanghai, you might well have loathed it as ugly, ruthless, a Moloch, and the rest—but it got hold of you somehow . . . it was one of those unique places. You couldn't just dismiss it. Its span in history as a Treaty Port was so brief—hardly a century—yet how quickly it grew, so that it could be spoken of in the same breath with the giants, with London and New York, as a tremendous port and commercial center. I don't suppose many people actually ever loved Shanghai, but it was, in spite of everything, a great place.

Of those who did love it, there was, preeminently, the cartoonist of the *North China Daily News*, Mr. Sapojnikov, or, as we all called him, Sapajou. In his time, he was perhaps the greatest cartoonist in the world—he had offers from the great papers of many capitals, coaxing him to join them—but he was so enamored of Shanghai that he would never leave it, small as his salary must have been, little as he could be known.

A good many White Russians were truly attached to Shanghai, which was a touching thing, as most of them were poor refugees, and had a terribly hard life there. They arrived soon after the Russian Revolution, before the world went through its great seasons of displaced persons, before systems were evolved which were somewhat prepared for these catastrophes, before they could have the help they would now receive. No one needed a passport or a visa to land in Shanghai—who would have issued it? So of course it was a haven for the stateless.

Shanghai was always charitable, and it did try to help the refugees—but the problem was too great, disproportionate for the small foreign community. The Russian refugees, the first white persons the East had seen in distress, were to the Western communities people of a halfway house—some of them Europeans in a cultural sense, many almost Asiatics. They arrived destitute and desperate in a city where the Chinese could do almost everything cheaper and better than anyone else, and where most of the foreigners were tied to their own countries, hired and paid from offices in Europe and America. Local jobs for non-Orientals hardly existed. The Chinese did not help them—why should they? They did little enough for their own poor. So assimilation was extraordinarily difficult for them—yet among these people many were so gallant as to *love* Shanghai! A humbling thought.

It was Sapajou who gave Shanghai its daily measure of wit and cheer to start the morning. His cartoons, satirical but never malicious, amusing, never ugly, put everything in proportion. He showed us the Chinese soldiers of the warlord era, with their teapots and paper umbrellas, and the heroes of the 19th Route Army, standing staunchly against the Japanese; we saw the Japanese themselves, grinning toothily as they poured tons of smuggled goods over the customs barriers, or, as a beaming Japanese *amah-san*, rocking the infant Manchukuo in its cradle; through him we saw Albanians and Greeks, Italians subservient to Mussolini, we saw John Bull, Uncle Sam, sprightly Mlle la France, and a strangely young-looking Stalin, the prewar Stalin. We saw Trotsky and the Chinese figures who were caught in the communist web, we saw the vigorous men of the Kuomintang. When there were troubles on the northern frontiers, he would sketch appropriate figures for "Mlle from Tsitsihar, parlez-vous?" or "Way down upon the Amur River." He reflected in his swift, assured drawings, his trenchant comments, that world view which was a particular Shanghai prerogative in those years before television, when hardly anyone even had a radio. On the Coast, at that time, they weren't worth having, there was nothing yet, really, to hear.

Shanghai was a maze of races, nationalities, and tongues, as well as widely separated spans of thought-time. The best example of this that occurs to me was the chance remark of a brilliant child. She was five, the daughter of the Chinese mayor; her father was dressing for dinner, and she was in his room, amusing him. That night a prominent English merchant and a member of a European royal house were coming to dine. "Why are you putting on your dinner jacket, Daddy?" asked the little girl. "Because a Danish prince is coming," he answered. "Oh," she said, "Hamlet, I suppose."

You wouldn't say that remark was typical, but it was a city where bright children could be extremely precocious, in the most attractive sense, because the place was such a paradox, such an odd mixture. It is often described as a center of vice, a really wicked town—but to most of us it was where our fathers had their jobs, where we lived as best we could, where the children went to school, where we made music, found friends if we were so fortunate, and kept our heads above water amidst the rising storms of the advancing century. For what security had Shanghai? What tenure? Who was really responsible for this far-off port? How could you put down roots?

The many different nationalities partook of the troubles and animosities, of the pride and dismay, of their own home countries, while China, as the Manchu power waned, became more and more unstable. Then after it fell, the Republic, contrary to the fervent hopes of so many Chinese, proved unable to control the country, where in less than a century there had been two decisive wars with the European powers, the T'ai-p'ing Rebellion, the Mohammedan Rebellions, the Nien Rebellion, the Japanese War of 1894/95, the Boxer Rebellion, and then the collapse of the Ch'ing. All these foreign wars had been defeats for the Chinese. Then came the warlord era, World War I, the Russian Revolution, incessant trouble with the Japanese, and the split between the Kuomintang and the Russian-oriented group, while throughout there was pressure from the foreigners—economically, politically, socially. The communists formed their party, grew in strength, and withdrew to the countryside—incessant civil war followed. The Japanese attacked in 1931, and again almost fatally in 1937. The people fled inland. World War II began. There were devastating floods, famines, epidemics. All these catastrophes, and many more, added up to a great mass of woe, with millions killed, millions displaced, confusion beyond description.

And on the edge of it, deeply involved, was Shanghai, building itself up on its muddy, isolated delta, tugged in every direction by opposing interests. The ordinary person just hung on. If he were a foreigner, generally he lived in that superficial comfort many good servants assure, but all too often the very ground seemed to quiver, even while he rang the bells for the boy, the cook, the gardener, the coolie, the *amah*, the chauffeur.

While Shanghai was in its hey-day, the press was still the great organ of communication; news agencies like Reuters, the Associated Press, the United Press, were of the utmost importance. I believe it is true that at one time Shanghai was rated as the third center of the world as a gathering place for news—it was far away from the powerful, ordered West, but it had a special significance. It had many papers of its own, too, some of considerable quality. There was the *North China Daily News*, the British organ, the *Journal de Changhai*, the American *Shanghai Evening Post and Mercury*, as well as Russian periodicals, and those of many nations, besides the Chinese papers, and their "mosquito" press. People took papers from home, though these would be weeks late— you saw copies of the *Times* of London, *Le Monde*, *Die Welt*, papers from Berlin, from San Francisco and New York, on desks wherever you went. They were another sign of the vitality of the city, which, while seldom intellectual, was often highly intelligent, with a wide, international curiosity.

Continuing to list Shanghai's virtues—not only was it charitable, vital, curious—another feature which marked it was that it was brave. Time and again it was exposed to the physical hazards of war, it was shelled, burned, looted—more in the suburbs than within the city—and suffered economic near-disaster, but every time it would stagger to its feet and begin again. Even when standing in great danger itself, its doors were always open to the wretched refugees who flocked in from the countryside. Aside from its many places of ill-repute, its smuggling rings and opium gangs, it established and maintained, without flinching, a plethora of schools, schools for the poor of all nationalities, as well as for the more fortunate, and continued to build hospitals and clinics, and to labor for the public health.

Considering its difficulties, the medley of peoples there who were basically transient, and the conditions, seldom of their own making, they had to endure, it was not entirely a cultural desert. It had a symphony orchestra, people learned to dance, paint, fence, ride; there was this robust multilingual press. The world's great artists traveled many weeks to play there, in bare halls and for little recompense: Kreisler, Pavlova, Heifitz, Moisevitch. There Alekhine came to play blindfold simultaneous chess—and there was a chess club to receive him.

Though the name "Shanghai" means "on the sea," the city is not on the Pacific, but lies well within watery deltaic country, some miles up the Whangpoo, the Yellow Creek (Huang Pu). The place was originally a fishing village and a smugglers' nest. At the mouth of the Whangpoo is Woosung, but even that is not on the sea. When your liner at last reached the ocean it was not a great moment of exhilaration, either (though you might have been looking forward to this leave for many years), because the coastal waters were dark brown with river mud and silt, for hundreds of miles out into open sea. Most of this came from the Yangtze, a muddy, turbulent, tremendous river. Both it and the small Whangpoo are difficult rivers, dangerous for many of the craft that live upon them, and then exacting every year a heavy loss of life in storms, typhoons, mishaps. They were crowded with shipping, absorbing as a spectacle, the junks with their rich brown sails making them beautiful and pictorial.

Dredgers were always at work on the Whangpoo, making it as navigable as possible by the vast merchant ships which called at Shanghai, as well as by the different navies which came and went. Large vessels had to anchor at the mouth of the river, off Woosung; people would then be brought up to the city by tender. Pilots were essential in these waters, and it was an honored calling. The Yangtze pilots, and the men who navigated the lesser rivers leading to Canton, Shanghai, and Tientsin must have had much in common with the men Mark Twain described, who worked the Mississippi in the old days.

When the first Europeans and Americans came to Shanghai after the treaties were signed, each country had its own strip of land, following the old "factory" system the East India Companies had evolved in India. It was soon evident that here this was impractical and costly, every country being obliged to arrange for the same services, and except for the French, the other foreigners banded together to form the International Settlement, run by a Municipal Council of local magnates, elected by the ratepayers. It was in many ways a sort of city-state, an oligarchy. Together these nationals managed a police force, the water supply, roads, sanitation, and established a court of justice (the Mixed Court). They felt it essential that the Western offenders should be tried under their own systems of law, and not dealt with by the harsh Manchu courts. This was one of the most important features of extraterritoriality; without it most people would probably have refused service in China.

The French stood aloof. They were determined to run their own area according to their own ideas, and they continued their French Concession with their own separate services and government. This tossed another language into our urban council orders and enhanced the flavor of the city. It gave the French, too, on occasion, very distinct advantages. For example, the Japanese, by far the most numerous foreigners, used the International Settlement as a base when they fought the Chinese in and around the city in 1931–32 and 1937–38, and took advantage of many other privileges, in spite of all our protests. They had little command over the council, as they were mostly too poor to be ratepayers, something they fiercely resented. But they had no foothold at all with the French, who could keep them right out of their Concession. That is, till the outbreak of World War II and the fall of France.

The whole essence of the city lay in the fact that it was a great port. It was a strange thing that the Chinese, having turned their backs on the sea, should now through the vicissitudes of history have come into such close contact with those peoples whose soul and chief joy (at that time) lay with ships and the broad bosom of the ocean. The old Manchu Empire, with its elaborate and tyrannical facade, yet crumbling within, had come head-on into collision with the bold seafarers of Europe and the New World, when the tide of these nations, one after the other, was at flood. The Chinese were to witness the races of the clipper ships, the advent of the steamers, the presence of long grey warships. These, as the concessions multiplied, the dynasty weakened, and trade expanded, were to edge farther and farther inland, upriver.

It wasn't all the fault of the Manchus. After the great rebellions of the T'ai-p'ings, the Nien, and the Moslems, the Ch'ing were at a loss within themselves, and turned over more and more power and responsibility to the Chinese. But it was too late; encumbered by the system, the new administrators could not sufficiently alter the direction of the state, even if they had known how to do it, or what, exactly, to do.

When I look back at Shanghai, I always feel that the sky was our luxury. That, and the light which always pervades deltas, where the great arc of the heavens is uninterrupted. In summer we had an endless procession of massive cumulus clouds passing above the horizon, swelling or light, tipped with colors, accompanied by slight, minute, fleecy *apsarases*, each with its own particular background of pale green-blue. In that season also, we experienced many fierce typhoons, and there was not much notice to be had, though the Jesuits' observatory and meteorological station at Zikawei did what it could. Ships were not infrequently lost at sea in typhoons—not only junks and small craft, but also large coastal steamers, would disappear. At these times the low-lying city would be inundated, trees uprooted, and sometimes the Bund itself was littered with shipping, lifted up and deposited there by the tremendous winds.

Though people who came from beautiful places like Switzerland or the Lake Country often found Shanghai intolerably ugly and bleak, yet this part of the delta, with the hinterland which stretches away westward, is not devoid of loveliness. Inland, not far away, is Soochow, once a very pictorial town, renowned in Chinese eyes for its beauty. Much of this had disappeared after the destruction of the T'ai-p'ings, but the region in itself is potentially a soft, genial setting. This was recognized by Chinese artists like those of the sixteenth-century Wu School, who worked here as well as in the neighboring province of Chekiang, painting the creeks, the local shipping, the low hills, the flowers, the walled towns. And in default of anything else, at Shanghai we had these skies, soft, open, and luminous, pouring out penetrating light, enriching everything we saw.

Shanghailanders

W HO LIVED in Shanghai? Who were we?

Chiefly the Chinese; in a city of four million the foreigners, though they were conspicuous, came to only a few thousand. The Chinese flocked into the little fishing village, once it became a Treaty Port, till in less than a century it became a great metropolis. It represented to them opportunity and a haven.

The politically conscious Chinese, the nationalists, resented the city's status deeply, but nevertheless they found it irresistible. They came for education, for the free clinics, for their own growth. Like it or not, it was *the* city of the Coast in their lifetime.

The order of the Settlement and the Concession, their relative safety compared to the chaos prevailing over so much of the country, was an immense attraction. This was true not only of Shanghai, but also of Tientsin, Hankow, and the other ports where the foreigners were able quickly to create conditions in which trade and industry could develop. Shanghai, being the biggest of these towns, offered more opportunities, more jobs, more social services. Places like the YMCA were very important in Shanghai and Tientsin, for instance, offering young Chinese adult education, athletics, and science lectures, setting up museums, in fact, opening up a new world to the eyes of many hitherto almost cloistered persons.

Many of the laborers who came remained bitterly poor, slaving

43

for a pittance in the factories, but a great number managed to advance themselves, beyond the limits their villages would have afforded. There was hope in Shanghai, hope of success. It was more than the usual lure of the city for the country boy—the contrast was greater here.

There was another type of Chinese who found these ports, and particularly Shanghai, the place to seek. This was the revolutionary who, for a little while, within the foreign enclaves, might find a refuge from the Manchu government and their secret police, from the immediate dangers of inimical secret societies. Though the long arm of these organizations would eventually discover and seize him, yet here he had at least a respite. In the twenties of this century the scope of this situation was enlarged. It was then that persons began to arrive in Shanghai who were to be of extraordinarily wide influence, men who thought on an international level. They were the agents of the Comintern.

As for the foreigners, aside from the consular people and the missionaries, nearly everyone came out as a businessman. They came for the export-import firms, for the oil companies, the tobacco companies, for tea and silk, for the railways and the banks, for the waterworks and water-conservancies, as architects, engineers, lawyers, doctors, teachers. The French came to work for the tramways, the Danes for the telegraphs, the Swedes for the Swedish Match Company, and there were hosts of people in the shipping firms. Regiments were sent out to be ready to defend the ports in case of need—the Welsh Fusiliers, the Infanterie Coloniale, the U.S. Marines. The Sikhs came to police us (as a British force), as did the Annamites, brought by the French. Red Russians came to spread their doctrine and for their consulates—they were only a few, whereas thousands upon thousands of White Russians had arrived as refugees. The Japanese came in thousands because they were so crowded at home and could make a living here. Also because it suited their government's policy to have them settled in China; Japan wanted, hoped, intended, to have China for much of the colonial period. Then, as the Western phase of the city's life was drawing to a close, waves of German Jews, fleeing from the Nazis, arrived. The great bait for the refugee, as for the agitator, was that you didn't need a passport or a visa to enter the city. What authority could have issued one? On whose behalf? It would have been impossible.

There were already a good number of Jews in Shanghai, even a few, a very few, Chinese Jews, as in China this people had nearly died out, or been lost through assimilation. (The only well-known Chinese Jew of modern times, I believe, is Liu Shao-chi, and he is not a Jew by religion or culture.) The Jews in Shanghai had come rather recently—that is, after the Russian Revolution—from Russia, or they had come in the early days from Baghdad and from India. At the very beginning, when there was a tie between the East India Company and China (based on opium), certain Bombay merchants had taken an interest in the opening up of the China trade. With them modern banking came to the Far East—with the establishment of such places as the Agra and United Service Bank, and the Commercial Bank of India. We had in our midst financiers like the Kadoories, like Hardoon, Sassoon, Cama. These people, with their genius with money, built widely and started many enterprises; they were charitable, and left their stamp on the city. A good many of them held British passports.

Shanghai absorbed everyone it could. Once there you generally couldn't go much farther, you had to make do with it—unless you were already destined for a mission inland, or a branch of some firm, or a minor consulate. There was certainly less opportunity for the foreigner up-country, when he had to start from scratch as a refugee—if there were any opportunity at all.

So it was that Shanghai (and to a lesser extent the other Treaty Ports) had almost every religion, ideology, language, custom, of the globe.

The navies of the world called at these ports, and patroled the waters of the China Seas. All the great newspapers had their correspondents here, besides which the city came to have a very respectable showing in the world of journalism on its own account.

Everyone was always learning languages—generally on an individual basis. Learning them, or teaching them. Not only the usual European languages and Russian, but also Chinese, and at that, there was the question of subdivisions—were you learning the standard Mandarin, or Cantonese, Hakka, or even the horrible Shanghai dialect? Shanghai's speech was the worst in the country, it was taken almost as a joke. *"Shanghai hua pu shih hua"* as a train conductor once said to me, laughing with comfortable contempt, knowing that he, a Nanking man, spoke *"kuo yü,"* or the standard speech—"Shanghai's speech isn't even speech"—it was in fact a sort of cockney or Platt-deutsch, hasty, amusing, bold, slovenly, a dialect of the fisherman and of the coastal villages near the mouth of the Yangtze.

This was too bad from the point of view of those of us who ought to have learned Chinese as we grew up. That was usual for the children who were born in Peking or Tientsin, and many places up-country; but in Shanghai our parents were always warned not to wreck our potential capacity for learning the language by starting on this basis. The servants were instructed to speak to us only in pidgin English, so, like our parents, most of us never learned to speak Chinese at all, (unless like myself they took it up seriously later on in life). We were hurried instead into French lessons, German lessons.

Shanghailanders enjoyed speaking pidgin English, a garbled speech, containing words from many languages, which amused everyone and could be picked up without the slightest effort. The hide-bound, imperialistic, dyed-in-the-wool "old China hands" always insisted that studying Chinese drove people mad, and could always produce splendid examples.

The marvelous, intricate, baffling structure of the Chinese characters and the richness of the language attracts those who do study it, partly because it is so different from anything else, really rich and strange. At first it seems quite easy, and the student makes rapid progress, gaining command of enough words and characters to feel he has entered a new frame of reference. Then comes the conviction that he is thousands of characters and years away from any true grasp of his subject. But by now he is in its toils, he can't escape it.

There is a great divide between the spoken and the written language; the characters, so formidable to remember, make a barrier. People could sometimes speak Chinese very well, but never read it, much less write it, which calls for special skills in handling the brush. There were plenty of local jokes about studying Chinese, like that of two language students who were walking together in the Western Hills outside Peking.

Such students were always urged to speak to all the Chinese they could, so when they came upon some countrymen they stopped to pass the time of day with them. One old farmer remarked to another: "Isn't it strange, how similar these foreigners' speech is to Chinese?" "Listen, old man," said one of the students, "I *am* speaking Chinese." The farmer burst out laughing. "Can you speak foreign talk?" asked the student. "No, can you speak

Chinese?" was the reply. The student gave up. "No," he said. "Isn't it curious, we still understand each other perfectly," mused the farmer.

I finally studied Chinese in the British Chamber of Commerce School in Shanghai, and in a few months took the First Interpreter's Examination at the British Consulate—not a difficult test, involving only some five hundred characters. After that I went on by myself, with a teacher, till I left China, learning several thousand characters and reveling in them all. Nothing is more provocative than a character, it seems to tease you to pull it apart and discover why it is as it is. And they are so beautiful to look at! People who feel this and who would pursue them with vigor and absorption would perhaps seem mad to those outside the charmed circle. It is hard to keep them in mind, you must constantly refresh yourself and keep working at them. But once you have mastered the use of a dictionary—which is not a simple step, as there is no alphabet—you can, if you will, plunge into T'ang poetry and start translating.

The Chinese institutes which are now so numerous abroad, and which have trained so many Chinese speakers, did not exist till comparatively recently, but we had in China some excellent textbooks, written by sinologues, consular people, and military attachés. Priests too had done their share in this work: you can find their old Chinese language books phrased in Chinese, Latin, and French.

Chinese is complicated by the many tones used in the spoken language—four in Mandarin, or Kuo Yü, nine in Cantonese. These have to be learned. Every monosyllable is susceptible of these different shades. The written language, too, has many versions— the Classic, Great, the Small Seal, the Grass, and so on. And now there are all these new international words which have been added to it, after being somewhat sinified, and as the effort today is to simplify characters there is the question of the old style and the new. To romanize a language like this is nearly impossible, if it is to be satisfactory, though it has often been attempted. Now there are many romanizations, but in my time we used the standard forms, drawn up by the eminent Sir Thomas Wade, who had aspired to making his romanization fit all the commonly used European languages, with such dreadful results as may be imagined. It was because of Sir Thomas that you had to learn the romanization as though it were almost a separate language.

When I went to the language school everyone had a tutor to

himself. These old-style gentlemen, dressed in long gowns, and very ceremonious in their ways, guided us through the textbooks which were thought best at the time, and rehearsed us in tones. There were not many pupils, and we sat there and intoned, each with our own *hsien sheng*. Three successive American military attachés, stationed at Peking, had produced in turn three books on studying Chinese: Major McHugh, Colonel Aldrich, and Colonel Ratay. These volumes were very good indeed, and beautifully printed, with large clear characters. Though of a rather military flavor, they did not neglect ordinary useful themes; if you had mastered Ratay you had a workable knowledge of the language, and could take part in most discussions.

Everyone was conscious of the necessity to speak French, with the Concession part of the city, and so many of us living in it. German as a language waxed and waned in importance, according to the condition of the home country. When the Ports first began, Germany was not even united—but there were Hansa representatives, and envoys from the court of Prussia who came out. When the country became a strong power it was ambitious in China; the truculence of its Minister in Peking, von Ketteler, at the time of the Boxer Rebellion, cost him his life. With the First World War Germany's star waned in China as elsewhere; it recovered, and many Germans, mostly businessmen, came to the country again, for Siemens and I. G. Farben and such firms. Their Lutheran missionaries were much admired, in particular for their noble work among the Chinese blind.

Then came the German Jews, flooding the city with the language. Meanwhile, the Russians, numerically strong, presented their own linguistic world, as did the Japanese, the Portuguese, the Sikhs, the Annamites. The Chinese on the ground learned, in their own way, whatever language they needed, including their own dialects. They are good linguists, and could find work in many foreign houses, speaking sufficiently well whatever speech Missy used. English was the most common lingua franca among the Westerners—the British were the dominant nation.

This was an accepted fact, reflected in makeup of the Municipal Council which governed this polyglot, cosmopolitan outpost: it contained (in the thirties) five British members, five Chinese, two Americans, and two Japanese. The Chinese had only lately been allowed to appear on it in such force, and the head of the Council was, I believe, always an Englishman. He was also often the head

of the most significant and prestigious foreign firm on the Coast—
Jardine Matheson, the "princely *hong*." The original Jardine had
come out to China very early indeed, and everyone always said
that the company had been founded on opium, and then turned
respectable, building mills, acquiring a shipping fleet, exporting tea
and silk, establishing a great commercial empire, with a "royal
family" of its own as its senior staff. The British were the most
influential foreigners among us all in the Yangtze Valley, and Jardine's incorporated what this meant.

In 1935, according to the Shanghai Municipal Council Report
for the year, there were in the International Settlement under
forty thousand foreigners all together. Among these were
(roughly) 6,500 British, about 2,000 Americans, 3,000 Russians,
and over 2,000 British Indians. The Japanese, by far the most
numerous, came to over 20,000, including those who lived on the
"external roads." These figures do not include the residents of the
French Concession—taking that area into account, the Russians
(and almost all were Whites) came to 12,000, the British 11,000
(with the Indians), the Americans numbered 3,400, and the
French 1,430. Besides these nationals there were Scandinavians,
Netherlanders, Belgians, Germans, Finns, Spaniards, Italians, Portuguese (in quite large numbers), Koreans, Austrians, enough people from East Europe to allow a flourishing League of Danube
Women to be formed; one could go right on through the whole
list of countries. And there was a very large colony of Eurasians,
some listed under the nationality of the father, if he had been
European. There were also, nearly always almost unknown and
unseen, a considerable number of Western women who had married Chinese, and were living in the Chinese parts of the city—in
Nantao or Chapei.

The Japanese, numerically so strong, but generally individually
of modest means (with a few notable exceptions), were very
dissatisfied with a franchise based on ratepaying ability and land
regulations, which kept their Council representation limited to
only two members. They repeatedly tried to alter the rules, but
without success, as the other foreign nationals were persuaded that
the system worked well enough as it was. If they had so wished
the Council could have formed itself solely from the British and
American communities, but they wanted to have other voices on
it, as minorities. By 1940 the Japanese were so infuriated by this
situation, and were in so aggressive a mood (having conquered the

whole Coast), that they determined to alter the representation to include five Japanese, two British, and two Americans.

The Japanese were then pouring into the Settlement in increasing numbers, and felt they could take over the Council, but the British and Americans, by splitting up voting units with a good deal of dexterity, managed to defeat the Japanese in the elections of that year, and maintain the same proportion of councillors. Soon after this result was announced, following the custom of introducing new councillors to the public at a ratepayers' meeting, a dramatic event took place, entirely in the spirit of the Japanese martial feelings at that time.

These people had been holding Japanese Association meetings, and were fired with such indignation, national pride, and recklessness that on this particular morning, with hundreds of persons convened in the open air, at the Race Course, they were ready to assert their convictions in a way they felt suitable. The meeting was held in front of the public stand, because so many people attended, too many for the Town Hall or the Grand Theater. In the full view of all these persons, a Japanese called Hayashi drew a revolver and shot at the Chairman of the Council, Mr. W. J. Keswick, also the head of Jardine Matheson, a young man, well known to everyone and generally popular. Fortunately he was only wounded, and not seriously. The assassin was sentenced to two years' imprisonment and sent to Japan, but was never made to serve his term. He was, in Japanese eyes, a hero.

The Mixed Court, after the Revolution of 1911–12, had come under the control of the various consuls, and the magistrates were paid by the Municipal Council. This was an improvement, as previously, though foreigners were judged by foreigners and their own law, the Chinese came under Chinese jurisdiction, and often suffered conditions incompatible with our concepts of justice, even though theoretically they were subject to our control. Now justice could hold a more impartial sway, and the treatment of prisoners could be bettered. There was a lot of respect for the Mixed Court, as well as amusement. Everyone was delighted when one morning, while the court was in session, two workmen came in to repair the large clock which was fixed over the magistrate's desk. They put up a ladder, detached the clock, and solemnly bore it away, no one restraining them. They were professional thieves and the clock was never seen again. It was impossible not to admire their aplomb.

In 1927, when the Kuomintang became the recognized government of China, a Provisional Court was set up, instead of the Mixed Court, and certain adjustments were made. In 1929 this was succeeded by a District Court and a High Court, which, it was always assumed, worked well.

It could be argued that to impose extraterritoriality on China was outrageous, while the powers tolerated having their nationals live in many other countries, no better managed, without such special protection and privileges. The foreigner in Turkey, Mexico, Russia, and other lands ran the risk of very grave eventualities if he fell foul of the legal system pertaining there—he could not be assured of justice. But in these places there had not been the peculiar chain of circumstances which had permitted the other powers to act in unison, demanding enclaves where they could administer their own government, drawing up a framework of law acceptable to themselves.

For a long time, though some of the Chinese were hostile to the unequal treaties and the economic grasp the foreigners had on them, they were not ready to make a stand about it. They were preoccupied with other problems, they blamed their situation on the Manchus, they came to see that their own incredible weakness was blameworthy, that they must modernize themselves. They would admit, privately, that they gained something from extraterritoriality, too.

But after the yoke of the Manchus was thrown off and the country became more nationalistic, achieving the beginnings of a stable government, it was obvious that eventually extraterritoriality would have to go. It was a question of "when." Naturally the conservative foreigner was loath to relinquish it; it was difficult for him to feel the country was safe for trade without it. In point of fact, it seldom was. But as the years passed it was increasingly evident that the time was approaching when China must have full sovereignty over her own ports. The troubles of 1925, '26, '27, '31, militated against the first steps being taken. Those were the years of the communist strikes, of the Kuomintang takeover, of a Japanese battle inside Shanghai. Even the Chinese were then often glad of the protection of the foreign settlements.

A great deal of furious criticism has been leveled at the gunboats, those small, low ships which anchored in the rivers, and which were on these waters, ready to protect foreign nationals in times of disorder, only because of the provisions of extraterritoriality.

Many people—a lot of them missionaries—needlessly lost their lives at the hands of unthinking mobs when these little grey boats were not at hand. In the last decades how many foreign nationals, either without trials, or with faked-up, pretended tribunals, have been sentenced to imprisonment (solitary confinement, torture, endless suffering) because they could not appeal to the jurisdiction of a fair court? That was what these boats were intended to prevent, and in fact often did prevent.

Extraterritoriality cannot fairly be taken out of its context. To understand it some historical events must be weighed—not only the slogans of the opposition. For instance, as a small example, one might remember a letter which was sent to London by the British minister in Peking, when that city was under fire, with the Empress Dowager's blessing. In the dispatch was this sentence:

> I should be astonished to learn that while the Chinese Minister in London was preparing his communication his Legation was under a constant fire from British troops, yet it is in a situation analogous to this that the Foreign Representatives at Peking find themselves placed. [August 8, 1900]

When the Settlement had been legally brought together, under the Land Regulations of 1869, it had been recognized that the Council must have its Chinese members, but it was felt that this would have to be deferred, as they were then so inexperienced in the very procedures of such a body and had no background of democratic administration of this sort. The French then took the same stance, and in the same way deferred its execution. It was not till well into the twentieth century that the issue was raised again in a practical way, some of the more progressive elements among the foreigners welcoming the idea of Chinese participation, but the conservatives, now firmly entrenched in what they felt their inalienable rights, opposing such a move. Gradually, as the twenties advanced, the necessity of Chinese representation became more and more favored, and by degrees accepted, till at last in 1930, their number on the Council reached the same figure as that enjoyed by the British.

The history of the administration of the Settlement makes very interesting reading. Though certainly strongly weighted on the side

of the Westerners, it still was in many ways what it claimed to be—
a "model settlement." The problems confronting it were so vast and
it had basically so little ability to exert pressure, that it is really
remarkable how much it accomplished and how fair in the main it
was. The problems of revenue alone were complicated beyond
belief.

The Chinese themselves administered the areas surrounding the
Settlement and the Concession, as well as Pootung, which lay
across the Whangpoo. These sections together comprised a territory and included a population very much greater than those
under foreign jurisdiction. Their mayors were (after 1927) appointed by the Nationalist government in Nanking, and their
powers were wide. Mayors like Wu Te-chen and O. K. Yui were
well-known, highly respected, and much-liked figures in the
whole of the city.

With this background, and even though Shanghai was philistine,
living for trade, it could hardly be dull. We had several New Years,
two Christmases, two Easters, at least a score of National Days,
with parades for Chinese New Year, for the Quatorze Juillet, for
local events like big funerals or marriages, and military parades
when troops landed or embarked. Besides all the different nations,
and the special features they brought with them, their own cuisine, their particular talents, every province in China was represented too—with its special cuisine, its accomplishments. The foreigners put on amateur dramatics which were often so good we
could compare them favorably with professionals, and the Chinese
had their opera, their entertainments.

To the poor Chinese who came in looking for work these pleasures at first meant little. What impressed him were the cheap,
clean tap-water, the drains, the trams and buses, the cinema, the
Chinese department stores, so ably managed, so full of things to
see. These patient, cheerful, hardworking, polite people would
generally enter the city on foot, balancing their baskets on a
shoulder pole. Within the confines of the old Chinese city, or the
foreign sections, they would seek out some lane where a relative
or a guild-brother would give them a corner to sleep in, and help
them find work. They would accept very humble employment, and
be content to live meanly, while cheerfully saving something and
sending it back to the family in the country. The rich came, of
course, in quite another way—but their paths need no description.
Some came for crime, too—to be pickpockets, gamblers, to peddle

opium, some were sold into brothels. There was a big Beggars' Guild in Shanghai; some of their people must have been recruited in the country.

Beggars were ubiquitous in China—in every city, town, and village. This was generally true of the Far East, and stemmed from the same tragic roots—too many people, no welfare on a sufficient scale, not enough work to go round, human exploitation. The beggars fell into two groups: the professionals, with their guilds, and the unfortunates who were obliged to beg or die, dispossessed by flood, famine, war, depression—the people at the end of the tether.

Everywhere you were besieged by them. The professionals were cruel—in order to excite pity, or to make themselves so repulsive that anyone would pay quickly to lose sight of them, they would maim themselves, twist children's limbs to make them seem even more piteous, have women carry starving babies, who would be hired for the purpose. This was part of that callousness toward individual suffering which could occur in a country which exposed its girl babies, sold children into slavery, watched with amusement prisoners being tortured, and was almost always hard to animals—callousness was accepted as an inevitable part of the human scene by the Chinese.

The situation was beyond amelioration from the private point of view, though most of us gave continuously to the swarms of suppliants. But the coppers we handed over could do nothing except buy a bowl of rice, and these people were filthy, ragged, verminous, diseased.

The refugees from areas which had been struck by disaster were easier to help—except that they also were so numerous. These people we would try to help find their feet, we would give them work—we could reach them mentally and plan together. They had skills, too. But altogether the problem was of catastrophic dimensions.

Some of the Shanghai Chinese became our wonderful, faithful, intelligent servants, the servants who were also our friends, who made our lives so superficially easy, who gave us our leisure. They gave us a way of life which is, I am sure, what many people most remember when they think of Shanghai—the comfort it offered.

The poor worked in the factories and mills, for long hours and almost no pay—men, women, and children. The foreign firms drove hard bargains with them, through their Chinese overseers. They worked on the docks. Most of these poor laborers preferred to work for the Europeans rather than for their own people, however—conditions were a little less inhuman in a Western firm. Sometimes a foreign concern would be really good to its workers —up to a point, a paternalistic point. They would put in dispensaries, and occasionally there would be someone in charge of labor relations who would regard these poor people as his brothers, and suffer for them, though his board of directors usually was lacking in any evidence of practical humanity. Business without controls has never been distinguished for its good-heartedness throughout history. And who was to control these businessmen? The Council had no authority of that sort, or very little. It was created and sustained by and for these very people, who sat on its committees.

"Much wants more," the proverb runs, "much wants more."

If the newcomer had some education he might become a clerk. There were plenty of firms, both Chinese and foreign, ready to employ him. However, he faced competition not only from other Chinese but also from Eurasians and Portuguese, who often held such posts. A clerk had to be really effective to keep a job. Still, the Chinese would work for less than anyone else, and they worked well, whatever they did.

They worked in the shops, they swept the streets, they learned to drive cars, buses, and trams, they built, painted, planted, sewed, embroidered, worked in the post offices. They mended everything. Now when it is almost impossible to get anything mended at all, I often look back and marvel at that period, when you sent your lamp to be repaired, and it was back the next day better than ever for a few pennies. Your books were bound, your china riveted together, your furniture kept in perfect order, your quilts recovered, after their down had been aired and shaken, or the cotton teased, your clothes were refurbished, the hems put up or down, your husband's suits turned. It was a world of total service.

The Chinese who had some capital opened their own firms, played the market, bought land, became rich. Some were *compradors* for the foreign businesses, managers or go-betweens between them and the people of the country. In a big firm, like Jardine's, this meant a great position. Their children went to the local schools, and then abroad to study. But Shanghai itself came to have good universities, for the Chinese, St. John's for instance,

Shanghai College, Aurora College (which was French), Futan University, the Shanghai College of Law (which were private), and national universities like Chiao Tung.

The town came to be full of students. As the unrest in the country increased and became more aggressive, these scholars made Shanghai on occasion turbulent, a characteristic at that time of Eastern countries seeking change. The Westerners, unseeing, little realized that our time for this phenomenon was coming. China, however, possessed student bodies inflamed with a more genuine urgency than most of us know—the country was in so parlous a state, and the number of literate, informed persons (even slightly informed) was relatively so small.

But by and large most of us didn't come into contact with these students. Their teachers did, and the people at the "Y," and the missionaries, but forty years ago the different nationalities didn't really mingle very much. The French always kept pretty much to themselves; the British and Americans were fairly close, sometimes very close; the Germans, politics permitting, were generally friendly all round, as were the Swiss. The Japanese we didn't know (*we* being the Anglo-Saxon element), nor most of the White Russians, the Spaniards, the Italians, the Indians, though we were all living side by side. We met only if we were tied to some common interest—like sport—there were then too many barriers to surmount, we felt—religious, economic, traditional—to make social contacts easy and natural. That would not be true today, but this was before World War II—and we saw always before our eyes the unhappy marriages between races, the results of people defying conventions and regretting their acts.

Yet we were so few and the place was so remote and intense that some of us were inevitably swept up into currents far more important, deeper, more significant, than we would have otherwise encountered. Many found themselves in positions much more responsible and lively than they could have had elsewhere, both in their work and in their interests—even in our local entertainments, where we had our own stars.

Some of Shanghai's amateur dramatic performances were extraordinarily good. There were sometimes a few professionals who had somehow come to the city for trade, and who gave their evenings to this old love, training the rest of us. People had the leisure to rehearse, because of the servants. *The Barretts of Wimpole Street*, which was produced in Shanghai about the same time it was running in London, was superbly done. Later, when we saw the movie with Charles Laughton, many of us thought that our Mr. Crane had been as convincing and appalling as Charles Laughton; and we all lost our hearts to Mary Hayley Bell, with her scarlet muff, and her defiance, an unforgettable Henrietta.

Tom Jones, The Mikado (superbly costumed, with beautiful geisha kimonos), and other musicals delighted us, through the quality of some of the singers who had happened to come to the city—they sang too in oratorios, and on special occasions. When *Lady Precious Stream* was interesting the theatrical world, it appeared in Shanghai, mostly acted by Chinese, and most people who had seen it in London preferred our version. We had the advantage in our rich harvest of "return students," who on this rare occasion were willing to be with us.

Then there was *Dear Brutus*, which attained the level of a really great performance, with Rosalind Welch as Margaret. When the artist realizes that she is nothing but a midsummer night's dream, the actor's anguish was so moving that I doubt if anyone who saw the play has ever forgotten it. Now that I have seen so many second- and third-rate plays running in the great capitals of the world, I marvel at our Shanghai amateur theatricals, and wonder how many sitting in the audiences would not themselves be doing better on the stage. So many people can act, but so few have the opportunity.

A few people enhanced careers here, which they would have had in any event, but which China furthered. They seldom stayed in the country, but they came as explorers, collectors, art experts. Langdon Warner and Horace Jayne were among these, coming to examine the Wei sculptures, to go on to Tun-huang—but they never tarried on the Coast or wasted time in Shanghai. Dr. Osvald Sirén was another, coming here to look at Chinese sculpture, gardens, and paintings. He was in and around Shanghai in the thirties, before he became the greatest Western authority on Chinese painting, whose books were to become the standard references. I even heard him give a lecture on the Tao of painting, which I never forgot, and the notes I took then I still have. Lectures like that were rare indeed in Shanghai. I was enraptured by his theme, but remember nothing of the man himself.

Orvar Karlbeck, another distinguished Swede, was then already deeply engrossed in the study of bronzes, and was buying some of the best in the country for the Crown Prince (now the King) of

Sweden. Mr. Karlbeck was a friend of ours. He had come upon this great interest in an apparently fortuitous way, literally almost stumbling upon it. A railway engineer, he was living up on the borders of Anhwei, in a very lonely district, when some of the workmen on the line began to unearth, in the fields through which the railway would run, those great bronzes of antiquity, the priceless treasures of the Shang. He fell in love with them at once, and became one of the most knowledgeable of connoisseurs in this glorious chapter of Chinese art.

James Plumer, who worked for the Customs, had about this time decided that Sung porcelain was really the object of life, and was filling up his house with shards, broken pots he had found at Ch'ing-tê-chen, the old pottery center, and occasionally collectors' pieces. He gave a lecture on this theme once, urging his small but eager audience to start collecting shards, assuring us that you didn't need to have much money occasionally to pick up a real Sung dish, only an eye. He had on the table before him several of his own favorites, one a pale blue, egg-shell thin, almost moonlight-fragile bowl, faintly incised, of Yung Lo ware.

Two of the greatest sinologues of our time never set foot in China: René Grousset and Arthur Waley. They knew the world of antiquity too well, the wonders of the Chou, the Han, the T'ang and Sung, to wish to risk seeing the country in modern times, but their writings are a priceless heritage for us all.

Paul Pelliot was the greatest scholar of all the Frenchmen on the ground. This brilliant figure was as versatile as he was intellectually endowed. He was a member of the French Legation during the siege at Peking, and seems to have made a certain mark then, though only in his early twenties. One evening he climbed the barricades and disappeared, to have, as it transpired later, a dinner with the Manchu dignitary who was in the close confidence of the Empress Dowager, Jung Lu himself. He told Jung Lu that the legations were in good shape, but that some fresh fruit would be welcome, and returned safely to the battered headquarters with some very fine peaches.

Between 1901 and 1906 he was a professor at L'École française d'Extrême Orient in Hanoi. It was after this experience that he went on those expeditions into central Asia and northwest China which made their mark on the world—his discoveries at Tunhuang were of monumental importance, as far as the West was concerned, opening our eyes to the wonders of the Buddhistic caves. His numbering of the caves was so significant that even today the Pelliot numbers are cited as auxiliary identifications. As the editor of *T'oung Pao* he guided and formed European knowledge of things Chinese for decades, being besides a curator, a translator, and a tireless historian, with an inspired understanding of Chinese art. He lived till 1945—one of the men who opened the way for future generations.

One of the most significant of his contemporaries was the great Berthold Laufer, associated both with Germany and the United States. Born in Cologne, and educated at the universities of Berlin and Leipzig, it was the Field Museum of Natural History in Chicago (where in 1915 he was appointed Curator of Anthropology) which became the setting for his publications and research. His writings on jade, on Chinese pottery and porcelain, have remained classics, though his great interest was in the peoples living on the borders of China. He was a man whom everyone loved; speak of him to an "old hand" and you encounter a smile of real affection.

Then there was the Canadian, Bishop William Charles White, who, aside from his evangelical work in China, made such great contributions to our artistic, archaeological, and ethnic knowledge of the country. It was he who first began to probe the issue of the Chinese Jews, and what had happened to them at K'ai-fêng-fu.

But you could have counted such people almost on the fingers of your hands, in the ports. There were more of them in Peking, a leisured place, always an artistic center.

What most of the foreigners were interested in in Shanghai was sport, athletics, having a good time, parties, dinners, dancing in the beautiful old Majestic Hotel, or the Cercle Sportif Françias, or the nightclubs. Most of the nationals formed their own clubs, where they could swim, play tennis, and entertain each other as they liked. The Chinese came to be very angry about such places, because they could not join them. But, of course, that's the nature of a club—it is created on the basis of selection, including persons of a certain category, with specific things in common. The Europeans in China were often homesick and lonely, many of them never had any understanding of, or sympathy for, the country in which they worked, and in their free hours they wanted to be by themselves, speaking out freely, without fear of offending those of another race. They wanted to be at ease. And they often excluded persons of their own nation, of whom they disapproved, snobbishly, economically, politically. This is a commonplace of life. But the Chinese, with their new and terribly sensitive nationalism, took such attitudes personally.

Most of the clubs began quite early in the life of the foreign settlements, before the Chinese wished to meet us socially, before they had any wish to play games themselves, when swimming in a common pool would have revolted them, even if they had ever dreamed of swimming at all. The pattern once set was hard to break; it was a pity that nothing could be done to soften these barriers, which came further to exacerbate and bedevil the relationship between us all.

Until very recently both races frowned upon mixed marriages, though they existed, for the most part unhappily. And if young people come together at clubs, of course some of them will marry. Once barriers of this sort have been swept away it is not easy to imagine how fierce they could be, how deeply people took them to heart. The exclusiveness of the Westerners' clubs in the East was not intentionally a mean gesture, it was part of its century.

City Streets, Establishments, Attitudes

WHERE THE SOOCHOW CREEK met the Whangpoo was the best site on the Bund; here stood the British Consulate surrounded by green lawns. For many decades this Consulate was the most important one in the country—probably that was true of it during the whole period of Western dominance on the Coast. It was a source of power, prestige, and control.

In the Treaty Port era, and almost up to the outbreak of World War II, all over the world, in any event, consuls were important people; the Chinese consular service was, among all these, particularly significant. Ambassadors had not yet proliferated in number only to decline in effectiveness, and most world capitals at that time had no more than a Minister in a Legation. The British Consul General in Shanghai was locally felt to be a great man; the post carried a knighthood and was an onerous responsibility.

Not far from the Consulate, on the Bund, facing the river, was the Hong Kong and Shanghai Bank, an imposing domed building, approached by wide steps, which were guarded by two large bronze lions. It was a superstition that touching these would give strength, and passersby kept their paws and flanks bright and glistening.

On the Bund, too, stood the Customs House, which in the thirties had been given a new building, a fine place with pillars and pediments. Colonel Hayley Bell told me of a conversation which he had chanced to hear when he was the Commissioner of Customs after the new building had been opened, between two old countrymen who had come into the city and were looking about the Bund.

I should perhaps first explain that our money was reckoned in two units—either the dollar, or the *tael*. The dollar had originally come into the country during the Ming, as the Spanish *peso*, and from Mexico, on account of the intricacies of trade. Though dollars were now minted in China, and officially called *yuan*, the usual term for them was still "Mex." The *tael* was worth slightly more than the dollar, and was used in such transactions as rents and buying land, and reckoning up large amounts. Both *taels* and *yuan* could be exchanged for solid silver, as *sycee*, in ingot shaped like a boat, and which the Dutch had called *schuyt* for this reason; the Anglo-Saxons pronounced this as "shoe." The Chinese name for these lumps of bullion was derived from the fact that the silver was ductile enough to be drawn into fine threads.

Though the dollar was only worth, much of the time, about an English shilling, this did not necessarily mean that everything was correspondingly cheap. Land in Shanghai, particularly on or near the Bund, was astronomically expensive, even comparable with the cost of ground in New York City, astonishingly enough. This was partly because people were reluctant to build outside the foreign enclaves, partly because the rich merchants, like Sassoon, for instance, could pay such prices, and get their money back with good interest.

There was not much land to spare in the Settlement and the French Concession—of course it was expensive. Labor was cheap for building, but there was a severe construction problem, due to the marshy nature of our ground. Shanghai was right on the water level, and always saturated with moisture—if you dug a pit three feet down it would soon fill itself up with water, so that building had to be done on a type of raft, a costly procedure.

Some of this would have been understood vaguely by the two peasants whose remarks arrested Colonel Hayley Bell. They were standing looking up at the Customs House, awed by its size and appearance, admiring it, speculating as to its cost. "That place," said one to the other, "must have cost a thousand *taels*!" In a sense he was not so far off the mark—accustomed to reckoning his own purchases in coppers, he had named a figure which to him was beyond the imagination.

The whole structure of the Western position in China resting on trade, the question of duties, tariffs, and the management of the revenue arising from them was naturally of first importance to the newcomers. The issue had been resolved by the development of the Chinese Maritime Customs Service, a unique instrument.

This organization came into being during the T'ai-p'ing Rebellion, when the region around Shanghai fell into rebel hands. The three senior consuls of the city (the British, American and French) decided that the best thing they could do would be to take control of the local Customs House, in order to prevent it being captured by these soldiers. That was in 1854; the Rebellion would not end for another ten years, with the fall of Nanking in 1864. In 1858 rules of trade were drawn up as a part of another, larger, treaty, which stated that the dues levied at the various open ports must be uniform, and that foreigners would take part in the administration of the revenues, with the agreement of the Chinese Government. Not very long afterward Robert Hart (later Sir Robert) was appointed inspector general of the Service, a post he held for nearly half a century.

Before this time customs dues had been subject to extremely arbitrary and personal levies, all over the country. An unscrupulous official or the government itself could, and did, exact heavy fees wherever and whenever they liked.

Robert Hart, a man of integrity and high intelligence, was very sympathetic with the Chinese, and throughout his long career was always conscious that in this post he was their servant. He directed the Customs in the interests of the Chinese Government, which came to repose great trust in him, and it was a relief to the people of the country that these funds were handled with perfect honesty, becoming a source of income upon which Peking could count. The Westerners gave themselves preferential treatment in the matter of duties, but they must have more than compensated for this through assuring that what was paid came through to the last copper cash.

The Customs Service was wholly international, but modeled on the British Civil Service. No one particular nation was ever permitted a preponderant share in its control, and side by side worked British, Americans, French, Germans, Scandinavians, Russians, and many other nationals. It was an honor to belong to the Customs Service; its employees loved it and were loyal to it.

They all had to study Chinese, and most became very proficient in it.

Sir Robert Hart himself became so identified with the Chinese scene that when the Boxer Rebellion was about to break out, he could not bring himself to believe that what did in fact come to pass, was possible. He lived in Peking, where for many decades the main administration of the Customs was located, in order to be close to the Chinese Government.

The Chinese staff was for a long time limited to very junior posts, but eventually this was altered, and these people took their proper places beside their colleagues of the other nations. The fall of the Manchus, the Russian Revolution, and World War I disrupted to some extent the personnel of the Service, when the Germans, Austrians, and Russians were obliged to leave it. After 1927 the Customs Service came under the direct control of the Chinese, under the inspectorate of Sir Frederick Maze.

If it was unjust for the foreigners to protect themselves by fixed low tariffs, it must be also admitted that the financial stability and the possibility of continuing trade (which was of advantage to everyone) in that turbulent era was enormously promoted by this well-run, absolutely honest, effective Service. It was above the convulsions which shook the country, and could withstand the power of the warlords and other temporary quasi authorities.

The Customs also took care of the lighting and buoying of the Coast and many of the inland waterways, maintaining a fleet of vessels to assist them in this. The harmony within the Service was proverbial, and a comforting element in an environment where there was a great deal of discord. The perquisites were great— men could have as much as two years' leave at a time, it was an interesting, well-paid job, not too arduous, and offering many opportunities to see the country. A post in the Customs was a plum, in fact.

One of the "great" commissioners was Sir Francis Aglen, who served from 1910 to 1927, years of notable service, but it was Sir Robert Hart who embodied the Customs; he was looked upon as an oracle, the figure who had managed to cement strong and felicitous ties between the Chinese and the West. Years after he was gone, if anything alarming suddenly befell us, people would say that it was Sir Robert turning over in his grave.

The Salt Gabelle (salt tax administration) was another institution which the foreigners managed for a long time, working with

Chinese, in a friendly and mutually advantageous way; the postal service was also in this category. Ventures like these represented a form of tutelage, but when they were formed, the Chinese had need of that sort of guidance—they could not then have done it nearly as well alone. They had missed too many centuries of development in this sort of competence through their own determined seclusion.

Going downtown in Shanghai meant going toward the Bund, generally by Nanking Road, the major artery, but there were a half a dozen other parallel roads leading to the river, each named after a city: Peking Road, Kiukiang Road, Foochow Road. The streets at right angles to these were called after the provinces: Szechwan Road, Fukien Road, Honan Road, and the like. All these ran between low buildings—few structures in Shanghai were more than four or five stories high. All the Chinese shops, which far outnumbered the Western ones, had their names painted in huge handsome characters on long panels overhanging the sidewalks, greatly enhancing the look of the area.

The foreign shops—Whiteaway Laidlaw, and Weeks, which were small department stores, Kelly and Walsh, the booksellers and publishers (whose volumes are collectors' pieces today), Bianchi's, the Italian restaurant, Sam Lazaro, the music shop and piano importer, made much less of a show with their horizontal signs tucked away up over the show-windows. The Roman script is beautiful when it is well done, which is seldom; in the ordinary way it can't hold its own against the Arabic or Chinese. It's much less pictorial, much more practical.

The Commercial Press had an office downtown on Nanking Road, too, but this represented only a small part of it. This was a very remarkable firm, dealing primarily but not exclusively in Chinese books, and was an indication of how far literacy had advanced in the country. Beginning in 1896, established by a few Chinese who had been trained by foreigners in Shanghai, it so quickly made its name by its excellent performance that by the late twenties it covered twenty acres of ground in Shanghai alone. It had then 1,500 agencies.

By that time it was estimated that there were over seven million Chinese children in school, and the Commercial Press printed a great proportion of their textbooks. It was keenly interested in the many different plans afoot to combat illiteracy, and published books on a wide range of subjects: science, mathematics, history, geography, art, ethics. This firm printed newspapers and magazines, sold paper and games, and generally showed itself to be a lively, effective, and very important firm, a great firm. We used to buy art books there with reproductions of Chinese pictures, on soft paper, all the commentaries of course in Chinese. We would buy Chinese writing paper there too, beautiful paper, with long indentations to guide the characters, each sheet decorated with orchids, blossoms, mountain scenes, the classic subjects of the Chinese artist.

The downtown streets were always jammed with traffic of all kinds: some cars, many, many rickshaws, bicycles, hand carts, huge carts pushed and pulled by straining coolies, lorries, wheelbarrows, laden with anything from vegetables to silver bars, and carriers with shoulder poles balancing full baskets at each end. Often these baskets would be full of squawking chickens, or hissing geese. Itinerant restaurants were carried by on the shoulders of their cook-owner, ingenious paintable arrangements, containing everything needed to prepare tea, rice, and noodles, from a brazier to the bowls.

More pitiable, even, than the rickshaw coolies, were the men, women, and children whose existence depended on their being almost literally beasts of burden—pulling carts, pushing carts, hauling loads, either in company with each other, or in the country beside a mule, a donkey, a buffalo. Their ranks included the old and children, who would take their places beside a vehicle, shouldering a rope, or putting their fragile weight against a wheel —though they appeared fragile, and their weight was small, they were nevertheless strong. In this way almost everything imaginable was moved; in the cities like Shanghai, Canton, Hankow, Tientsin, there were many trucks and trolleys, but there was never enough motorized transport to begin to compass the demand, and it was more expensive than coolie haulage.

Coal, lumber, bales of everything, earthenware jars full and empty, pipes, machinery, country produce of all sorts from vegetables to bamboo furniture were heaped up on carts or wheelbarrows—anything that could be pushed or pulled—and propelled for a pittance by these desperate individuals, who were always on the ragged edge of destitution and exhaustion, but who carried on. They also performed the horrible task of pushing the carts which took night soil out of the towns and cities to the fields.

Though they suffered all too obviously, they still worked to the last ounce of their energy, uncomplainingly, even cheerfully, and with a visible pride of achievement. This is characteristic of the race. Somehow they manage to perform this sort of task without loss of self-respect (that is reserved for other causes). And all this remains true today—motor transport is still too costly and too little in China to meet the need for transport, and people must do it—the old, the disregarded, the unfortunate—women and men.

Driving amidst this throng, which also included carefree pedestrians who much preferred to walk in the middle of the road, took very special talents; you had to be calm and careful to an unusual extent, and of course most people weren't. The extreme type of driver simply pressed on regardless, roaring down Szechwan Road or Avenue Edward VII as he does every place else in the world. There were a lot of accidents.

The new Chinese drivers had no idea at all of how to gauge speed, any more than did most pedestrians. They weren't used to it then. Their teachers learned to make novices sit beside a chauffeur and be driven about for a full month before they ever touched a wheel themselves, simply to try and grasp what it was all about. On the roads most drivers never took their hand off the horn, while people darted across their path with the most hair-raising disregard for what might happen. It was lucky to have a close shave, they believed. You cut off devils in that way. The small craft on the river had the same notion, and would cut across an oncoming steamer's bows for the same motive, often with fatal results.

The average Chinese had then a tremendous inheritance of superstition. The lower sort of Taoism had fostered it, but it was probably so much a product of the countryside and legends that it would have thrived without priestly help. You were always aware of this trait about you. For instance, in the towns you would see on thousands of roofs, bottles so arranged that their open necks lay outward, ready to catch any troublesome demons which might want to mischief the family within. Spirit screens still blocked the old-style type of Chinese entrance, to cut off these evil spirits which, being basically stupid, traveled only in straight lines.

Szechwan Road and Kiukiang Road were particularly busy though narrow streets, full of open-fronted small shops. Some of these were, in a fashion, banks, and spent much of their day changing money. Until, late in the Kuomintang era, money really began to be stable, there were constant fluctuations in the rate of the currency from one place to another—a dollar in Shanghai would be worth somewhat more than a Swatow dollar for instance, and the number of copper cash you could get for a penny also varied. We called these divisions "small money."

This business of the exchange was reflected on the international scene by the exchange brokers, who handled the buying and selling of different moneys as people made their contracts. After he left the tea trade, my father became an exchange broker; it was exciting business, limited to only a few people, working between the banks and the firms. The brokers went about in traps, the ponies galloping down the roads, the *mafoos* driving with great style, and their employers standing up ready to spring out and dash up the steps of the Banque Belge pour Étrangères, or some such place, to catch a favorable rate. It was the quickest way. Though the brokers had a very short day, they changed their ponies three times, twice in the morning, once in the afternoon, all for darting about so small an area. These traps further enlivened the medley of traffic of the downtown streets.

Most of the Chinese shops were open-fronted, closed completely by long shutters at night or in troublous times. As you passed them you heard the loud, firm click of the abacuses, reckoning everything up. The streets rang with sounds—bicycle bells, peddlers crying their wares, horns, people yelling at each other to get out of the way, ponies' hoofs, and beyond them this click-click-click, from the shops. In among big places were many small shops, which somehow seemed to make enough to keep going, though the rents were certainly very high.

One such establishment, on Szechwan Road, was called the Axe Company, which sold haberdashery. Opposite stood the Freedom Company. Here my father became rather friendly with the proprietor, over the purchase of ties and socks, so much so that one day he asked him why the place was called the Freedom Company. The owner explained that for long years he had been an employee of the Axe Company, and when he was at last able to leave it and set up on his own, he felt he must have a name expressive of his new-found joy and exhilaration.

Places such as this were interesting in advertising, and often sent out masterpieces like this:

MAJESTIC
DRY CLEANING AND DYEING WORKS
570 Szechuen Road (Opposite Chinese Y.M.C.A.)
Telephone No. 19666
Shanghai, China

Shanghai————

Dear M

How glad that spring has come! the earth has been asleep, and is now awaking to life again. The days are growing longer, the sun rises earlier each morning and the weather will be warm.

Everybody will change their wearing, but it was dirty already. Which it will mildew in the moldy season. So it is must dry cleaning or dyeing and after keep in the case, that will be nothing appear.

Who will holding it? the MAJESTIC dry cleaning and dyeing works, will undertake anythings. So that we informing to you. If you are set in order, that only give a telephone or a letter to our office. Then we will send the bearer to your dwelling, that you are saving your times and expenses.

We remain

Yours very truly

Where Avenue Edward VII entered the Bund, standing on the embankment, very conspicuous, was the city's chief War Memorial, dedicated to the men from Shanghai (on the Allied side) who gave their lives in the First World War. The wide bronze wings of the angel on its high pedestal were silhouetted against the river and the shipping. As it was placed just on the dividing line between the French Concession and the International Settlement, it marked, also, a change in the nature of the foreshore, even to an extent, of the ships. Often a French gunboat lay at anchor here, like the *Henri Quatre*, locally known as the *Angry Cat*. The French quais were workmanlike and busy, but unlike the Settlement authorities, the French had made no effort to embellish their river frontage. The Bund lost at once at this junction its proud, imperialistic, good looks, and took on something of the rakish, attractive, unkempt air of a small French port.

The European population of Shanghai suffered sufficiently in that war. Much of the British youth and the French left as soon as it was declared, never to return. To the Chinese, this conflict came as a great shock—that is, to the relatively few Chinese who realized what was going on. Those who had come to think that the

West, and perhaps also Christianity, held the key to the world's problems, were shaken, and doubted. The standing of the European, his morality, fell in their esteem.

The handsome War Memorial was an unusual gesture for Shanghai. It was seldom that anything was done that was not utilitarian, no one tried to make the city beautiful, and there were no civic elegancies. This was partly because most of the Westerners were transients, no one intended to *retire* in China. Most of the people who spent their working lives in the country would go back, in the end, to their homes, and feel nostalgic about China for the rest of their lives, missing it keenly, restless, unsettled.

In spite of this feeling of impermanence among us, the city grew by leaps and bounds. The rapidity of its growth, and the constant going and coming of its affluent Western population, its obviously temporary political structure, made it a place of hasty and expedient manoeuvres. It was remarkable, given all this, how much was done on a solid basis, how many schools were built, how much effected for the public health. To the Chinese coming in from the hinterland, these Treaty Ports like Shanghai or Tientsin gave a glimpse of something entirely new—a world of street lighting, of a *fire service!* The foreigners in Shanghai had not only a professional fire service, but, to supplement it, as it was small, a volunteer organization also, formed of enthusiasts who were always ready to rush to their engines at a moment's notice and do what they could to save some part of the town. This was an impressive thing to the Chinese, who in the old days, if they came from most country areas, were accustomed to seeing people come out with drums and cymbals when a fire started, trying to frighten the fire devils away, as all that could be done.

When you went downtown in Shanghai, as you neared the River, you often had the pleasure of watching a ship pass across your line of vision—the black hull of a coaster, or the high carved poop of a junk with its slanting sails, which seemed to glide over the cars on the road in front of you. On foggy autumnal mornings when the Bund was shrouded in mist, foghorns echoed down between the buildings, their melancholy, loud, reiterative warning reverberating on each side of the road. Sometimes we could even hear the thrash of a propeller. There was no radar then, and the foghorns never slackened as long as the mist endured, nor did the softer notes coming from the conch shells blown from the junks.

It was the River itself which was the essential physical feature of this cosmopolitan, burgeoning city. Everything seemed ultimately tied to the water then—everything except ideas, and ideas of course are everywhere, light as gossamer, strong as steel, constantly rebuffed, always returning, to be reshaped, rejected, welcomed back, torn to shreds, coaxed back once more. You can't do that to a river, it's easier to rest on in a way, though in the end, of course, it's not half as substantial, it's a flimsy thing, as time passes, and ideas change even its significance.

The coastal steamers and the Yangtze shipping tied up at the wharves, either on the Shanghai side, or across the river on the Pootung bank. Most of them berthed on the Shanghai side. Most of the warships, the cruisers, and destroyers moored in midstream, except for the little river gunboats. The great ocean-going vessels had to wait up in the roads beyond Woosung, but we never missed them, as the Whangpoo was always alive with traffic, with tugs, tenders, lines of barges being towed, with sampans bobbing about on the choppy brown water taking passengers or sailors back to their ships, and especially with junks, ocean-going junks and river junks, with their glorious rich brown sails, slatted lug sails, often patched in a variety of opposing colors, always beautiful. The river had no beauty of itself; it was about a mile wide, brown, running between flat banks, but the shipping made it a splendid place and one never tired of watching it. Country people clustered at the wharves and jetties, loading up flat-bottomed boats with huge jars of soy sauce, taking on or off great stacks of cabbages, baskets of chickens, rolls of mats, dumping down chickens with their feet tied together, putting a baby near a gunwale. The children were far too sensible ever to fall in. They sat placidly and watched the panorama of life as did we all.

The Whangpoo offered an endless variety—like the city itself. Vladivostok, Dairen, Tientsin, Chefoo, Wei-hai-wei, Tsingtao sent their products down to Shanghai, meeting here the northbound shipping from the Philippines, Borneo, Sumatra, Singapore, Hong Kong, Canton, Macao, as well as the old emporiums of Foochow, Amoy, Swatow, Ningpo. They met in these waters, too, the ships of the Japanese merchant marine, bustling, ubiquitous. At that time, and because labor was plentiful, most of these vessels were smart—the crews were always painting them, swabbing the decks, polishing the brass. The warships of course were gleaming with order and care. But they never surpassed the small Chinese craft in beauty and line.

The Chinese had an innate feeling for proportion and décor,

which was apparent even in the most casual sampan which ever came lazily down the Soochow Creek, ready to ferry anyone over to the other side. The canals and streams all over the region made their way to the creek, and thence down the river, and on them floated a myriad little boats, every one a theme for a painting, graceful, brownish, honest as the wood of which they were all made. They were nearly all propelled by the *ulow*, a great sweep at the stern, balanced on a pin, and worked by one person or half a dozen. If you tried yourself to handle a *ulow*, you found it wasn't nearly as easy as it seemed, the oar was always falling off the pin. But five-year-olds who had grown up on the water did it with perfect ease and success.

The junks varied in form and style from province to province, from river to river, suiting their capacities to local conditions. Most of them had great eyes, and were carved about the poop and cabin. There was a size of craft between the junk and the sampan, a long, low boat with a cabin formed by an arc of matting, which was also very prevalent. All of these vessels were plied by their sailors with a graceful, easy, unconscious dexterity, as they ma-noeuvred through the currents of the Whangpoo, or rode the tides. The boat people, lithe, unhurried, barefoot most of the year, could bring their craft inshore with a turn of the wrist, while someone else aboard minded a little brazier at the stern, fanning the charcoal while the rice boiled. The junks made little gardens of potted plants aft, and you could see their cats, the washing hanging on a bamboo pole, a bird in a cage on the foredeck—it made you long to go aboard. These people lived on their boats but in Shanghai we had no floating city of boatmen, as in Hong Kong or Canton.

We who were used to these active waterways, with cargo cease-lessly passing on them, find it hard to understand why in the West so many rivers are idle, almost empty. The roads have robbed them of their traffic and the cheerful life which went with it. Boatmen are generally less anxious and careworn than landsmen—they have learned to go with the stream, and so much of their round lies at hand. Your bowl of rice is ready on deck, and as you eat it you can watch the shore slip by and see a flock of ducks being herded up-stream, there's that wonderful blend of move-ment and change, and still a settled home. These people didn't worry about their children missing an education—they didn't ex-pect such bounty then.

Anchored in midstream or tied up alongside the jetties were the

liners. Only the largest had to wait in the roads beyond Woosung;
the Whangpoo was full of ships which had crossed the Pacific, or
come from Europe via the Suez Canal, our indispensable water-
way. Everyone used it who went west except for the lightly-laden
who followed the Trans-Siberian route—some people had been
through the Canal as much as thirty times, or more. The very idea
of its being closed would have been horrifying to us, unthinkable.
It was a necessity for freight, mail, and people.

A great deal of the freight was loaded manually, and here, as
everywhere in the country when the coolies were working together, they would lighten their task with chants. A leader would
half-sing, half-call out some sentence, and the others would repeat
a few tones. The themes chosen by the foremen were essentially
impromptu, and would be like "Oh look at this funny-looking
foreigner coming down to the docks," and they would reply knowingly, in short sounds whose rhythm helped their toil. There were
plenty of cries of "*Ai ya!*" How hard they worked! Often their
burdens would be too hard even to leave them breath for a chant.
But that terrible pressure of so many people wanting work never
let anyone slacken, though they didn't appear to hurry or bustle.
It was just that it was almost unremitting.

Light, portable restaurants, selling noodles and rice, would always be near the docks, ready for travelers or coolies. They sold
tea and twisted bread fried in deep fat. But generally you would
see the laborers, to whom even a few coppers were a great expense,
squatting in a circle, each holding his bowl of rice, with a common
dish of cabbage or small fish set in front of them all—meager-
enough rations for such active men. Yet their strength seemed ready
to meet any demand. Their muscles, under that glistening amber
skin, delighted the sculptor.

Summer was the typhoon season. The Jesuits out at Zikawei
would tell us when one was coming, and the big ships would leave
the river to ride out whatever was coming far out to sea, if they
could. The small craft tied up and hoped for the best. People
remembered great storms. There was one my parents used to
speak of, when the whole Bund was covered with tugs and junks
which had been simply lifted out of the water and hurled ashore
by the force of the wind. That must have been even before World
War I—my father came out in 1901, and my mother as a bride in
1906. These catastrophes marked the years, as they do everywhere. At the time when the Japanese were advancing on Shang-

hai in 1937, there was a particularly terrible typhoon in the South China Seas, which wrought great mischief in Hong Kong. One huge liner of 30,000 tons was tossed up on the rocks in the harbor, something which was locally a cause for rejoicing, as it put a dock company, much in need of work, on its feet.

There was a semaphore tower down on the Bund, which used to run up signals to warn us of how strong the winds might be, and which got its information from the Zikawei Observatory and the Jesuit meteorologists. They would also fire a warning gun or maroons. A lot of lives were always lost in typhoons—how many, who could know? The unnumbered poor living afloat, how many of them may have disappeared? When a coaster simply disappeared that was known of course, with awe and consternation. On shore things were knocked this way and that, and the city would be flooded, it was so low anyway, but that didn't disconcert us. The Chinese were resilient, a typhoon cooled the city and cleaned it, it was exciting. People will rise to a storm.

Today the significance of being a maritime city has been muted. The air has done away with many of the differences between inland and coastal regions, but then everything seemed to depend on the port itself—the mails, cargo, people. We felt not so far from Manila, Singapore, Colombo; we knew that wood oil, tungsten, soy-beans, and hundreds of other things were going east, and paper, oil, machinery, were coming in.

In downtown Shanghai was the Cathedral, presided over by a Dean of the Church of England, with a Boys' Cathedral School nearby. There was a Girls' Cathedral School, too, but farther out on Yates Road. The most distinguished pupil it ever had was Peggy Hookham, whose father worked for a tobacco company. Even then her dancing on special school days excited comment, but most of us did not take such remarks seriously, alas. We did not realize that there in our midst sprang and glided the future Margot Fonteyn.

The Cathedral was a patriotic and religious center for the traditional part of the British community, including the forces, military and naval, but the most memorable wedding ever celebrated there, I think, was that of the Chinese film star, Butterfly Wu, who, to everyone's surprise, said she was a member of the Church of England.

The ceremony took place one Saturday in the mid-thirties, and made something of a local sensation. We all wondered what Dean Trivett really thought of it. Butterfly Wu was a great name in the Chinese world of the cinema—beautiful and talented—also married. Even the Westerners knew of her. The cinemas in Shanghai boomed, we were all fans, but most of the films were Hollywood pictures, which the Chinese also attended with enthusiasm.

What had happened to her husband, we wondered, hearing that she was now uniting herself to a handsome young modern Chinese in the traditional Western way, in white with a veil and orange blossoms.

White is the Chinese color for mourning, and to change over to it as a bridal symbol was quite an important step in the modernization of Chinese women. The day of the scarlet-clad maiden, carried to her new home in a fine sedan chair with a procession of liveried flunkies carrying her trousseau, had not yet passed; we still often heard gongs beating for these parades, and would see the freshly-varnished bridal furniture being carried down a road, with piles of bright quilts, handsome vases, and the traditional wedding geese.

Perhaps Butterfly Wu had had something of this sort once, but this time she had arranged things very differently. She had a long train of attendants, the chief flower girl being designated in the papers as the Chinese Shirley Temple. The wedding was to take place early in the afternoon; long before that the church was filled with Chinese guests, who, as they would have done at an ordinary Chinese wedding, passed the time in gossip and laughter, even eating oranges and spitting out sunflower seeds in the pews, while boys kept them supplied with hot towels, if the papers were to be believed. Shanghai shuddered or laughed at these heresies, described with great gusto by a delighted press.

In accordance with the old Chinese custom of a shrinking bride, Butterfly Wu was about an hour late on purpose; during this time the unruffled bridegroom and his eight ushers, all of whom wore huge, bright boutonnières on their white flannel suits, paraded up and down the main aisle of the Cathedral, to help keep the guests amused. Shanghai wasn't experienced in the flamboyant ways of film stars, but it was a sign of the times, it showed that even in the International Settlement patterns were changing, and not always with violence and ill-will—sometimes merriment had its day, too.

Water

S HANGHAI'S DOWNTOWN AREA first included a rather small section
bounded on three sides by water: the Whangpoo, the Soochow Creek, and the Yang King Pang. The Soochow Creek was a
part of the Grand Canal, and an integral part of the water-borne
traffic of the region, where most of the towns and villages relied on
creeks for their transport, rather than roads. The Soochow Creek
was always full of junks, long lines of barges being towed by tugs,
sampans, ferries, and other miscellaneous craft, among these
(within the city) the sculls of the Shanghai Rowing Club.

The Yang King Pang, a particularly filthy and malodorous piece
of water, was finally filled in and turned into Avenue Edward VII,
marking the boundary between the Settlement and the French
Concession. The tea firm for which my father came out to China
was on the Yang King Pang, near the Bund. The family lived
upstairs, and it was here that my older sister was born.

All these streams and creeks and rivers, like practically all the
waterways of China, were polluted beyond the imagination. This
seemed unavoidable in a country like China, which was, except in
a very few cities, entirely without running water, drains, water-
borne sewage, or any proper facilities for the disposal of waste.
Anyway, down there on the delta all the water was inevitably
muddy, heavy with silt. The modern homes in the Treaty Ports,

and slowly in a few other cities, came to adopt modern plumbing, but the country as a whole never did, nor has it now.

As for the ordinary disposable articles, every tin, every bottle and jar, every scrap of cloth or old shoe that was thrown out, then began its life of real usefulness, to someone. There wasn't as much to throw away as now, in that things weren't packaged, there wasn't this vast sea of plastic. Your napkins and handkerchiefs were of cloth, generally linen, if you were a Westerner, and monogrammed, edged with lace, and washed and ironed by *amah*. Your food arrived in a basket, hanging from a bamboo pole. Up-country many purchases would be wrapped in lotus leaves. Of course there was some paper around things, but that was used in laying the fires, not thrown out.

The city creeks, the canals which nourished the towns and moats—and in our delta many places were as watery as Venice—were dirty and even foul, unless like the Soochow Creek they had something of a current, a little occasional push of the tide, to keep the water moving. China wasn't *clean*—it was too crowded, too poor, there were too many flies, cockroaches, rats. People were personally clean if they could manage it, according to their own standards, doing what they could with limited water, which had to be carried in by bucketfuls, which was too often cold and not pure to start with. By and large hygienic standards were low; the country was still fundamentally medieval; beds and clothing were frequently verminous. There was no tradition of daily public bathing, as in Japan, though there were bathhouses. The women were almost invariably neat, modest, as groomed as circumstances would allow, even dainty.

It costs money to be clean. Missionaries have told me of the joy with which humble women in their parishes would welcome a clean, cheap, respectable bathhouse, if one were built for them. Then they would delight in washing their babies, and revel in the hot water for themselves. Much of the year in their poor homes it was really too cold for them to bathe their small children. But there were never enough people to set up bathhouses of this sort for them.

From the point of view of the friendly and curious stranger, it was a great drawback to have the native inns and facilities so dirty—it meant that even if there were a season free from nearby banditry or wars, you couldn't go off and explore, particularly if you were a girl. Where could you spend a night? The answer was often houseboating. But that took a lot of arranging and was an expense—and it kept you apart, out of touch with people on the land. All this medievalism, this absence of machinery and appliances made the country very delightful to the eye—no water towers, no gas tanks or hard roads, no noisy pumps—but there was the other side to the coin, and that was a hard one for the people who really had to live with it, the poor countrymen themselves.

The people washed their rice and drew the water they washed themselves in from the creeks, if they lived in the country villages, unless they had, perhaps, a convenient local well—a well probably of doubtful purity. They emptied their receptacles into the same thick, muddy waters, on which the boats passed. What else could they do? They had found, over the centuries, that it was better to boil the water they drank, whether or not they could afford the luxury of tea leaves—they were not drinkers of fresh water. All this, however, began to change as the Kuomintang started their massive plans for public works, plans so cruelly checked by the attack of the Japanese.

At that time infant mortality was still staggering, but those who survived infancy had an almost unbelievable stamina. A German doctor, long in the country, who gave much of his time to a free clinic, used to tell my mother stories of how men would come into his surgery in the last stages of tuberculosis. If they had been Westerners, he said, they could not have sat up, let alone walked to see a doctor. They did not possess anything, not even the barest necessities of life, they would not have a change of clothes, they never had enough to eat, they lived in dreadful slums. Yet they would not only survive, they would recover under his treatment.

Still, in spite of this, even with the testimony of the endurance of their soldiers (when properly motivated and cared for), it was also true that the average life expectancy of the Chinese was only twenty-seven or twenty-eight. The enormous toll of the infants partly accounted for this, along with the recurring famines, epidemics, and wars.

How terribly hard life was for these people! Fully aware of it, often basically pessimistic and melancholy, they would seldom betray their anguish. On the surface they were a smiling people, laughing uproariously at jokes, full of mockery and humor, civil and easy in their ways—up to a point, up to that sudden savage breaking point, when they would throw off every restraint, and let themselves go in murderous impulses. "So kind up to moment of their cruelty," was a true summary. No people ever worked harder, and more cheerfully, under conditions which were from time immemorial harsh, unjust, and ill-rewarded.

Tea

THOUGH IT DECLINED in relative importance as time passed, tea was always a significant part of the China trade. Most of the old foreign tea firms were on Peking Road, near the Bund; sometimes as you sat inside a *hong*, sipping and tasting, you heard not only foghorns, but even ships' bells, as the vessels went by a few hundred yards away.

The ceilings of the *hongs* were immensely high, because it was necessary to have huge windows, boarded up nearly to the top, with an open funnel left through which the pure north light poured down on long counters where the tea was measured out and studied for the color of the leaf. This design had been evolved long ago, and no one ever altered it. As the busy season for the tea merchant is in the summer, the high ceilings, with their rotating fans, were a boon to everyone working there, in those unairconditioned days.

The two important points with tea are the leaf, and the cup. As for the leaf, the best description for it was written in 780, in the *Tea Classic*: "The best quality leaves must have creases like the leathern boot of Tatar horsemen, curl like the dewlap of a mighty bullock, unfold like a mist rising out of a ravine, gleam like a lake touched by a zephyr, and be wet and soft like fine earth newly swept by rain." Good tea is like that still—that was not too much to ask. But you had to be on the lookout for these characteristics.

A Chinese teaman would come in from Chekiang or Fukien with samples of the new season's crop. These people were known and on good terms with the foreign *hongs*, everyone was pleased to meet again. This being an old-fashioned country trade, these men still wore gowns and soft shoes and had ceremonious manners.

Exact amounts of the new crop would be weighed on a small balance, and then put into little handleless white cups, which were ranged round a circular table, and a precise amount of boiling water would be poured on them. The taster would sit at the table, swinging it round, and tasting from one cup after another, and spitting out the tea. No one could drink all that tea at a time. After a time he would be clear in his own mind as to which of these shone out like a star. The color of the leaf had also to be considered, and the color of the tea once the leaf was infused—subtle distinctions. The fragrance of the tea, both before and after infusion, was judged. All this was art, and meant that tea was almost a profession, much more than just a trade. My father, who went out to China in 1901 for a tea firm, was very conscious of this and used to delight in the niceties involved in the final choice of brands.

At one time the trade with Russia was immensely important to the China firms, and a number of Russian merchants lived in the country—very comfortably, too, in great houses, in Hankow and Shanghai. The Revolution stopped this abruptly. Before that most of the foreign teamen, many of whom spoke Russian (among these my father) went every year to Moscow and St. Petersburg, during the winter when the trade was quiet.

I well remember, as a child, my father setting off on these long Trans-Siberian journeys, and I can remember him studying Russian and practicing it when he could. He would come back with the most delightful toys for us children—round red wooden boxes, full of miniature wooden bijoux—tiny pieces of furniture, beautifully polished, bottles, fantasies. He brought, too, large crystal eggs from the Urals, yellowish like alabaster. When you tilted them they swam with light.

The Russian market lost, people cast about for another. The British had their tea gardens in the Lower Himalayas, long since established, following Robert Fortune's bold stroke in getting a few of the plants out of China; they did not take up very much of the China trade, not nearly so much as in the beginning. The

Japanese had captured much of the American market. Now the Shanghai firms turned to North Africa, and began sending great amounts of green tea to places like Casablanca, Oran, and Tripoli —unfermented leaves, suitable for pious Moslems.

Once I worked for half a year in one of these firms on the Peking Road, making them a cable code, which though it was in English, was still practical for both the Arabs and the Chinese. Cables had become a vast expense. No one wanted to write letters —but they had to have some cheaper way of communicating than using the ordinary codes.

I had no experience whatsoever in the making of codes, but as it happened, I had recently worked for a time in a firm which imported Swedish newsprint into China. The manager of this concern had gone off on six months' leave, and asked me to fill in for him. The Chinese *comprador*, Mr. Lin, knew all about everything, all I was there for really was to provide the necessary English, and give an impression of status. I didn't know anything about newsprint either, but as in everything else, all one really ever needs is the opportunity, and then things fall into line. This firm used a good, simple code; when the tea firm asked me to make them one, I remembered it, and my friend was kind enough to lend me a copy, so that I could take note of how it was arranged.

Mr. Lin and I got on well together, in our long consultations over the cables from Malmö, the tenders from Stockholm. Dealers would come in to buy, long-gowned men evidently full of secret thoughts. The atmosphere was not nearly as much like that of a club as it used to be in the tea firms. Mr. Lin sometimes told me about these men, particularly cautioning me against one of them. "Be careful of Mr. Chu," he said. "He is like a tiger in a grove of sheep!" During that fall, Mr. Lin gave me the delicate present of a cricket in a bamboo cage, a small, tuneful creature. He told me it was called Fairy Bells, remarking, "Spring is the season of the eye, autumn of the ear."

To put this paper code into perspective for the tea firm, I had first to learn something concrete about the trade, beyond my childish memories of my father's *hong*, and its swinging tables, with those white cups reflected down into the shining surfaces. I began to taste tea, spit it out into a tall spittoon, and try to discriminate. I sniffed the leaves, and delighted in their gradations of tone, under that pure cold light. I was there in the winter—the vast room was very cold, almost unheatable. But the firm was served by men who had spent their lives there, and had brought in their sons; they were friendly and courteous, very anxious to help me understand something of the mysteries of their calling. The owners were European, as was the *taipan*, the chief, but everyone else was Chinese. The chief clerk, Ah Chang, was a thin and melancholy figure, most kind and able. He alone dressed in Western style in a shabby brown suit; he seemed to me something of a Dickensian character, a universal type, such as that genius so often created for us in those novels which teem with all of us. Ah Chang's passion was for music, Western music. He had taught himself to play the violin by correspondence, and was playing regularly in a Chinese amateur orchestra.

Dickins was no stranger to the literate Chinese, who read widely and voraciously from his works. At that time, when many Chinese adopted foreign given names it was quite a common thing to encounter "David Copperfield Ku," "Paul Dombey Wong," "Oliver Twist Ma," and the like. English students struggled with the original texts, and one shuddered to think how hard these must have been for them—looking up the rich vocabularies of those immense novels, and their detailed colloquial descriptions.

But for those who only wanted to enjoy the novels for themselves, there was no necessity to go through this misery, as China had been singularly fortunate in having an astonishing translator of Western fiction, a man who seems to have been born to put Dickens into classical Chinese. Arthur Waley even preferred the Lin Shu (for that was his name) versions, which are not very literal translations, to Dickens in the original.

Lin Shu (1852–1924) was already a writer, when near the end of the nineteenth century a returned student, a friend of his, came to him with *La Dame aux Camélias* in his hands, and translated it to him aloud, spontaneously, on the spur of the hour. Lin Shu could not read French, nor indeed any foreign language. He was immensely excited by this moving story, wrote it down at once in literary Chinese, and published it. It was immediately successful; he realized that this was something he could do.

For the next quarter of a century he continued with this sort of work, translating very fast, and getting different people to read the originals aloud to him: a great many Dickens novels, and romantic tales like *Paul et Virginie*, *The Eagle and the Dove*, *Ivanhoe*, stories from Conan Doyle and from Washington Irving's *Sketch Book*. The Chinese seized upon them with avidity as they came from his pen—it was a type of writing, a sort of plot unknown to them, but they responded eagerly to it. It seems rather surprising that a man with so wide-ranging a sympathy, so quick an imagination (for he was himself totally absorbed in the stories, and suffered and enjoyed with their characters), would have turned to the old *wen-li*, literary Chinese, as his vehicle, rather than using the colloquial, the usual language for the novel in China. But this was the tool which was ready to his hand. His rapid and easy prose, his intense, even passionate interest in the plots, coupled with the ability of his translators (who were many and various, generally students who had lived abroad and were now finding their way once more in China), was one of those marvelous literary events. He did over a hundred and fifty of these translations. How delighted Dickens would have been had he known that his name would be a household word so far away— and how angry that he received no translation rights!

The Chinese were already (that is, the literate Chinese) well accustomed to reading foreign works in translation. World histories—English histories in particular—sold by the hundred thousand. The Chinese were fascinated by our biographies of famous men, and by philosophical works—Mills, Huxley, Darwin were much read. They were starved for these ideas, for a vigorous interpretation of life, seen through other eyes. All this began, seriously, in the second half of the nineteenth century, but it took a great deal of time before it was generally recognized. China's first envoy to England, for instance, Kuo Sung-t'ao, who dared to report that Western civilization went back two thousand years, was censured and ostracized.

So it was not unnatural to think of Ah Chang as a Dickensian figure. He was a practical man, as well as a musician and a judge of tea, always ready with solutions to office problems. We had, for instance, a canary of which we were all fond. It sang beautifully in that huge room; but I was worried about its situation at night, knowing that rats came into the *hong*, and though its cage hung high up, away from supports, rats can be fiendishly clever. I told Ah Chang of my anxiety, and was reassured by his rather unexpected reply: "That all right, Missy, one cat come night-time looksee canary."

Bob Schlee, who owned the firm, was one of our greatest friends. He played the violin, read, rode, entertained, and delighted us with his conversation. His people had long ties with China and with the trade—he himself for very many years divided his time between China and England, spending six months in each country, and generally journeying via Siberia. He had a large family which was being educated at home. As a young man he had taken part in the first war, and he would be involved in the second; between these two events he had many dramatic experiences in the course of his work—in Russia, in North Africa, in Europe. He never learned any Chinese, being a Treaty Port man, but he could speak fluent Russian—he had lived in Moscow when he was a youth, in order to learn it. That was in the days when the Russian trade was so important to the teamen. Of an easy and genial nature, taking life as it came, he found friends in all sorts of different milieus; he used to make music with White Russians in Shanghai, he knew all the *taipans*, and he also was at home with unworldly people like ourselves.

Going West on Nanking Road

THE BUND behind us, let us go west on Nanking Road, away from the river, down towards the Race Course, turning aside only to look once more upon what were probably in their day the best silk shops in the world, Lao K'ai Fook and Lao K'ai Ch'uang. On their wide high shelves lay bolts of crêpe de Chine, luscious satin, thick silk, silk gauze, brocade, chiffon, in pure white, ivory, rose, robin's egg blue, Nile green, Moslem green, turquoise, russet, salmon, nut brown, palest fawn, and black so lustrous you could see reflections in it. There were striped silks, silks interwoven with the country's emblems and symbols, like the everlasting knot, the double-cash, the lotus; there were taffetas; there was silk shot with iridescent colors, pink and mauve; there was pongee and Shantung silk; there was every range of gold—gold satin, gold gauze, after the old tribute gauze, a harking back to the imperial colors.

All these were as strong as iron and would last for years. Silk for men's shirts used to be something like thirty Chinese cents a yard, pongee was cheaper, even satin was only a couple of dollars —seldom more than four. Taffeta was so cheap you could have your French windows curtained with it. People made presents of bolts of crêpe de Chine—a handsome present, but not uncommon. Except for the very poorest, silk was worn by almost everyone— even the people on the ragged edge of poverty could manage to wear it on special occasions, even if it meant hiring a silk gown.

86

Except for rayon, synthetic fabrics had hardly begun, so the choice within the country really lay between silk and cotton.

There was almost no woolen cloth made; most Chinese wore padded cotton in winter—the rich lined their garments with fur. There was no linen, though there was a fabric that resembled it, the shining slippery grasscloth, suitable for the men's long gowns in summer, dazzlingly white, very crushable. It was made into embroidered teaclothes for the foreign trade, but altogether it must have been a rather small affair. Most of it came up from Swatow for Shanghai.

None of these materials was to be found in Lao K'ai Fook and Lao K'ai Ch'uang—they stuck to the great traditional product of the country, the fabric of which China had been from earliest antiquity so justly proud. Silk remained something of a cult still— no one forgot that it was China which had discovered and jealously guarded over so many centuries the mysteries of the silkworm.

It was hard to choose between so many glorious bolts; the patient clerks, in their long grey gowns, foil to so much brilliance, would bring down from the high shelves anything you wanted to see, shaking out the lustrous folds in sumptuous piles on the counters. Once the decision was made they took out their round-handled Chinese scissors, which look clumsy but are not, and nick the cloth, afterward tearing it across with that marvelous ripping sound which so enraptured a wanton concubine of long ago. All the reckoning was by abacus; a slim hand clicked away with the brown and black beads which, as round as water chestnuts, made a pattern within their frame, and your bill was ready. No adding machine could have been faster. These shops ran on traditional lines, but were totally efficient.

Away from these treasures and back on Nanking Road, were the Chocolate Shop, a popular American rendezvous, where you could buy ice cream and sodas (then a rarity in the East) and near it Sun Ya, a popular Chinese restaurant, much patronized by foreigners. Beyond them were three large, entirely Chinese, department stores, modern, well-run, and always bursting with Chinese customers—Wing On's, Sincere's, and the Sun Company. Many of their patrons had no money at all, but came to enjoy them as though they were museums in an almost museumless land. They rode the elevators—free!—and felt themselves part of the great world. There were many Chinese specialties to be found there, things like hundred-year-old eggs and ducks' tongues. These stores were almost entirely aimed at the Chinese trade in the way of clothing, but the foreigners found a good deal to buy in them, especially at Wing On's. Outside Sincere's, a more wholly Chinese-oriented shop, stood very large brown and yellow Soochow tubs, with tall palms growing in them.

Then came the Race Course, about which so many bitter things have been said. It has been a special target for attack by those who feel today that colonialism and imperialism were essentially evil, and particularly of course by the communists, who are quite good at practicing these forms of government under other names.

Certainly it was unfair in that limited area, with all the races paying rates, to set aside this large piece of ground in the heart of the town for the Westerners. Even the authorities were uneasy about it; they knew it was unfair, and late in the Settlement's existence decided that they would break down this discrimination by having everyone, of whatever race, pay a little to enter any public park or enclosure. Whether this was ever put into effect I do not know; I rather doubt it.

But even so, you could make out a strong case for the Race Course, in its own context, looking back at the nineteenth century when it began, and remembering that change comes very hard. The Race Course was no center of privilege, like so many of the clubs—it was open to every foreigner, and a great boon to those who were not well off, and that meant most of them. It wasn't only a race course, the track ran round it, but the center was devoted to every sort of game: tennis, football, baseball, cricket, bowls, swimming, golf, hockey. There was a polo field. Runners ran round the race track when the ponies weren't on it; it was always full of people who liked exercise, athletics, sport.

When it was started no Chinese had any interest in, or ability to do, any of these things. Their civilization did not include this sort of recreation—they might like to watch people engaged in sport but never dreamed of the pleasure it gave the amateur himself. It was a long time before this attitude changed. The YMCA was one of the instruments which broke down these prejudices, as were the mission schools, but that was a slow affair. So when that large piece of open ground was set aside for this purpose—recreation and a place for every sort of sport people might want—the Chinese had no wish to become a part of it.

The openness, the wide view of the sky, was a boon for everyone, a breathing place in the middle of the city. The various sports-
men formed themselves into clubs, or not, it wasn't necessary to
join or pay. I used to play golf, during the long luncheon break,
on the Race Course—there was a little clubhouse, but it didn't
cost anything. There were fine golf courses outside the town,
but those were luxurious. Those of us who played on it loved
the nine holes of the Race Course; it made a great difference to us,
to be able to go there and play so freely and simply.

Most people came out to work in Shanghai as young men. They
were there for years, and without some provision of this sort,
would have been entirely cut off from the way they had been
accustomed to spending their leisure.

The foreigners were so few, that had our parks—and there were
not many of them—been thrown open to the huge Chinese population we could not have used them. The Chinese ideas of hygiene
being very different from ours, and they being so many, would
have in effect meant that we had no parks at all. The countryside
being so often closed to us through the local wars, people would
have been confined to their own gardens, if they had them.

The actual racing was all by amateurs, and was a keen pleasure
to the young men who came out for the firms and found that they
could afford to race, as they could never have done at home. For a
long time the local firms even closed their doors for a week in
spring and in fall, so that everyone could devote themselves to this
important occupation. The Chinese lined the course, as it ran
through the city, betting and watching with great eagerness—the
Chinese then were, almost to an individual, ardent gamblers. A
small contingent of the foreigners would be in the stands watching, making it a social affair; most of us were at home, enjoying a
holiday, not caring about the racing in itself at all. Some of the
more bigoted missionaries frowned on the Race Course, missing
the innocent pleasures it offered so many, looking upon it as an
incentive to gambling, a bad example for their flocks. It's very
hard to please everyone.

Past the Race Course, going west, Nanking Road became Bubbling Well Road. There was a temple and a bubbling well in a
square coping. Here every spring, under a sea of mat-shed roofs,
used to be held a splendid bamboo fair. On the other side of the
road, for a long block, stretched a high red brick wall, enclosing
the estate of the immensely wealthy Mr. Hardoon, a Jewish mer-

chant from Baghdad, who had married a Chinese lady. She was a great patron of Buddhism, who was helping that religion to achieve a revival. The Hardoons were extremely charitable, and not only toward Buddhism—being childless themselves, they had adopted a dozen White Russian orphans, all of whom lived there behind that long wall.

The fair used to go on for several days, and as I look back, it seems to me that it was nearly always raining then, but it was a warm and gentle rain which, falling on bamboo, could not hurt anything. Everything there was literally of bamboo. The booths were made of bamboo poles and matting. Matting was sold in itself: fine matting for beds, coarser matting for the floors. The most fetching articles were the baskets, of which there were thousands, of all shapes, sizes, and weaves, every one a delight to see. There were shallow grain baskets, some as large as six feet in diameter; homely market baskets, capacious and comfortable; elegant, high-handled flower baskets; fruit baskets, clothes baskets, waste baskets, everything. There was bamboo furniture; there were vases made of sawn-off joints of a large bamboo; there were chopsticks, brushes, fans, and toys. The toys were irresistible, made of thin shavings of the bamboo—tiny grasshoppers, praying mantises, fierce tigers.

It was the whole world in bamboo: shining, clean-lined, fragrant, pure, of muted and delicate colors—the color of the bamboo itself, unpainted. Not one article was tawdry or discordant, they were all made by hand, and they cost almost nothing—most of them. (The sleeping mats and the big baskets could be quite expensive.) Every year we were amazed once more by the skill and artistry, the innate good taste of this race, and at the profligate gifts of nature, exemplified in this beautiful tree.

The bamboo, like silk, is more than just a marvelous item in China—it is important to their world of art and imagery.

My sister and I used to have dancing lessons, when we were children, at the old Burlington Hotel on the Bubbling Well Road, where on certain afternoons the sweet, pretty, and graceful Miss Newcombs rented the ballroom and held classes. We loved these hours, and looked forward to them all week, practicing our foot positions, our arm movements, and our curtsies. Every child brought a bright chiffon scarf, which she swirled in the air in time to the music, a special pleasure. (No doubt the chiffon had all come from the great bolts of Lao K'ai Fook.) Another pupil here became a great friend when we all grew up, the gifted Nansi Pugh, a writer, a wit, and possessed of a loving, loyal heart. When she passed away not long ago in London, the obituary notice in the *Times* said of her, justly, "dearest friend of so many." She was also, at that stage, a blithe, supple little dancer.

The rival establishment to that of the Miss Newcombs was Miss Sharp's—they were the same sort of place. The Russians meanwhile were teaching ballet, and probably very well, but most of the British and American children were not sent to them. At that time Sadler's Wells had not brought this art back to the world to enrapture the Western public, and Russia itself, with its great ballet schools, was under an eclipse.

The French Concession

As for the constant and excitable spirit of the French
with their perpetual struggle among political factors,
they resemble the age of the Former Ming Dynasty.

HSUEH FU-CH'ENG

THE FRENCH CONCESSION, being slightly less given over to commerce and industry than the Settlement, was more residential, and many of the foreigners had homes in it. We would receive our municipal notices in French, roads changed their names, and the police force, instead of being manned by Sikhs, was made up of Annamites. Other Annamites came to the city in the service of the Infanterie Coloniale, whose regiments would come up on tours of duty from l'Indochine.

You would begin your day in a section where there were signs like "*Route Barrée,*" "*Défence de stationner,*" "*Défence d'entrer, danger de mort*"; where streets had names like Rue du Cardinal Mercier, Rue François Xavier, Avenue Pétain (then a great hero) —and then go off to places like Seymour Road, Edinburgh Road. The Chinese characters for everything were written up beside the Roman script, and the Chinese pronounced these names in a Chinese way. All this we enjoyed.

The French, keeping themselves to themselves, as is their wont, were not personally much in evidence in their Concession—not nearly so much so as were the White Russians who settled there, and who greatly outnumbered them. Russian restaurants and dress shops lined Avenue Joffre, the most important street, which we came to call the Nevsky Prospekt.

There was a French park, near Route Vallon, and a club—the Cercle Sportif Français, which (paradoxically) was easy for any foreigner to join, and was devoted to good food, tennis, swimming in a fine long pool, and dancing (on the roof in summer, *thés dansants* and dinners in winter).

One year, late in August, I had the opportunity to go up to Peitaiho, a resort on the Gulf of Peichili, and then on to Peking. I took the next boat, which happened to be a shabby old coaster, with only two other passengers traveling on it—dark Mediterranean types, of whom my father remarked, laughing, as he saw me off, that they looked like the essence of the Cercle Sportif Français, the complaisant French club.

The trip took two or three days, so I came to have a good deal of conversation with these gentlemen—or rather with one of them, as the second (and much more attractive) personage, a Colonel Lodi, kept himself in the background. The one who talked to me was Count Ciano, then Consul General in Shanghai, already Mussolini's son-in-law. Countess Edda Ciano, the Duce's daughter, I had often seen in the nightclubs of Shanghai, though I had never noticed the Count, who cut a less dazzling figure. She was a beautiful young woman, her Roman features recalling the profile of Mussolini, and pictures of her, with her growing family, sometimes appeared in the press.

Count Ciano was then riding high on waves of success, power, and ambition. He was soon to go back to Italy, and was glad as, he told me, he despised Shanghai, and particularly, he added, the members of the French club. I remembered my father's parting remark. No shadow of doubt ever appeared to cross Count Ciano's mind as he spoke of the world situation and the role Italy and he would soon play. He was a natural, total egoist, but in other ways a man of quick intelligence. He and the subdued Colonel Lodi ate by themselves and seemed to concentrate on potatoes doused liberally with oil. The Colonel already showed in his shape the dire results of this diet, but the Count was still slim and agile.

When we reached Peitaiho we said goodbye, and never met again.

During World War I, many Germans resident in the French Concession were obliged by the authorities to leave it; unwelcome also in the Settlement, they had to find places to live in the Chinese city. We once rented a little house in Rue Ratard when I was a child, which was being vacated, with great bitterness, by some of these people. They took every bush and flower from the garden with them—the lady of the house explaining to my mother that it was not a gesture against her personally, but to show their resentment. Gradually in the late twenties and in the thirties the Germans came back, till they formed a large community of some thousands. The Kaiser Wilhelm Schule was in the French Concession, in front of their war memorial, a replica of a trophy from the *Emden.*

When we left Rue Ratard we lived consecutively in two large houses on the edge of the Concession, by the Zikawei Creek, which was bounded by the Route de Zikawei, and led on to the village of the same name, where the Jesuits had established their meteorological station and had their cathedral.

The first house, which was ugly and jerry-built, stood in about an acre of ground (seven *mou*), delightfully laid out and called Jardin Caprice. Behind the house were stables, built long before the house. Next to us was a long garden with well-kept lawns and flower beds, and without a house, seldom used by its owners.

One day a Korean gentleman called on us asking if he might have the use of this neighboring property on behalf of his school, so that they might celebrate there the approaching Korean National Day. We helped him to arrange this, and the fête took place with great enthusiasm—we were invited to join them, and found ourselves being led to seats on the platform. These Koreans were exiles, who refused to go back to their homes as long as the Japanese were in occupation there.

They were intensely miserable in being the vassals of the Japanese, and were inculcating in their children a strong sense of national pride, identity, and independence. Meanwhile they kept alive by importing apples from their country, and a strong, brightly colored cotton fabric which we called "Korean cloth." At this time the occupation had been in effect about thirty years—none of the children had ever seen their own country. The Koreans were good, quiet denizens of Shanghai. On this national day they made patriotic speeches, ran up their flag, and the children sang special songs, ran races, danced—there's not much variation in these affairs between one country and another. We felt ignorant of Korea ourselves, and were glad to have a chance to talk with them. People sometimes used to go on walking tours to the Diamond Mountains, but it was rather an expensive holiday—few persons had much to do with the country, considering how near and how interesting it was. We felt an aversion to what the Japanese were doing, anyway; we didn't want them to give us visas for this land which they were wrongly claiming as their own.

There was another sort of Korean, much featured in the press. When the Japanese, as their hour of darkness drew near, used to set the stage for "incidents" in China, the immediate cause for these disturbances was very often traced to a figure dubbed "a Korean *ronin*." His was the hand which threw the rotten pear, which created panic, which in its turn roused a mob to fury, which the Japanese then had to quell, so that law and order would be restored. These *ronin*, masterless soldiers of the feudal legends, did exist—they were thugs, assassins, desperate characters. The Japanese Intelligence hired them, exploited their excitable nature, set them provocative roles. Their actions were easy for the Japanese to disavow, if they became an embarrassment to them— clearly these trouble makers were not Japanese.

Nothing could have seemed further from such behavior than the gentle ways of the Koreans who watched their children with mild pride in that garden on the Zikawei Road. Korea, like Poland and other lands placed in a geographically tempting position between powerful and aggressive neighbors, produced persons of unusually disparate nature—the mild, calm, enduring type, and the revolutionary.

Jardin Caprice contained many beautiful great trees, and flowering bushes. My mother enhanced the garden, putting in a great many bulbs and English flowers, setting out a path with daisies between the stones. Shanghai was not a good place for bulbs, though—they would come out in profusion the first year, but after that tended to fall away—the summers were too hot, the winters neither long nor cold enough. Our long banks of multicolored, astringent hyacinths, which gave us such keen pleasure that first spring, never reproduced themselves except in the most attenuated way. The *mei hua* was especially good there though, and the forsythia and jasmine. There was a tennis court; it was a garden to live in. We had many meals set out under those spreading trees, and spent many long summer nights, stretched out in flat grain baskets from the bamboo fair, watching the stars.

Around us were open fields; it was a quiet area. Just behind us in a large enclosure was a soya sauce factory, a very silent industry. There were a few small sheds, which never appeared to be the scene of any particular busyness—the activity was centered in the yards themselves. Here were row upon row of huge earthenware jars, covered with large conical straw hats; in them the thick, fragrant, black sauce ripened and matured. From time to time the whole area was pervaded by a delicious scent of burnt sugar. That was all. We would look out from the upstairs back windows of our house, onto these hundreds of vats, sometimes covered, sometimes open to the air, a scene of great placidity, apparently no trouble to anyone. We liked having them there.

Some years later we moved a few blocks farther down Zikawei Creek, to its intersection with Route Ghisi. At the end of Route Ghisi a bridge crossed the creek, and then you were on Chinese territory. Not far from here, on the Chinese side, was the house where the Panchen Lama stayed when he was in exile from Tibet— a very important person indeed.

The Route de Zikawei was not much used. In the morning and evening wheelbarrows went down it in a long stream, carrying factory girls to the mills beyond the bridge. Pretty, slender, chattering creatures, in short jackets and trousers of figured cotton, their braids swinging, they would perch five or six on a side, enjoying the ride, enjoying a few moments of inactivity. They must have worked for the meagerest wages, but they gave the impression of being carefree. Perhaps the mill was better to them than their homes.

The sides of the creek were steep. Narrow boats passed below on the muddy brown water. In troubled times when warlords drew near the perimeter of the city, *chevaux de frise* would be placed up and down the bank of the creek, to discourage stragglers from some disbanding army from entering the Concession. Afterward we sometimes picked up bullets in the garden, stray shots fired at random; once we even had to leave Jardin Caprice till an army had withdrawn to a more convenient distance.

That second home, on the corner of Route Ghisi, was one of those places you always carry in your heart. It was a large old house, with fine paneled rooms and molded doors, lying in a very beautiful garden of twenty-one *mou* (about three acres), which was large for the city. This had for a long time been the official house for the manager of the Russo-Asiatic Bank—the last occupant, in that role, had been George Candlin, an Englishman. None of us suspected when we moved into Route Ghisi, that years later, this very brilliant man, who spoke Russian and Chinese, and whose career had been sadly thwarted through the dissolution of the bank after the Revolution, would be "Uncle George" to me—I married his nephew.

After the bank gave up the property it became the house where the head of the French police always lived. These gentlemen seemed able, after about three years in Shanghai, to retire in comfort to France. The house when we moved in reeked of opium.

But the garden was older than either of these periods of tenancy, having been laid out at least forty years before by a German horticulturalist, with great imagination as well as botanical expertise. He had assembled here rare trees, laid out terraces, landscaped it all, put in a wooded section and a vegetable garden behind a high rounded hedge. There were long paths lined with star lilies, there was wisteria over the portico, and a round swimming pool. The servants had a good building to themselves, on two sides of a cobbled court, modeled on some Tudor lodge.

When we rented it, it belonged to the Jesuits, great landowners in Shanghai as elsewhere. They could not make up their minds what to do with it in those uncertain times, and, while hesitating, were willing to let some tenant have it at a low rent, without a lease. We were these people, and through this good fortune, spent several years there—till 1937 and the Japanese War.

The trees were especially remarkable. One botanist among the fathers used to come out sometimes to examine them, and make note of their progress. There were Himalayan cedars, paulownias, tulip trees, several sorts of magnolias, gingkoes, bamboos, plane trees; the list was long. There was a circular drive, where the cedars (which were huge) had been planted; under them stood a martial stone figure, and two stone horses, all larger than life. Every window opened onto a beautiful view—it was one of those miraculous places, doubly miraculous in Shanghai.

We were the last family to love and cherish it. I came back to the city during the Japanese War—by then my mother was living in a small house in Route Frelupt, not very far away. One day I went out to see what had happened to our old home, to find that it was being dismantled and taken down. The trees were being cut; it was a dreadful sight and I never went that way again. I hold it in my mind as it was on summer afternoons, with the tennis balls thudding against the rackets, the bowls rolling on the lawn, the flowers so sweet and tall, or on moonlit nights, when there were such deep shadows lying over the terrace. We had four stone dogs, the traditional *chi-lin*, which we had bought up-country, who guarded certain low flights of stone steps, and looked particularly magical under the moon and stars. Changes never touch this sort of memory.

My mother, who had lived as a child in the Canadian Northwest, and had as a young woman been a serious mountaineer in the state of Washington, used to think her life in China sadly lacking in many essential elements. She felt her children were deprived of the wild, free, vigorous contest with nature that she had known, and tried to make up to us for it, as she could. We, cosseted little creatures, did not miss what we did not know, and were perfectly content to learn about the heights and depths of the universe from the books which we read as soon as we woke till someone put out the light over our protests.

But Mother did what she could. She made bonfires in our gardens, day after day, in the autumn, and sometimes cooked something over them—this was long before the days when barbecues became fashionable. We had our meals outside as often as we could. She helped us to make a house of woven bamboos in one garden, large enough for us to enter and play in. She would sometimes even hire a carriage and take us all the way to Jessfield Park, taking along a brazier and charcoal, so that she could make breakfast in the open, without any servants. We enjoyed these occasions, but they awoke no stirrings for the wild in us, and my father would never go to Jessfield to sit on the ground and eat an egg. He had no feeling for that sort of thing at all, being entirely city-bred.

When we were small my parents beggared themselves so that frequent visits could be made to my grandmother in California. The long sea voyages, two months almost, coming and going, were a great change from our Shanghai life, but just the sight of the open sea was not enough for mother's active spirit, and when we were in America she would take us into the hills or by the sea as often as she could, teaching us to row and to build fires. But circumstances were against her—we grew up without any wish to rough it in the wilderness, however beautiful that wilderness might be.

My maternal grandfather had been a minister, with a parish

church in Ontario. Tiring of this, and, I surmise, possessed of that same call for the wild that my mother had, he responded to an offer made by the Canadian government, offering a square mile of land in the Northwest to anyone who would settle on it. He set off by train with his large and reluctant family (there had been eleven), finishing the last stage of the journey—some eighty miles—by covered wagon. In the vast cold plains, where they found their property and built their house, the pleasures were great but few, and the difficulties became in the end unsurmountable.

Their nearest neighbor was a great distance away, as they realized when their fire went out and they had to borrow a coal; they had no matches. They could get no help upon which they could count—the Indians who lived round about would never work for more than a day or two. Grandfather had no knowledge whatsoever of farming, and it was not an easy country to farm. But it was a sportsman's paradise: when we had duck for dinner my mother used to remark that at that time it never would have occurred to anyone that you could have less than a duck *apiece*— the idea of sharing a duck would have been as bizarre as cutting up a cherry.

The grown-up daughters hated being exiled; the boys hated having to work with father. The winters were terribly hard; they had a drought and lost most of their cattle; they had a fire. It was a romantic idea which could not stand up to its expression; they gave up and abandoned their claim. The new settlers who came to live in the area were all in the same case; many of them were younger sons from England or Ireland, who hoped to become landed proprietors, who loved the hunting and the spaciousness of it all, but who could not cope with the problems. One of my aunts, the beautiful Belle, whom I never knew, married into one of these families. My mother was a small child when this venture began, and had throughout a glorious time. She was considered delicate, so no one tried to burden her with lessons. She was simply given the run of my grandfather's large, excellent library, and when she was not galloping over the prairie on her pony, she was voraciously reading everything she could, and remembering it all, so that when they returned to civilization, and she was sent to school, she won, that first year, a state medal.

But it was not much of a preparation for life in Shanghai.

She and my father met in rather unusual circumstances. He was traveling on the West Coast, and soon to go to China. She was teaching in Seattle, and had been down the coast on a trip with a friend. It was 1900. When they were on the return journey it was discovered that there was a smallpox case on board, as a result of which everyone on the ship was obliged to disembark on a small spit of land near the Canadian border, and spend three weeks in a camp. All their clothes were taken away to be fumigated, and they landed wrapped up in blankets. This long pause was very unwelcome to many of the passengers, but some of them, including my mother, did not mind at all. They were young, and plunged into the many activities the stranded ship's company improvised. They made friends across a fence with the Canadian soldiers, who used to sing them martial airs, like "The Soldiers of the Queen"; and they set up a whist club, a baseball team, and such amusements. My father played whist; my mother did not, and they never met till the very last day, when they happened to walk together to or from the dining hall.

By this time many of them had been given nicknames: my mother for some forgotten reason was "The Child," and my father "Collars and Cuffs." This was because he had plenty of clothes with him, unlike most of the others, who had set out on what they thought would be a short trip.

After that first encounter my father kept in touch with my mother, writing her long letters from China, which she never answered. Finally he asked his cousin, an artist, Charles Bobbett, to look her up and see if the letters had arrived. Charles accordingly did this and reported that she had said yes, they had.

On his visits to the States my father always went to see her, and sent her carnations. After six years she finally did say "Yes," and they set off to China together. He gave her then a jade ring, inscribed "Sept 6 1900–1906," as it was on that September day that they had met, and throughout their life together he always sent her carnations on that day—that happened thirty times after their marriage.

My father was a curious mixture of the conservative, the Victorian, and the really forward thinker. He loved Gauguin, Corot, Daumier; he read continuously when he was not playing chess, and his only sport was the old-fashioned type of bowls, with the great big wooden balls. He read and reread Gibbon, Samuel Butler, Conrad, the English essayists, Ernest Bramah. This last was somehow typical of his attitude towards the country where he lived so long. He loved Bramah's highly stylized elegance, and through Kai Lung acquainted himself, in a thrice-removed fashion, with a quasi-Chinese literary outlook and flavor. Some of Kai Lung's aphorisms he used to quote so often that they became household sayings with us, like: "When compelled to share a cabin with a tiger, one learns to stroke fur in the right direction," and ". . . is like pursuing an active goat along a rocky path by moonlight where the certain risk outweighs the doubtful profit."

We all read constantly, even at meals and going to and fro, morning, afternoon, and in the evenings. My father used to say that if any of us were sentenced to the scaffold we would go cheerfully, a book in one hand. He was a great raconteur, with a fund of humorous stories, which we loved to hear over and over again, and he was very musical though he did not play. His mother and his brothers had been the performers in his family. He read Russian, French, and Spanish, but in the thirty-six years he spent in China he could hardly have learned more than five words in Chinese. Still, he was delighted when I took it up; my mother was so fired by this event and with my enthusiasm that she began to study it herself, with a Chinese teacher coming to the house.

When we children were young my father used to read to us while we had our supper, choosing French books and translating them as he went along, which we enormously enjoyed, though we did not know why we would so often hear such shrieks of laughter from my mother who was in a neighboring room. In this way we first encountered the whole of *The Count of Monte Cristo*, and other classic tales.

My parents were certainly not at all typical Shanghailanders, if there were such persons. Probably there were not.

There was one of my father's chess friends of whom we were particularly fond—a Finn, Mr. Keijola, who came often to play, roaring up past the stone horses on his motorbike. He was the only person we knew in all Shanghai who would have used such a vehicle. It must have been a godsend to him too, as he lived far away, in Hongkew. To us he was in many ways a mystery, though not a mystery to which we gave thought—we were simply full of affection for this big honest man, no longer young, with his greying blond hair, who could converse so well on a variety of subjects in his good, strongly accented English. He was musical, too, and sometimes after dinner before returning to the chessboard he would sit down at the piano and play us some tinkling Finnish airs, and he made note of our progress on our instruments.

When a quartette was in progress on an evening when he came he was very well aware of what we did, occasionally lifting up one big hand and beating a few bars, absently, as he considered his next move.

He used to urge us to go to Finland to spend the summer. It was so easy to reach, he would say, just over there, by the Trans-Siberian, and it was so clean and light in the long summer evenings when the sun never went down. There were the lakes and the blackberries. We could walk and walk. It did sound lovely, we always wished we could. And certainly, once you got there, it did sound extremely cheap.

Mr. Keijola's grown family was in Finland; I think they had never been in China with him. When we knew him he had a small plywood factory, as one of his interests. He had done many things, he had been a sailor and a missionary, and he clearly knew immensely more about China than we did. That would not have been difficult. Once he remarked, considering our simplicity affectionately, that not one of us had any idea of what was really passing in Shanghai—no doubt that was true, and no doubt he himself did know. He spoke very good Chinese. Perhaps he had some sort of intelligence job; but we never asked, and if we had he could not have told us—something held us back. He remained a true friend, even after my father was gone and there was no one left to confront him at the marble chessboard, even after we had to leave Route Ghisi.

That chess table, with its carved central stem, the mottled white and henna-colored marble, and the black edges where the captured men would stand, was one of the pivots of our home. My father's chess set had been given him by his mother, when he was thirteen; he kept the pieces in a blue velvet bag with a silken drawstring. Every few years it would become worn, and my mother would have a tailor down on Yates Road replace it. The presence of two figures facing each other, silent and watchful over the board till one of them would slowly raise his hand and make a move, was a characteristic element of our evenings—just as a knot of musicians working round the piano was another (most of these being only amateurs of the impassioned sort who will slave away without much hope of any real accomplishment).

Sometimes there would be a restless player at the board, a man who would get up, thrust his hands in his pockets, and stand back from the table, scowling, studying the pieces from all angles. Mr.

J. E. S. Green, of the Asiatic Petroleum Company, was a rapid and nervous player who used to read while my father considered his next move. J. E. S. Green ("You can remember the initials," he said, "by just thinking of Jesus") contended that he was the best-educated man in the world, having been a soldier, a Cambridge don, and now a businessman. There was something in it, too, but this viewpoint was not an easy one for his employers to accept; he fell out with them, and was asked to resign. "I won't resign; you can fire me if you like," he said; which they did, so that my father lost his cherished opponent, and the rest of us a sparkling conversationalist at the dinner table. He went to Africa, writing us long and perceptive letters from that continent.

White Russians

> Presently the sounds of a flute coming out of the open window of a lighted upstairs room in a modest house interrupted his dismal reflections. It was being played with a persevering virtuosity, and through the *fioritures* of the tune one could hear the regular thumping of the foot beating time on the floor.
>
> Lieut. D'Hubert shouted a name. . . . The sounds of the flute ceased, and the musician appeared at the window, his instrument still in his hand, peering into the street.
>
> CONRAD, *The Duel*

THE WESTERN NATIONS may well have been nibbling away at China as the silkworm does the mulberry leaf, to use the local parallel, but the country which was really making ready for a thundering impact wasn't one of us—it lay to the north—Russia. Ideologically and physically its aims were much more succinct and inclusive. The makers of the Revolution, long before they had really consolidated their own position, turned their ardent attention to the desperate land which lay to the south, over that long frontier with its disputed border provinces. The first clandestine meetings, laying the ground for the formation of the Communist Party in China, began only four years after the Revolution, in 1921, when a few men under the chairmanship of the Dutchman, Maring, met in a house in the French Concession in Shanghai. The French authorities were alert to the danger this implied, but few of us had any knowledge at all of it.

But everyone was aware of the turmoil in Russia; the White Russians who were pouring into China as refugees bore eloquent witness to the disruption of the whole way of life in that vast region. We watched, too, the demise of the old tsarist enclaves in Hankow, Shanghai, Tientsin, Harbin. The Russian merchants who had been so successful in tea, furs, and silks, who had had behind them the resources of the Russo-Asiatic Bank, lost everything. The business vanished, the bank was liquidated.

It had been only a dozen years before that Russia had had extravagant hopes of at last acquiring her longed-for warm water port, of establishing herself on the Pacific at Dalny (which the Japanese, taking it over after the Russo-Japanese War of 1904– 1905, called Dairen). The Russians wanted to transform this little place (named Lü-ta by the Chinese) into a Far Eastern Paris, and busied themselves in drawing up grandiose schemes for it. They intended to keep a fleet at nearby Port Arthur, and in their brief hour of exuberance began to build themselves fine stone mansions, and to live in style. But their disastrous campaigns in the field soon enough disabused them, and like the Chinese, they had to see Danly become Dairen and a bustling Japanese city, right there on the Liaotung Peninsula.

After 1917 Russian influence on China changed its outward mien, but penetrated the country on a greater scale than ever before, looking for different rewards. In less than a decade, so subtle and effective were their agents and propaganda, they nearly had the country. After their setback in 1926, however, they had to wait over twenty years before they finally regained their losses. But they were not discouraged—the communist doctrine is in the hands of people who are prepared to wait, if need be. The relationship between the Chinese and the Tatar, that of invading, being invaded, repelling invasion, goes back over two thousand years. The tactics of the struggle had changed, not the basic principles. Now the weapons were ideas, influence.

This sort of influence emphatically did not come from the White Russians, the outward symbol of the rejection of the new system, as they stumbled in amongst us, desperate and desolate. They came through Harbin, halting at Mukden, finally reaching Shanghai as the last stage of their long trek from St. Petersburg or Moscow. If they could find work or shelter they stopped on the way, but as generally there was nothing for them, they pressed on to Shanghai, hoping it might be more promising—which was saying little. A few came in by Central Asia, trading in horses, traveling with the caravans.

The Russian refugees fell, broadly, into two categories: those who went westward into Europe, and those who turned east, crossing Siberia, a terrible journey. Those who were able to go to Paris or London or Switzerland were generally the more Europeanized, who spoke the appropriate languages, and sometimes were so fortunate as to have true friends in the countries to which they went—even bank balances which were not in the worthless double-headed eagle rubles. But the others, often poorer, less-educated, less-privileged, but equally determined to flee the blessings of communism, struggled toward Asia. They were frequently obliged to beg their bread—and in poor, arid places where there was none to spare, and little charity for these strangers.

Once they reached the coast, and the shelter of some town, how hard a place it was for them to settle in! Yet what else could they do? At least no one asked them for papers. They could stay if they liked. The problem was to make a living. But China was supersaturated with people, with labor—industrious, patient, civil workers, willing to accept the smallest wage, to sleep on a bare board if need be, to live on a handful of rice and a leaf of cabbage.

The good jobs in the big Western firms were filled at home, except for that of the *comprador*—and he had to be Chinese as the go-between. The clerks, shop assistants, and like posts were filled by the Portuguese, long resident on the coast, and by the very large colony of Eurasians. Local boys had small opportunities, but even they would stand before the Russians. The Eurasian population, English-speaking, well-versed in the ways of the city, undemanding, already housed, seemed infinitely more employable than did these large, blond people, shabby and emotional, importunate, far too often recounting doubtful tales of "my father, the colonel." The Chinese had no wish to see the Russians as possible competitors, and were astonished to see white people in such a position. They saw no reason for putting themselves out for these poor destitutes, having already far too many of their own whom they were allowing to perish without succor. The new world organizations to help displaced persons were not yet in being, but there was the Red Cross, the Salvation Army, and the help of many private individuals. The Russians had in their ranks many who were brave, indomitable, and resourceful—these managed to find their feet. Others turned to crime, something for which Shanghai offered many inducements.

It is a proof of their talents and energy that after only a few years, these people, few in number, literally penniless, shaken by terrible events, had yet made a strong mark on the coast, enriching the lives of many people in the Settlements in unexpected ways. Because of them, we had much more music, horsemanship improved, their dress shops made it possible for thousands of women to be stylish, their restaurants induced people to dine out, to enter more into the life of the town, their nightclubs became world famous. The men became bodyguards, watchmen, sometimes soldiers. They taught, they ran printing presses; one by one, with heroic endurance, they made niches for themselves. Living so close to utter want, it was inevitable that many became problems for the police; the wonder was that the community as a whole remained so respectable. They were, in the main, very pious, very God-fearing; several Greek Orthodox churches were built in Shanghai alone in those few years they had before the Japanese War began.

The Greek Orthodox churches were well built and embellished, to the extent to which these poor people could manage it. The singing there was always splendid, and much of Shanghai, Russian or not, would go to their Christmas and Easter services simply to hear the choirs. The midnight mass of the Easter cycle was particularly moving. Everyone carried tall white tapers, and the crowd was always so great it was a wonder no one was ever set afire. They would even have to build matting annexes to hold the overflow. Everyone stood, of course, with his lit candle in his hand till at midnight the cry arose: *"Christós voskrési!"* to be answered by everyone *"Vo istinu voskrési!"*

The foreigners in Shanghai craved music; we never had enough. This was long before the days of hi-fi, though there were good gramophones and a lot of amateur playing. Great artists could visit the city very seldom. The White Russians did a great deal to fill this need. The Municipal Orchestra—a brave venture on that shore—soon was almost entirely staffed by Russian musicians, and very able they were. The conductor and the leader were Italians— Maestro Paci and Achille Foa. Signor Paci was a good musician, very much the Latin in his mannerisms, very lively on the podium, fond of opera and of Respighi. Signor Foa was a dandy, slender and conscious of his good looks, but he was also a good violinist, and with the talent which they assembled round them, Shanghai had something of which it really could be proud. The concerts were well-attended, though there was the usual civic difficulty in paying for the orchestra every year when the cost came up for discussion. All the players gave lessons; Shanghai was a hive of music teachers. The Chinese were fond of Western music; there must have been thousands of music pupils in the city.

Teaching music is a precarious profession, but the Russians had little option, and for some of them it was in any event their true calling. Among them were musicians who had studied in the conservatories of Moscow and St. Petersburg, and were eager to impart what they knew. One of the best teachers I ever had was Mr. Leibensohn, from St. Petersburg, who taught after the Leschititsky tradition, and was enamored of John Field. He used to tell me all sorts of stories about Field and his delicate playing, of the white nights of St. Petersburg, and the cracking of the ice on the Neva, which had inspired his tender, dreamy nocturnes. The exhaustion of poor Field, too tired even to pick up his cane if it fell on the pavement, was a living thing to Mr. Leibensohn. He seemed exhausted enough himself, to me—he was hardly five feet tall, slight and fragile as Lob. I could scarcely imagine how this man, no longer young, apparently without any worldly interest or capacity, could have become so aware of what was passing round him that he would have left the city he loved, the conservatory and all that went with it, to undertake the terrible journey to China. Still—he had.

This was perhaps due to his wife, a much less impractical person, who kept their flat orderly and clean and saw to the meals. They had learned a little English and rented an upright; quite a number of pupils came to their door. Mr. Leibensohn had been intended, he told me, for a concert career, but the strain of such performances was unbearable to him; his genius lay in actually enabling his pupils to play with feeling and delicacy. You had to teach well in Shanghai, there were so many gifted people doing it too—Czechs, Germans, Poles. The best pupils were, as a rule, the Russians themselves, but teaching them was like the islanders taking in one another's washing. Compared to most of these children, whose parents were putting on performances of *Boris Godunov*, playing in Jessfield Park on summer nights and in the Lyceum in the winter, as well as in nightclubs and cabarets, we as children felt ourselves musical clods.

Every Christmas the different schools in the city would send groups of children to sing their country's special songs at the

Town Hall. The girls from the Cathedral School in their neat uniforms, the Americans dressed anyhow, the earnest, erect pupils from the Kaiser Wilhelm Schule, the children from the Lycée, and finally some little White Russians, would assemble and take their turn on the podium. Most of these performances were deplorable, but, in spite of that, touching—no one demands that Christmas songs be sung with great art. Two groups sang really well—the Germans and the Russians, and it was the Russians who led the field, every time. They transformed the event. We would begin, as a rule with "The Holly and the Ivy," go on with "O Little Town of Bethlehem," and "Es ist Ein Ros' Entsprungen," and at last the moment came when the White Russians filed up to the platform.

They were the smallest and stoutest of us all—and shabby, though their mothers did the best they could by them; their shoes shone, their braids were tied up with bright bows. Without any whispering or jostling they came forward; with real aplomb, almost in a professional manner, they took their places, and a hush would fall on the audience. The Russian colony wasn't much respected, but these waifs commanded our attention. They were themselves obviously extremely happy, ardently longing to begin, fixing their eyes on their conductor. He lifted his baton—and at once they would burst into four-part singing, as true as bells chiming together, and as moving.

We were all touched, even humbled, by this performance. They lifted us into another dimension, and they always won the acclamations of that audience which, seldom very musical, prejudiced in favor of its own children, could never resist this splendid outpouring of talent. That was the era when music teachers gave recitals, and with dread and reluctance most of their pupils exhibited their "piece" to an invited audience. But it was not at all like that when the pupils were Russians. Here again, they were eager to begin, even though they were performing singly. They were confident, they knew they could do it, they were overjoyed with the music, with the sense of occasion and festivity. I have seen really small children, as young as four, rush down the aisle, be picked up by their teacher and lifted onto the piano stool, which would have been raised to a proper height for them by piling a few big books on it, and then, legs dangling, chubby, strong hands poised high over the keyboard, they would begin at once, *forte*, *con brio*, with a few rousing chords. Everyone was always laughing with pleasure. It was reassuring to feel that there was such joy for these poor people, washed up on that remote coast.

Till they came, people didn't go out to restaurants much. With the best servants in the world at beck and call, and food at home so good and cheap, with a long period free in the middle of the day so that most of the men came home for tiffin, why use a restaurant? And in the early days most people weren't interested in Chinese food, Chinese eating places. The Russians changed this. We all began to have beef stroganoff or chicken à la Kiev in their little restaurants on Avenue Joffre, to have their bliny at Easter, to have the pleasure of hearing a violinist go round the tables, playing. It was inexpensive, and these places became a feature of the town.

Then there were the nightclubs, where Russian girls, many of them very beautiful, worked as dancers, entertainers, hostesses. In other circumstances most of them would probably never have dreamed of undertaking such posts. But what were they to do? To work in an office as a typist, an ill-paid job indeed, demanded a good command of English, better than most of them had in those early years. And of course they all wanted husbands, husbands with passports, through whom they too could have passports— British, French, American, any kind—and stop being stateless. There were a good many marriages between these women and the troops, and other persons, but more broken hearts. These nightclubs were garish and glamorous, but they were sad, too.

The Russian women who had a flair for sewing and cutting were probably the most fortunate. They mobilized the expert Chinese tailors, and started up salons. There was a lot of entertaining in Shanghai, cloth was cheap, and now there were people who knew how to cut. It was a hard and exacting profession for them, and they couldn't charge much, or people would fall back on the unaided but clever Chinese tailor—still, they were successful. They became also a hallmark of the coast.

It was worse for the men; it could not be wondered at if many turned to dubious professions. They could, if they were fortunate, find jobs as guards, watchmen, bodyguards (for warlords, or people who feared kidnappers), and a few hundreds were employed as a part of the Volunteer Force, in a White Russian detachment, which paid its men. They started papers, ran printing presses, taught riding—there were Cossacks in some of the riding schools. They taught Russian, if anyone wanted to learn it. Most of us were too preoccupied with French or German to realize how much we should have availed ourselves of this opportunity—it would never be so easy for us again. Those shops on Avenue Joffre with the signs in Cyrillic didn't tempt us to decipher them.

Most of these people could do little more than hang on, but as always, there were a few who understood the mysteries of trade so well that nothing could hold them back. One of these was a Mr. Blok, who would say, looking out over his lumber yard: "Look at me! A few years ago I arrived in Shanghai without a kopeck in my pocket, and now I owe the bank two *lakhs!*" (A *lakh* was worth $100,000, a lot of money in those days.)

Though of course the storm had been brewing for so long, though the Russian scene had been threatening some great catastrophe for decades, yet when it came most people were unprepared. You get used to living on a volcano. The pitiable thing about many of these refugees was the suddenness with which disaster had come upon them. Madame Ivanterre, who taught French in the American School, had been out of Moscow visiting a sister who was having a baby when the Revolution broke. She never got back to her home, never saw her husband and son again. Everything disappeared under her feet. She was brave, and we admired her, though her French classes were a trial. She wanted everyone to learn every conjugation, every tense, every mood of every irregular verb, *first*, by writing all these out, singular and plural, person by person, positive and negative, affirmative, and as a question. Of course it was beyond endurance to roomfuls of young Americans, and the consequent indiscipline was bedlam, though the school was normally extremely well-behaved. Looking back on it now, it appears the height of docility—but not in Madame Ivanterre's classes.

Others, like Madame Mouzykant, who also turned to teaching, had had to take a complete fall in their standard of living. Madame Mouzykant, whose husband had been a tea merchant and who lived in great comfort and style, suddenly found herself with nothing. She did not have to undergo the miseries of flight, but it was painful to have to be so poor, in a setting where she had known only abundance. On feast days she had always had her big house full, high cakes set out beside the samovar, her monkey capering about; now all that had to be forgotten. Her monkey was a character. She used to take him in the old days, every autumn, to a wool shop, and tell him to choose the skeins for his new coat. He would skip up the counter and run up the shelves, looking till he found just the shade which matched his own pelt.

Thanks to the refugees Shanghai became a great place for chess. Chess clubs sprang up, and you would see people playing in the cafés along Avenue Joffre. This was a great pleasure to my father, who had so seldom found anyone to play with, and it was through these clubs that such matches as that with Alekhine were arranged.

So, slowly, in all these ways and a myriad others—fencing schools, dancing schools, haircutters, little shops—the White Russians found their way into the heart of Shanghai. I think few of that first generation could have been happy there, but their children were fond of it. Their parents, too poor to send them away —even if they could have gone without passports—were grateful for the local schools, and some of that younger generation, sensibly going on to such universities as St. John's or the French Catholic Aurora, had excellent educations. They did much better, in this way, than the offspring of the class-conscious foreigners, who thought their boys would be forever damned if they had to say, later in life, that they had attended, say, the Yü Yuen Road School. But these graduates of the local colleges have now more in their hands than those more fortunate boys who went to Harrow, while their fathers struggled to find the fees in Shanghai and often did not see their sons for five years at a time.

An English boy in the Tientsin Grammar School in 1927 had a conversation with some White Russians, which could hardly have taken place with the members of one of the other national groups.

In Tientsin an athletic field had been laid out for anyone who wished to use it, Chinese or foreign. In the event, this meant, as a rule, the schools. It was called the Min Yüan, or People's Park, and, something like a third of a mile in circumference, required looking after—the work was given to some White Russians. They cut the grass, rolled the ground, whitewashed lines, watched over the equipment, and gave it out. The men employed here were generally middle-aged, several lived on the site, others came and went. They identified themselves with the place, and were perturbed if the grass didn't grow properly, or if equipment was mishandled.

One winter afternoon when he was sixteen, this English youth went up to the store and asked if he might have the use of some hurdles. There were about eight Russians sitting round the coal stove in the corner, a samovar was hissing away, and they were drinking tea. They invited the boy to sit down and join them. One of them then said to him: "We have been having a very serious discussion, and we have differences of opinion. But before I explain what they are, tell me, do you believe in God?"

"Yes," replied the schoolboy, "I do, but why do you ask?"

"I am glad to hear you say this," answered the man, "but I wonder if you would say that so promptly if you had seen what we have seen, and gone through what we have experienced.

"That man, over there," said the Russian, pointing with his glass, "says that all this has happened because God is angry with the Church, which has mismanaged and perverted religion."

It was true that the Greek Orthodox Church in Russia had often had a poor record, many priests identifying themselves with the harshness of the tzarist government, even allowing monasteries to be used as prisons. The conversation continued as one would expect, vexed with the insoluble quandary of trying to reconcile good and evil in the old theological framework, but it left its strong impression on the boy's mind, due to the earnestness of those men. Of course, one of the reasons these people had fled the Revolution was the communist stand against religion.

Just about that time our friend Bob Schlee was coming back to China over Siberia, on the Trans-Siberian Railway. A Russian Boy Scout got into the carriage at some halt and they began to converse.

"Tell me," said our friend, "do you Scouts have the same sort of rules that ours do in England? For instance, do you do a good deed a day?"

"Oh yes," answered the Scout.

"What would you call a good deed, as an example?"

"Well, for instance," replied the child, who was perhaps ten, "there are still people in Russia who believe in God. We are taught not to despise them, but to pity them."

In those long hot summers, which so many of us, from the vantage point of comfortable homes and green gardens, so much loved, the White Russians had to endure small airless rooms down Chinese alleys; they knew that the clubs were full of people playing tennis, swimming, enjoying themselves—they were cut off from it all, they were so poor. Shanghai was a place for athletics and sport, but it was some time before any of them could enjoy any pleasures at all. Yet their children came to know all these things. When in the forties the British and other Allied nationals were interned in Shanghai in dismal crowded barracks, some of these Russians, remembering their old teachers at such places as the Thomas Hanbury School, would go down to them with parcels of food. The White Russians were not interned—they had no status anyway, and strangely, the Red Consulate extended to them a sort of protection—they let the Japanese know that these people, of the same blood as themselves, were not to be roughly handled.

Two children I remember in Shanghai, who went for a short time to the Shanghai American School, had a name to be remembered. They were Red Russians, not White, and in the middle twenties aged perhaps nine and eleven. What happened to them I do not know—they must have gone back to Russia with their father, after the failure of the Communist wing of the Kuomintang in 1927—they were the children of Borodin, but used the name of Ginzburg.

Hongkew

NORTH OF THE SOOCHOW CREEK, and lying along the river, was Hongkew, once the "American Settlement." The American Consulate was here for a long time, as were many of the consular residences. The Astor House, once the best hotel of the town, was nearby, still in business though superseded by the new hostels put up to the west; but it remained until the Japanese took the city and, after World War II began for them in 1941, made it a prison for foreigners. Going north there were still some pleasant houses left, which had been built for the Americans in the early days, and a little park. For a long time there was an American School in Hongkew, first one run by Miss Jewell, then, afterwards, formally, the Shanghai American School. This institution eventually moved out to the French Concession and fine new buildings on Avenue Pétain. Many of its students have made names for themselves since, the intelligent children of missionaries who came to devote their lives to the study of China in one way or another—to the Right, to the Left.

Hongkew declined as a "desirable" neighborhood as it began to be invaded by more and more poor Japanese. When I was a girl there were thousands of these nationals there, and we thought of it as the Japanese part of Shanghai; they had shops there, restaurants, bars, places of entertainment for the sailors who frequented the area by the docks.

The Thomas Hanbury School where many of the White Russian boys studied was in Hongkew. The North Station was there, too, just on the borders of Chapei, the next district to the west, yet north of the Soochow Creek. North Station was bombed and burnt out by the Japanese both in 1931 and 1937. Into Hongkew came, after the Japanese had fired it in 1937, the German Jewish refugees. At least here, among the blackened and charred ruins, there was some free space for the poor creatures. It must have seemed a nightmare to them after the beautiful though cruel cities of Germany.

In our ordinary lives, aside from wars and such things, the important thing about Hongkew was its magnificent market, very large, very effective, serving the whole city. Here at booths presided over by jolly (and astute) countrymen, whose produce had only that very morning left the farms, you could buy marvelous vegetables and fruits, so cheaply, almost as though from a cornucopia. There were chickens and ducks, geese, pheasants, snipe, bustards, baskets of brown eggs, bamboo shoots, water chestnuts, lotus roots, beside all the familiar vegetables of the West, in their season. There were mountains of artichokes, of peas, of cabbages, of new potatoes. The prawns and shrimp, the mandarin fish and yellow fish, the shad and mackerel, would be lifted out of a tank for you, still swimming; there were pumeloes, Javanese mangoes, lichees, pomegranates, lemons, bananas, persimmons, in one brimming stall after another, in a glorious orderly confusion. There were special sections for this and that—the Japanese part reeked of radishes in pickle, and there you could buy prawns just fried in batter, huge prawns, fresh from the sea.

There was a part for flowers, with pails of daffodils, roses, sweet peas, gladioli, chrysanthemums—whatever the time of year yielded. Upstairs a Japanese gardener sold dwarf trees—tiny, twisted pines, *pyrus japonica*. He had there a gnarled cypress, not two feet high, of dramatic lines, which was five hundred years old, he told us. This old man was an artist—his miniature gardens, laid out in glazed oblong pots were truly exquisite.

It was a long way from the French Concession where many of us lived to the Hongkew market, but rewarding in every sense.

Broadway ran through Hongkew. Here were the shops which made and sold camphor chests, here you could watch them being carved, while deciding which one you would like to buy. They were fragrant from the lovely scented wood, most of which came from Formosa. All of them were destroyed in 1937 in the fires the Japanese set. This craft was in the hands of the Chinese, but round them worked, amicably and easily, as far as one could see, many Japanese. These poor people were too occupied in keeping alive to have time for senseless quarrels.

Mikawa, a shoemaker of genius, had his shop down in Hong-kew, and here came his clients, Western ladies, no matter how far away they lived. There was no one else to compare with him on the coast—or in the world, I have sometimes thought since then. He had learned his art in Boston, and had afterward come back to this poor district, to his little, unadorned shop, which somehow had acquired immense renown within its own orbit. He never advertised.

You had to have your shoes made in China, as hardly anyone imported them; Mikawa performed an important function. When you went there first he would take your foot in his hand, and look at it silently for a long time, make a sketch, measure it, ponder, and then ask if you had brought any pictures of the shoes you liked. You produced these. Then he would go through them, saying, "No, you cannot wear this sort of shoe, your instep is too high," "No, your foot is too thin for such a pump," until he decided what would do. Then your future, as far as shoes went, was in his small, dry, competent hands, and you never looked back. He stitched your wedding pumps into elegant patterns, he covered your dancing shoes with different silks, and it cost no more than any other place, and not a fraction of what it would have in a Western country.

Sometimes a child would wander through the shop, a baby tied to its back. "How many children do you have, Mikawa?" someone once asked him. "I don't know," he answered casually, "thirteen or fourteen."

So he must have needed his long list of customers. Among these were some world celebrities, people who came to Shanghai on luxury liners, and having heard of him, would make their way out to his humble establishment. One of these ladies was Mary Pickford, if report be true, who would order twenty or thirty pairs of shoes at a time, all to be sent to Hollywood.

When you came back to Shanghai, after having been to Europe or the States, you took your new shoes down to him to be copied. His shop was not only bare and poor, but in winter was terribly cold, the only heat coming from a small pile of smoldering char-

coal which lay deep down in a high earthenware jar. While waiting for my shoes I used to hold my icy feet over its feeble glow,
hoping to survive. Mikawa didn't notice discomfort, apparently,
like a true Japanese, and he knew well that his clients would have
come to him if he had worked outside on the sidewalk. He was an
artist, and had that strange sort of concentration and luminosity
about him that marks the breed, in his queer, small, bent Japanese
way, sucking in his broken English between his teeth.

There was a hat shop on Broadway we used to patronize too,
this being an era when people wore hats. It was called Mode Élite
and sold Gage hats, which were very good indeed. Mode Élite
sent out wonderful circulars to lure us down to its out-of-the-way
establishment, like:

Give Your Beloved One a Gage Hat at this X'mas

Our special purchase of brightest winter hats has just arrived.
Each one is ultra different and distinctive! Each one is the achievement of a master artist! See the clever lines, curves, or slopes built
into the crowns or rims by original French blocks created by
master artists, which depict the authentic trend of fashion as prevailing today in Paris, New York and London. Compare these
fascinating models with those domestic made hats which women
are wearing. You'll find what a contrast! Those tucks, creases, or
gathers which you find on domestic hats absolutely non-existent
on the last-minute styled Gage hats. Why let your beloved one
mar her appearance by donning in such a wrong styled hat at this
X'mas, and it not only mars her appearance but does injustice to
the beautiful fur coats or luxurious garments which you've bought
for her!

A correctly-styled hat is the crowning glory of a lady. If her
hat goes wrong no matter how rich it may be made, she looks
lack of good taste and personality in the eyes of style conscious
persons. Why be penny wise and pound foolish? Why let
your beloved one go out to an important party with a hat that is
not right in style?

To avoid such a sad disappointment, the house of Mode Élite,
established since 1918, 60 Broadway, Shanghai; 20/22 Kayamally
Building, Hongkong; 33 Sankiao Street, Hankow, offers to women
of good taste these fascinating model hats by Gage and other
famous makers at a price within reach of every budget.

Give her a Gage hat and then you'll win her for whole 1937.
Even a grandma will be brightened in one of our fascinating

models. We invite your comparison and critical judgment before you buy. Don't mar the appearance of your beloved one with mere headcovers such as wrong styled hats are.

Special show of Gage in Paris winter hats including exquisite cocktail and afternoon hats and turbans luxuriously trimmed with veils or gold or silver quills or furs or brilliant ornaments, and cleverly styled fur felt and suede tailored hats at Ram-Singh Silk Store, 220 Chun Shan Rd for four days commencing from 21st Monday to 25th Friday instant, together with a lovely selection of gifts for men, women, and children.

Come with your friend and select the best. We give 30% discount for inducement.

Next Hongkew, if you were making your way up Soochow Creek, was the large, entirely Chinese suburb of Chapei. There was a good deal of industry here, and warehouses. The Commercial Press had part of its plant here. But in general it was a poor area, and aside from that, it seemed marked for devastation. In 1931 when the Japanese fought the Chinese 19th Route Army, Chapei was the battleground, and much of it destroyed. In 1937 it was once more the scene of Chinese-Japanese fighting, and this time it was shelled, bombed, and burnt out. It was not a part that the foreigners visited; it was unknown ground to most of us.

That was not true of the "Chinese City," as we called Nantao, the old original part of the town, once walled, which lay on the far side of the French Concession, separated from it by a wide, dirty street known by the grandiloquent name of Boulevard des Deux Républiques. Here was the famous but not really attractive Willow Pattern Tea House; here we went to buy, amidst its labyrinthine streets, porcelain, pictures, jade, furniture, curios. Very much in evidence here, as in the foreign parts of Shanghai, and, indeed, nearly everywhere in China, were the varnished ducks. These had been preserved with a particular gleaming, golden-red-brown glaze and were strung up along the walls, or suspended from the ceilings, of food shops. They were so prevalent as to be a characteristic sight of the streets and were very decorative, as well as good to eat.

It was an exhausting place, noisy, dirty, bursting with people, interesting. Here we went to replenish our blue-and-white dishes, to look for amber fish, or jade archers' rings; the setting was anything but glamorous, but it abounded in treasures.

These districts—Chapei, Nantao, Hongkew—presented far

more than they showed on the surface. Here lived and worked a great proportion of the poor and humble part of the population, that was clear enough. But here too the secret societies met and made their plans, the communists gathered, and the Kuomintang, as they came to strength. Here were the gangs, the rackets, the warlords' sources of income.

All these different sections of the city were separated one from the other in times of civil or international strife, by barriers of barbed wire and sandbags, and manned by the volunteers, the local citizens who were always ready to go to the defense of the town, and who would on these occasions man these posts, check on the people passing for arms, keep order. They were often called up, so turbulent was Shanghai, like a pulse quickening as the country stirred. The police couldn't handle such emergencies alone, and the different militia were few in number. Besides, if you called on the Welsh Fusiliers, say, or the American Marines to keep out a mob, you were much more likely to provoke an international incident than if you just used the young men from the banks, from the tea firms, and the YMCA. But in ordinary times all the streets were open, and everyone passed freely, all the motley crowd of workers, beggars, clerks, country people, communists, agitators, sailors, whoever they might be, of all these nations, each with his niche somehow carved out in that haphazard, remote, complicated city.

In a way, we all shared each other's holidays. The Chinese festivals were based on the lunar calendar; their New Year, which came, ushered in with many firecrackers, long after ours, was a period of the banks closing, of bills being paid, of new clothes being sported. It came in the cold, but after it spring would be almost upon us, with the Feast of Lanterns. Then the temples used to hang hundreds of lanterns on high masts before their portals, and the children would pull lit lanterns along the sidewalks at dusk, lanterns of comic fantasy—paper rabbits, dragons, flowers, each holding its candle. In the north these were sometimes made of ice.

Such events gave pleasure to everyone. The lunar calendar, flexible, often seeming almost prescient, was attuned to the sensitivities of the rural scene—every sixty years, so they said, there being a repetitive cycle. The Day of Excited Insects, for instance, did always seem to be heralded by a lot of those unwelcome creatures we had half-forgotten, but could not but be amused to see, turning up in their swarms to disport on their special day.

The British took note of Empire Day, besides the race weeks they gave themselves in the spring and fall. The French always organized a huge parade for the Quatorze Juillet, and had their park beside Route Vallon decorated, lanterns hanging from the trees, lotus-lanterns floating on the lake. This evening of Bastille Day was one of the great pleasures of my childhood. My sister and I, dressed in thin white frocks with wide sashes, would be allowed to stay up, and when the stars came out would be taken to see the familiar park, turned into a fairyland of soft lights. We would also, on the way, watch some part of the procession, which always included a huge dragon as a compliment to the host country. All the nations preserved and cherished their National Days and celebrations jealously, most nationals being very patriotic.

The foreigners in the Treaty Ports entertained constantly, being as transients given to quick and generous hospitality, and also because with plenty of good servants, and abundant cheap food, it was easy. There were dances all year long, but the National Balls were preeminent even among some very festive occasions. The St. George's, the St. Andrew's, the St. Patrick's, the George Washington Ball, were important events. These were held, as long as it stood, in the Majestic, one of the most beautiful of hotels, with a ballroom shaped like a great four-leaf clover. These parties lent themselves to national display: St. George and the dragon dominating the one, the pipers and the wearers of the kilt another, who also took care to have plenty of haggis on the banqueting tables, haggis brought out by sea from Scotland. The Irish airs, the shamrock, made St. Patrick's Ball sentimental and lyrical. The Americans sprinkled their tables with tiny hatchets, and experimented with red, white, and blue ice cream. These affairs, nurturing national solidarity, awoke no rivalry; we all enjoyed them.

The Rickshaw Men

THE RICKSHAWS, and the poor men who jogged between their shafts, or trembled beside them on a winter's night, hoping for a fare, were a great feature of the Shanghai streets, as of those of every Chinese town.

The fortunate puller worked privately, providing the transport of a family. He would take the children to school, Missy to market and out calling, run errands. His employers saw that he had proper clothing and shoes, that his rickshaw was in repair, licensed, and with lamps in good order. He had a monthly wage, and felt himself a member of a household; he would give advice as to where to go for any special article; he knew which routes to take; he kept his vehicle clean.

Sometimes these men were highly informed politically and artistically knowledgeable. They might even know something of several languages. Circumstances had somehow pushed them into this lowly occupation—they didn't want to be house servants, perhaps they felt it was better than being in a factory—because it was in its way, more independent. They felt at home on the streets, but were unable to become drivers, having no one to sponsor them, often being afraid of the very idea. It was terribly precarious, but so was the lot of all the poor. It was physically almost killing, but for a strong, curious, uneducated man, it evidently was not altogether bad. These poor coolies felt the city was their world, and gradually learned not to take so many chances with cars and lorries. They had a great many accidents, however, partly due to the fact that the vehicle is clumsy and cumbersome in itself, easy to tip over.

My family had a great friend who was a rickshaw puller. His name was Li, and he lived and worked in Peking, a city he loved, and he was a true connoisseur of Chinese art. He spoke the Peking dialect, English of a sort, a little German, and perhaps other languages, I do not know.

When we knew him he was attached to a very successful curio shop which was popular with tourists, and sent a good deal abroad in the way of furniture, rugs, jewelry, ceramics, glass. It was owned by an American lady with a flair for business, who used to buy all these easily-procured Peking articles, assemble them in a clean, Western environment, slightly sinified (with a moon door, for instance), and sell them at a tremendous profit. The tourists, exclaiming at the cheapness of the rings or vases, compared to the prices they would have had to pay in London or New York, didn't realize that if they had gone a few streets away into the town, they would have found exactly the same things for a fraction of her figure. But of course it is the fate of the tourist to be fleeced; you have to buy your experience.

The person who had the experience and did much of the buying for this shop was none other than our friend, the rickshaw man Li. He had an eye, taste, understanding, discretion, and knew just where to find anything. He bought for his employer when she was out of the city (she lived mostly in Shanghai, where she had another shop—this was really helpful to tourists, as Shanghai lacked many of Peking's crafts).

In Peking this lady kept a little, charming, Chinese house, furnished and ready, for herself or for renters on a short-term basis, and with a full complement of servants. Among these, Li was the rickshaw puller.

Once my mother lived for a little while in that house, during which time she made a great friend of Li, so that whenever we came to the city he would attend us, advise us, and give us the pleasure of his company, while pulling us along the *hutungs*. He had so innate a sense of dignity that his occupation never seemed demeaning to him; when he picked up the shafts and started off he had the same attitude as a chauffeur who is your host and friend. While proceeding at a leisurely pace he would talk, explaining the nature of the district we were passing through, its history, the special places to see in it. Cheerful, resolute, interested in everything he was doing, he was a happy man.

He truly loved the treasures of the city, the temples, the walls, the ceramics and jade. He told us that he had these beautiful things so clearly in his mind that he could always see them, and if he were waiting with his rickshaw for someone, he would remember these objects, one by one, in detail. So, he said, he had no need to own them physically—he had them.

He not only bought for the curio shop, but he saw to the packing. He was the indispensable factotum and genius of the establishment, though I suspect his pay was small enough.

You only had to tell him the sort of thing you were after, and he would remember, almost at once, how he had seen such and such a piece outside Ch'ien Men. It was in this way that I was able to get the table I have taken with me across sea after sea ever since. It is a high, classical, black wood table—the one Li located had Ch'ien Lung's seal on it (not a fake seal, the real article; Ch'ien Lung's "seal" adorns a myriad nineteenth-century, and later, articles), and he bargained for me for it, brushing aside preliminary figures.

Most rickshaw men, obviously, were not like this. Many were horribly poor, and could hardly keep up the hire of their flimsy, dirty rickshaws. They were dreadfully cold in winter, underfed, exhausted, anxious, short-lived. But the majority were strong and cheerful; they ran fast, and if you were in company would enjoy racing each other on a wide road. They had splendid muscles. We were always sensible of their problems, paid them more than their fare, bound up their cuts if they asked us to. But they were too many for individual pity and concern; they epitomized, in their way, the vast insistent need of the country.

The rickshaw pullers had in Shanghai for very many years a protector, a Scot named George Mathieson, who devoted himself to succoring them through a mission entirely managed and inspired by himself. Though he called the shelter he built for them the Shanghai Rickshaw Men's Mission, he was not strictly speaking a missionary. He made no effort to proselytize, and no one needed to profess Christianity to receive help from him. He did, however, preach a short sermon to the coolies every night, being himself deeply religious and feeling this would help them.

He made this cause the great purpose of his life, supporting himself meanwhile by running a small tweed-importing business, an affair of one room, where you could buy Harris tweed, smelling of peat and the loom. He was a tall, thin man, whose red hair had become sandy-colored by the time I can remember him. I can remember how long and bony his wrists were, resting on a thick piece of greenish tweed, his big hands with their prominent knuckles covered with fine red hairs.

In appearance he was an archetype of the "Red Barbarian," and a total contrast to the short, yellow-skinned persons, with their hairless arms and hands, to whom he ministered. I don't know whether this would ever have occurred to the coolies, but I am sure that they, like everyone else, loved George Mathieson.

At the mission he dealt with each man individually, giving him all the help and comfort that he could. The rickshaw men could rest there, have a hot bath and a meal. If they could pay a few coppers that would be accepted, but they did not have to. Mr. Mathieson would buy them new rickshaws if they lost theirs through an accident, and would help them to regain their permits if they lost their licenses through some traffic misdemeanor. If a coolie saw a fare just across the street, it was so important for him not to lose an opportunity to earn that he often would dart across, regardless of traffic—this Mr. Mathieson understood, though he did not condone the risk it involved, and he would stand by them in court.

He urged the municipality to put out free *k'angs* of tea, equipped with bamboo dippers, on the streets in summer for these poor men, and they complied. This practice was adopted here and there by other philanthropists—but because of Mr. Mathieson there were more of these and every one was a boon. The public gave him generous support; we were all full of admiration, respect, and sympathy for him. At Christmas the papers helped him to raise money for the mission; people would give him a donation in lieu of sending flowers to funerals—it was an activity no one forgot.

The Door of Hope

THIS WAS another favorite Shanghai charity, run, I believe, by women, chiefly American women. Shanghai, being a port much visited by sailors, contained a great many brothels, places which were unusually tragic because of the nature of the country. The poverty in China was so overwhelming that hard-pressed parents would sometimes sell their daughters to these houses. At a time of crop failure, of flood or famine, of business depressions, if a family had more girls than they felt they could manage they would sell them even when still children to dealers in this traffic.

The Door of Hope set itself out to save as many of these poor little beings as they could. They arranged with certain Chinese to find them the girls and arrange with the courts that they might be taken out of the brothels and sent to them. The work must have begun early in the century—at any rate by 1914 they were a well-established, quite large organization, run by Christians who had complete faith that their financial necessities would always be met, as indeed they were.

Once the children came to the Door of Hope they were treated with the utmost kindness, rehabilitated, educated, and trained to support themselves. Some became teachers, some nurses, some "Bible Women," which meant that they would go into homes where there was an interest in Christianity, and read and discuss the Bible there. Some married, some stayed on to help the Door of Hope. The girls who had been rescued and had lived here had an enviable reputation for their behavior and talents, and it was not hard for them to find husbands.

Riding

You would not have thought, from the look of it, that Shanghai and its environs would offer a terrain at all inviting to the rider. But as the essential thing about the rider is that he has to ride, he will take immense pains to make his sport materialize. The paddy fields outside the city, cut as they were by innumerable small ditches; the "grips" which brought down so many ponies; the watery country crisscrossed by creeks, with those treacherous narrow stone bridges; the fields beset with graves—none of these obstacles deterred the *aficionados*.

When the Treaty Ports began, the world was still in the era of the horse and carriage; there was nothing particularly luxurious in the quest of the horse per se. In those early days the foreigners made their first acquaintance with the China pony, imported carriages, and very soon started racing and cross-country riding.

The China pony, a creature which came to be much beloved by some of us, comes from Mongolia, and descends from the equine troops which for centuries have run wild over over the northern plains, unbred, herded by Tatars, a part of that nomadic life which extended into Central Asia. These animals were rather small (thirteen hands was an average size), tough, wiry, capable of great endurance, plucky. They were scarred with wolf bites, and not at all smart to look at.

Every spring herds of them were driven down to the auctions in Hankow, Tientsin, and Shanghai, to be sold at the ring as "griffins" or unknowns (hence the common use of the word "griffin" for a newcomer to the coast). They looked exactly like those bewitching horses we see on Chinese scrolls, as well they should—from horses such as these the pictures had been made. They were generally not handsomely formed, but full of humor, knowing, paintable. When you had bought your prize, then you had to find out what destiny had sent you—a hack, a polo pony, a jumper, a racer. If he was not what you wanted you sent him back to auction. At this stage, they were not at all expensive.

Every spring and fall there were races, polo was played in the summer, in the winter there were hunts and cross-country riding, and every morning of the year the riders went out, rain or shine, for an hour before breakfast.

Cars were a little slow in coming to China: till the Kuomintang came in, there wasn't far to go in them—only within the enclaves of the foreign ports, where there were proper roads. People used carriages till well on into the twenties. We liked carriages, we liked their pace, their openness, allowing you to see the rich, full life of the streets, with the open-fronted shops. When my father was an exchange broker, he like all his colleagues tore about the business district in a trap, standing up, his *mafoo* driving as fast as he could. All this was colorful and exciting, much more so than any car could be. But the cars of course prevailed as the years went on.

Thirteen hands is enough for an animal which has to carry a modest weight, but a big foreigner was too much for them, they were not up to that. So people began to bring in Australian Walers, but seldom with much success. The country didn't suit them; they were clumsy in the field, fell at the grips, drooped in the heat, and slid about on the bridges, unlike the Mongolian ponies, who surmounted these hazards with aplomb. Then it was thought that cross-breeding might be the answer, and the Walers were bred to ponies, producing what was called a "Y" (the local pony being a "Z"). The "Y"s might have a height of fifteen or sixteen hands, and were up to a good deal of weight. It was quite a successful experiment, there were a good many "Y"s to be seen.

Most of the ponies were not, strictly speaking, beautiful—they were more noble than they looked. But once for a time I was loaned a very beautiful, exceptionally small pony, which had the head and shoulders of an Arab, and was graceful and fiery, a great pleasure to ride. For centuries—from Han times—horses were sent into China from Persia, Bactria, Ferghana. The Chinese needed mounts capable of forming an effective cavalry, with which they could confront their Tatar foes, and they were prepared to pay for blooded animals with great treasure: with silk. They could not keep up the strain of these horses, more always had to be sent in. Ming Huang of the T'ang had, they say, forty thousand horses in his stables at one time. The Toba Wei, the Golden Tatars, the Tatars under Genghiz Khan, were all ardent lovers of horses, always eager to improve the breed, discouraged that their horses degenerated. It is not surprising that the Chinese have been among the greatest horse-painters in the world, led by geniuses like Han Kan, Li Kung-lin, and Chao Mêng-fu.

Something of these splendid strains must have remained, so that a rare pony would arch its neck like a noble stallion.

The standard of riding was high and diversified. A Manchu prince used to appear every morning on Great Western Road, on the outskirts of the Settlement, an old-fashioned but very competent rider, standing almost straight in his stirrups. The Americans sat easily right down in their saddles, loping along; the British rode in the cavalry manner; the Germans had backs like ramrods. The Cossacks rode the best—they were dream-riders. People didn't talk about dressage then, but in winter, when it was too cold and unpleasant outside to do much, some of us used to go to their schools after the day's work, and in the dim light of a few lamps go round and round the ring, jumping. How inept these men must have thought us! They had done far better, instinctively, when they were still small children. But they were patient teachers.

People dressed well. The Indian tailors made our jodhpurs and breeches, and for the hunts everyone turned out in stocks and white breeches, looking very smart. Some of the men got their riding clothes (especially their pink coats) from London, even though the hunts were only paper-chases, and the country little more than divided fields. But riding is riding; it's like music— you're so happy to be able to do it at all, the setting is secondary. It brings out qualities of skill, courage, companionship, sensitivity. You want to be able to ride with a silken thread; you have to go on trying.

The best part of it was the regular early morning ride into the country, before we all went to work, when the light was so fresh and clear, before the day began to crowd in. Most of the world was awake, though, in China, where hardly anyone knew what it meant to lie abed.

Out at the far end of Yü Yuen Road the *mafoos* would be waiting with the ponies, having walked them out from their stables—sometimes as far away as the Race Course. The grooms would be waiting patiently, talking; they greeted us with smiles and cheerful looks, and seemed satisfied with their lot, which gave them company, time to open, no pressure, and the interest of looking after their charges. In winter the ponies' breath rose up in the frosty air, and the men would be stamping their feet, in their cloth-soled shoes, which were probably warmer than our leather boots. My feet used to be like ice on those winter rides, well do I remember.

The riders drew up in their cars; got out, measured the stirrups, tested the girths, mounted, and rode away for that magic hour which seemed every day to be the same, and yet was never the same. The air, blowing from the open fields, was sweet. In spring and summer the plane trees on the road cast their abundant, big-leafed shade; we would leave their coolness for some narrow path of hard-beaten earth, passing between low fences made of living willows, and then going out into the fields, on paths which were even narrower. Single-file we passed the paddy fields which were so brilliantly green in summer, and which alternated with crops of beans, cabbages, and the rape which was yellow as buttercups.

There were many hamlets, with thatch-roofed cottages and dirt threshing floors, and many creeks, where the willows hung low over the water. Mandarin ducks swam down them, and sometimes you would see a man with a boatload of cormorants, fishing, the birds taking off, and returning fish in beak. Their necks were ringed with a tight metal band, so they could not swallow their prey. Side by side, attentive, obedient, they would line the gunwales of a sampan.

By the creeks were waterwheels; in summer you would see the shiny black water buffaloes plodding round as they turned the wheel, bring up thin braided streams of water into the flooded paddy fields. They would be hard at work when we passed them early in the day, but if we came later we would find them wallowing in the creeks, taking their ease. The ponies seldom shied at them; they seemed to know what it was all about, and understood that the creaking wheels meant them no ill. They were, however, sometimes reluctant to cross the bridges—often we had to dismount and lead them over.

Once when I was crossing a bridge on a pony who was always ready for anything, my dear Kaweah, he saw at the far end something which alarmed him, and immediately began to turn around. The bridge being only a slab of stone, not more than four feet wide, he and I were instantly in midair. To my horrified companion it was "just like Tom Mix going over a cliff." But though dramatic, we both fell too lightly for serious harm, onto the soft mud, luckily missing the filthy water. Kaweah tipped me off as we fell, and was good enough not to land on me, so it was all over soon enough.

The rice fields, flooded in summer, were after the fall harvest allowed to dry out, with the old tufts of the plant still adhering to the clayey soil. When winter came all this froze solid, and the fields seemed as though studded with these low, yellowish knobs; we would gallop over them, rejoicing.

The fields were studded, also, with something more permanent —with graves and grave mounds. These were sometimes quite high—fifteen feet or more—you would calculate, in a hunt, whether it would be better to ride over or round a grave mound that might lie in your path near the finish.

It was estimated that an eighth of the arable land in the Yangtze Valley was lost to graves—something the country could in no way afford, but except under a tyranny these customs are hard to dislodge. In hilly land the family graves would be built on the slopes which were not terraced, and could be spared, perhaps; but down on the plains there was nothing for it but to put your ancestor right down in the midst of the crops. The poor could not afford more than the thinnest of wooden coffins, if that, and one's pony sometimes knocked aside a bone which looked horridly familiar. But these macabre appearances disturbed no one—no one was morbid about them. The Chinese felt on an easy and natural footing with their departed, to whom they made presentations, at the proper season, of paper necessities, burning these near the grave. These representations were lifelike enough, of suits of clothes, *sycee*, food. What they dreaded was the thought of changing a grave-site. When a fortune was told, peoples' minds would be set at rest about this, or the reverse, as the lot might fall. It all depended on geomancy then—not on a government edict.

The peasants we encountered were friendly, even genial, waving and smiling. In the winter they were punctiliously compensated if a careless horseman rode over their crops, and most of us were extremely careful not to damage anything. I never felt anything but goodwill in the villages—I do not remember a single hostile glance. Had I met with one I would not have been surprised—the contrast between people who could afford this hour of sheer pleasure, and these peasants with their life of unending, ill-rewarded toil, was so patent. Most of them, I suppose, accepted it as inevitable. They had never known anything else. Then, the strikes in Shanghai must have been very remote from them, in their villages.

Magpies, golden orioles, and bluejays flew over us in that short and captivating hour. How soon it passed, how difficult it is to recapture! The sky above the bamboos was almost white, there was that squeak of leather, there were the grey lines of thatched roofs, the soft grace of the willows. In the autumn blue smoke rose up from the braziers while someone made the rice ready; nearby women would stand on stools, holding the new grain high over their heads, in shallow baskets, letting it drift into the wind, winnowing it. Children would dart out to watch us pass. We were a mutual spectacle, the one to the other. You trotted on, someone in front would hold out his hand, calling back, " 'ware onions!" and you swerved to avoid the plants.

In the light rain of summer, in the frosty fall, and in the bright spring mornings we would meet and start off, with little speech, linked by an intense awareness of the present—just this particular path, that hedge, this opportunity to canter up to the bridge, the bridge itself. Riders are always on guard as to their riding—they have to be on the alert as to the terrain, the reins, the pony, but in so doing they forget themselves and let another guard down, so that you get to know each other without words. It's like playing in an ensemble, the nature of a person reveals itself, even in the way he picks up his bow, arranges the music, waits for the beat. There is a companionship about it, strong but inarticulate.

Banditry

In Chinese literature there is no permanent definition
of a bandit or non-bandit. The connotation depends on
time, circumstance, and subjective point of view.

LI CHIEN-NUNG

IN THE TWENTIES and thirties banditry was rife, indicative of the
condition of the country and the thin line separating the farmer
and the soldier from crime undertaken in desperation.

A famous instance of banditry occurred in 1923, when there
was really no central government, except in name. Nevertheless
the Peking government was held responsible by the Westerners,
who had to negotiate with someone, and in the end the twenty-
five-odd foreigners were rescued. The case was notorious because
it was so bold, and because so many nationalities were involved. It
was called after the railway station near which it took place,
Linching, in Shantung, where some bandits derailed the Tientsin-
Pukow Express, abducting certain passengers, who had been on
their way to Shanghai on the Blue Express, the best train on the
line.

Shantung was a particularly bandit-ridden province, full of ex-
soldiers who had no chance of employment. In the various armies
at that time in more or less loose formation in North China, there
were reckoned to be something over a million men, but they had
no zeal in suppressing bandits. Many of them had followed this

occupation, and might well do so again; they were unpaid, wretchedly clothed, hungry, unprincipled, undisciplined. On the mountainous borders of Shantung, where if need arose they could slip over a safer frontier, bandits could operate almost with impunity.

Linching was an almost ideal place for an ambush; here a thousand-odd bandits tore up a length of track, and then waited for the Express which thundered along in the middle of the night and was derailed. The bandits hurried aboard and forced about two hundred passengers off the train, not giving them time to dress, though they were quick about collecting their valuables.

The foreigners included British, Americans, Danes, Italians, Germans, and French, some of them on their way around the world as a part of a luxury trip; others were businessmen. Among the tourists was Miss Lucy Aldrich, whose sister married into the Rockefeller family. The bandits had no idea who she was, and as she did not prove a good walker and they felt in a hurry, they soon left her in a field. She made her way to safety; probably they never knew what a prize they had abandoned.

A friend of ours happened to be on the Blue Express that night, a businessman called Day, who afterwards told us a good deal about it. He was a good observer, being very calm and optimistic. He could not help being amused throughout by the bandits' naïveté and ignorance, even when he was distressed over what they were doing. He was upset at the plight of some of the women, who were pushed off the train in their nightgowns, barefoot, and made to walk over the rough fields, or mounted on donkeys, which they found almost as bad. Mr. Day was sure everyone would come out unscathed, but there were dangerous possibilities of accidents—the bandits were ingenuous, but they were also armed. One youthful bandit came up to him and took his watch, offering him at the same time another, very inferior one, which he had taken off someone else's wrist a few moments before. Another man approached him, his two hands cupped together and brimming over with rings, asking him to value them for him. The bandits took the whole situation as a perfectly normal thing, unlike their indignant and appalled captives.

The prisoners were taken to an old fort on the top of a mountain and held for several weeks, while negotiations went on between the bandits, the Chinese authorities, and the various consuls concerned. It was uncomfortable in the camp, and the captives were both hungry and bored. A kindly missionary contrived to send them all he had to give: some pork and a few copies of the New Testament, gifts which were rather ruefully commented upon by a Jewish reporter (who, however, gratefully sent the man of God a contribution for his mission, when the affair was over).

Colonel Aldrich's textbook, *Practical Chinese*, contains a number of phrases to be used in these contingencies, like: "The local militia's Adjutant General says 'We have already ordered a battalion of cavalry from Pao-t'ou to take along two motor cars and go to the rescue. It will not be long before the kidnapped persons are out of danger . . . I hope that this matter may have a most satisfactory conclusion.' "

It didn't always. Sometimes people were tortured, sometimes the imprisonment lasted a very long time, sometimes those who had been seized were killed. It was no laughing matter to be taken by bandits, however ingenuous they appeared.

The Tungchow

THE CASE of SS *Tungchow* was another example of what sometimes happened as people went about their business on the
China Coast, and why they were loath to give up extraterritoriality.

The SS *Tungchow*, a China Steam Navigation vessel, and part
of the fleet of Butterfield & Swire, an important shipping firm on
the Coast, was pirated in February, 1935, as she was on her way
from Shanghai to Chefoo, in Shantung. It was the second time this
one ship had suffered this outrage, but it was made famous, among
so many like happenings, because of the peculiar nature of her
passenger list. She was taking seventy children, between the ages
of seven and seventeen, back to the Chefoo School after their
Christmas holidays in Shanghai. They were the sons or daughters
of doctors, lawyers, missionaries, business people, who for one
reason or another had not sent their offspring home. Most of the
seventy were boys, aged twelve or under. This piracy was not
looked upon by them as a calamity, but as a truly marvelous
experience, one that filled all their contemporaries in Chefoo, who
had been so unlucky as to miss it, with deepest envy.

Like most of the ships on the coastal run, the *Tungchow* was
equipped with pirate grills—iron bars which enclosed the central
portion of the vessel, including of course the bridge, separating it
from the fore and aft sections. At these grills armed White Rus-

sians were posted, day and night, guards who held the keys to the grills.

It was afterward learned that the pirates, who went to work quite scientifically, had been informed by their agents that the *Tungchow* was carrying Chinese $250,000, in bullion, on this journey. They paid $4,000 for this intelligence, and the thought of so much booty made them exceptionally bold. They hardly waited for the ship to pass Woosung, at the mouth of the Whangpoo, before they acted. They had all come aboard, as was usual, as deck passengers, and were under the orders of a young but experienced pirate, who knew exactly what to do.

These coasters were, because of the deck passengers, and cargo often piled up on the hatches to be unloaded at small ports on the way, not as ship-shape as more conventional steamers were; it was possible for a certain amount of illicit movement to take place before anything was remarked. It only seemed some sort of minor scuffle, at first, when the pirates drew their pistols and advanced upon one of the guards, the gallant Sergeant Tihrivoff, shooting at him and at the locks. Sergeant Tihrivoff instantly responded, firing at the pirates, and then ducking down behind a skylight, where they could not aim at him. When he realized which man was the pirate chief he jumped up and drew a bead on him, but his pistol jammed and the others rushed him. He fought them off, as brave as a lion, but they were too many for him. He was a very large man, and stood, swaying, with several pirates actually on top of him, before he fell to the deck. Afterward one of the desperadoes put a bullet through his head, and he was dumped overboard.

This preliminary struggle was over so quickly that the alarm was not given, and hardly anyone knew what was going on, till they saw the poor sergeant groaning on the deck. Two children, however, watching, rushed down to the engine room and alerted a young New Zealander, an engineer, who came upstairs with them, perfectly calm and carrying the youngsters in his arms. He had been on the previous pirating of the *Tungchow* and seemed not to be in the least apprehensive—in any case, no doubt he wanted the children to feel that nothing very dreadful was happening. As he came out of a companionway onto the deck he encountered a pirate who shot him instantly, missing the children by inches.

The ship's company was by now aware of what was going on, and everyone assembled. The captain, Mr. J. G. Smart, and his officers gave up their arms, as the pirates demanded, and complied

with all their orders, because of the young passengers. These officers behaved from first to last with the greatest bravery and cir-
cumspection; they knew how emotional and senseless the pirates
might become if frustrated, and they knew, too, of course, that
even if they made no attempt to send out signals or defend themselves, the Company in Shanghai would remark upon their silence
and investigate it. They gave no signals to any foreign ships in the
offing, for fear of reprisals, and docilely turned the *Tungchow*
round (she was heading north) and set her course for that old
pirate's lair, Bias Bay, as the new masters of the ship directed.
They also cooperated in the scheme that the ship should be dis-
guised: they painted two white circles on the funnel, with a red
line between, and they changed her name to the *Tao Maru*, so that
she might be mistaken for a Japanese vessel.

Meanwhile, for many of the children, who knew nothing of the
shooting, the whole episode took on the aspect of A Dream Come
True. They were confined to the salon, but there had complete
liberty to rush about and do what they wished, and all the food
cupboards were flung open, so that they could help themselves.
The pirates, like most Orientals, loved children, and became
friends with them at once. They probably had no idea how romantic a cast they had given the journey in the children's eyes—so
much so that most of these boys, as soon as they had an inkling
that something unusual was afoot, instantly *knew* with intense
joy, that they had been pirated. And there was still another reason
for the children's enthusiastic cooperation: they looked upon
these men as benefactors, through whom they were going to miss
at least a week of school.

For the schoolmaster and the five lady teachers who were with
the children, each day was a nightmare. Pirates stood behind their
chairs during meals, with drawn pistols. Some of the children must
have been sensitive as to what this might imply, and it is recorded
that one little girl was in a constant state of anxiety about her
rabbits, as she was not allowed to go out and tend to them. But
most of the seventy had a splendid week, and were easy in their
minds, feeling the pirates were friends.

Very soon after the event, the owners of the *Tungchow* began
to suspect that something was amiss, and before long the British
fleet in Far Eastern waters was alerted. The aircraft carrier, HMS
Hermes, which was exercising off Swatow, south of Shanghai,
began at once to search for the merchant ship, but international

agreements forbade her planes flying over Chinese territory, so she was hampered in her survey. The cruiser HMS *Suffolk* and the sloop HMS *Sandwich* joined her, as did many other ships, in this quest. The whole coast buzzed with the news, and felt the same anxiety.

The pirates, having secured the *Tungchow*, were not long in looking for the bullion for which they had undertaken this crime. To their rage and disappointment they discovered that all there was aboard in the way of money was in the form of banknotes. There were five chests of these, but every note had to be manually signed when it was issued at destination, in order to have any value. (The banks had learned to do this through hard experience.) The pirates saw that their venture would be a financial failure, and were incensed. All they could do was to make the rounds of the passengers and collect what they could in the way of watches, rings, and cash. This was not much. The children's pocket money came to something like Ch. $7 a term. Altogether they took in no more than $3,000, not even covering their initial investment.

By the time they reached Bias Bay they were sick of the whole thing, and anxious to get clear of the ship. A few planes had been sighted, and they were nervous. They signaled the junks in the Bay, to come and get them; but the junks, through some mysterious grapevine, knew what was afoot, and that the British navy was after this vessel—they did not want to get mixed up with the pirates. At last one was bold enough to approach, and all the pirates could lay their hands on was hastily stowed aboard, while four of the villains boarded her. Just then another plane was seen overhead, and these four, not waiting for their companions, cut the rope which secured the junk to the *Tungchow* and went off.

This left four pirates still aboard the *Tungchow*, whom the captain agreed to put ashore in a lifeboat. They set off with five Chinese hostages, the chief officer, and the wireless operator, on a rather long pull. Bias Bay is very shallow, which has always been an advantage to its pirate community, who while tending their fields can see far over the water and escape into the hinterland if they see enemies approaching.

The lifeboat proceeded easily enough till one of the pirates, in a fit of bravado, or perhaps believing they were nearly at the land, shot a hole through the bottom with his Mauser. The sailors managed to bung it up, till they beached, when the pirates hurried away, only too anxious to disappear, while the *Tungchow* sent another lifeboat to pick up the escort.

The *Tungchow* then made her way to Hong Kong, a short run from Bias Bay. Meanwhile the children cut up the pirate chief's old tattered sweater, which he had flung them as a souvenir as he left, into small pieces, and divided them among themselves.

At Hong Kong everyone was fêted and cosseted till another ship was ready to take the Chefoo School contingent back to their proper destination. Not long afterward the children were writing essays on their great adventure, something they had known they would have to do, something they had wanted to avoid.

The deaths of Sergeant Tihrivoff and Mr. McDonald marred this otherwise happy outcome. Reuters' correspondent in Hong Kong cabled Shanghai, as the *Tungchow* entered the harbor: "No news since the end of the great war was greeted with such general relief by the foreign community as the tidings that the children were safe."

Houseboating

The bamboos envelop the inn by the bridge.

&

A boat lying idle the whole day long, as nobody
wishes to cross the river.

HOUSEBOATING FLOURISHED among the Westerners in the delta
country around Shanghai, because of the lack of roads and
inns, aside from the intrinsic pleasure of the exercise. It was a part
of the slow tempo of life, which made the world seem more harmonious and agreeable than it really was. To have most people
going about on foot, by wheelbarrow, cart, sedan chair, rickshaw,
pony-back, was romantic, though perfectly hopeless if progress
was to be made on the economic woes which beset the country.
Still, as the individual foreigner could do little to put things right,
he could at least savor the pleasures of the past as he went with his
houseboat through the canals of the hinterland. It was a way of
getting quite close to the heart of ancient rustic China.

A few foreigners owned houseboats, keeping them in the Soochow Creek by Garden Reach, or at Hen Li or Ming Hong,
where regattas were held. But you could hire a roomy Chinese
houseboat, clean and shining, beautiful with carved wood, which
did as well or better. You took your own bedding, drinking water,
and lamps with you, and your servants—a houseboat trip didn't
mean roughing it.

For Shanghai people the lovely countryside beyond Soochow was the usual houseboating milieu. My family used to anchor our rented boat near a village called Ch'ang Ch'o (Ch'ang Zo, in the local dialect), a poetic, dreamy sort of place where we never encountered any other foreigners. We went there, year after year, for a few days every spring, when the rice was sprouting and the rape already a brilliant yellow.

Soochow is a very ancient town, renowned for the beauty of its women and its soft speech. It was once a center for artists, and famous for its gardens. Some traces of these charms remained even in modern times, though as time passed it had become more known for the expert faking of pictures than for painting originals.

The T'ang poet, Po Chü-i, in 825 after he had held the governorship of Hangchow, was made governor of Soochow. He thought it would be a sinecure, and was greatly disappointed to find that his desk was piled high with old files. Never in his life had he been obliged to do so much laborious paperwork. After he had this backlog sorted out, however, he turned his mind to other things, trying to arrange a local performance of his favorite ballet, *Rainbow Skirts and Feather Fans*. He had managed to have this produced in Hangchow, but was transferred just as the troupe was trained—here he hoped to get another set of dancers and musicians together, who would have the interest to learn it. It was difficult to find enough talent in Soochow, and it is not clear whether the ballet actually did take shape in his rather short term of office. This throws a sharp light on the Soochow of the ninth century, this search for singers, for notations and music, for dancers—as well as on the character of the governor.

A thousand years had passed, and little of this cultural ambiance was discernible to the eager, but ignorant, foreign visitor. But it was a pleasure to reach the city, to see its maze of canals with their camel-backed bridges, its wall. We used to arrive there in the morning, having left Shanghai the previous evening, and having come through the Grand Canal all night with the tow, one of a string of other boats behind a tug. (The original Grand Canal, built under the Sui in the sixth and seventh centuries, began at Yangchow; this part was a later addition.)

At Shanghai we embarked at the Garden Bridge, and then moved out into midstream, waiting for the tow. As soon as we were tied up to the last boat, we felt the expedition had really started, and would spend the whole evening on the wide foredeck, leaning against the flat boards of the cabin. The city would fall behind us, with its lights and factories, and we would find ourselves passing through silent fields, everything peaceful and calm. The moon would rise; the water gurgled and slapped at the sides of the boat.

The servants were happy; they liked the change and the simplicity of it, and enjoyed being with the boatmen, aft, also watching the shore, talking. They made nothing of cooking over open braziers, which had been familiar to them long before they ever saw a foreign stove, and turned out course after course as perfectly as they would have done at home, excelling, like all Chinese, in *"pan-fa"* or the art of making things work out.

There was a stretch of open water as you reached Soochow, where the boats going only so far would cast off from the tow, and make their way alone, with the *ulow*. This was also a great moment; once more it seemed as though now we had really begun. The slight throb of the engine faded away, and we were left with only the gentle, silken swish of the oar, really back in medieval times.

There used to be many fine monuments in Soochow, but the T'ai-p'ings destroyed most of them. The pagoda was still there, and the wall; but we were absorbed in the waterways of the town (often called a Chinese Venice) and in the bridges whose smooth round arches joined their dark reflections to make perfect circles.

As we went slowly forward, the cry of *"Yang kuei-tze"* rang out at once, and people came running to see the foreign devils, crowding on the bridges, pointing. They used this term without hostility—it was just the name for us. Westerners were not really rare in that area, but the Chinese love to watch people, and our family having several red-haired members no doubt looked satisfactorily barbarian to them. We really were red, we confirmed a legend.

The houses edged the embankment, except for the many flights of stairs which led to the water, where people would be kneeling, washing, scouring things.

With all these crowds, we were as glad to be free of Soochow as we had been to enter it. Soon we glided out into the long still stretches of canal and creek which were the last stage of the journey, leading to Ch'ang Ch'o, and then to the foot of the hills. Now the trekkers would get out their yokes and ropes, fasten these to the mast, and go ashore to pull in a leisurely fashion, increasing our slow pace by some minute fraction. We would join them on the tow path, reveling in being in the country. When we reached a bridge a puller, making a bundle of his yoke and rope, would race up the steps to the arch and throw his harness right under the structure, darting across to catch it as it came up on the other side. I never saw anyone fail to do this with perfect adroitness. Even little girls took a sure aim, retrieved their rope, and came skipping down the steps, adjusting the light yoke as they did so. They all seemed to enjoy this phase of the trip; evidently it was easy to pull, no one bent to it.

About noon we reached a quiet place under some willows, as far as possible from any hamlet, and would tie up. To our left, beyond the fields, were lakes. Up above us on our right were the hills, where the azaleas and wild lilacs were coming out and the wisteria was in bud. Flights of stone steps led gradually to the summit, where there was a temple. It was a typical mild rustic scene of the region.

The next days were spent in the hills, visiting the temple, walking along the banks of the canals, or taking sampans out onto the lakes, where we would buy fish for our tiffin just as they were pulled out of the water. At night we fell asleep in the wonderful stillness of our creek anchorage on the lightly moving water.

The temple above us was a modest one, with not many courts. The roofs were of black tile, the walls whitewashed; a few slow-paced monks lived there, dreaming away the time. Not many people came to perform their devotions or light a candle before Kwan Yin. It was enough that it still functioned at all, and was respected by a few faithful Buddhists, in an era when so many of their temples were entirely neglected.

There was here one very beautiful architectural feature, the work of some unknown artist. This was a gallery which, open on its inner side to a courtyard of tangled bushes, plunged down the hillside in a few perfect, balanced curves. On the side facing the hill were a number of windows, each cut with grace and assurance, in the shape of traditional symbols—the gourd, the peach, the quince, the double cash, Buddha's fingers—out of the white wall. The descent of this gallery down the hill conformed to the rules governing the arrangement of gardens: that galleries must not be lacking, and that these should follow the curves of the ground, being sometimes visible, sometimes invisible. This would be understood locally, Soochow having been so passionately interested in gardens in the past.

It took us two or three hours to reach the temple from our canal-bank, on those lazy spring mornings. We kept on stopping and turning round to look out on the lakes and canals below, sparkling in the sun, and on the neat checkerboard of the fields, green with rice, yellow with rape. The servants always left before we did, taking what was necessary for the preparation of our lunch. This was not a strict temple, and the cook could do what he liked—they did not demand that their guests be vegetarians. Afterwards we wandered about in the hills, picking wild flowers, admiring the gallery, watching the birds.

Going downhill in the afternoon we passed again on the lower slopes of the mountain a number of grave sites, sometimes meeting family parties which had assembled to tidy up their mounds and to burn paper money, clothes, and food for the use of the ancestors. Easter coincides with *Ch'ing Ming* in some years, and it is this festival which concerns itself with these duties. The families were always cheerful; the Chinese have generally taken the transition of death more lightly than we have—it is the "life partings" they have found unbearably sad. The grave enclosures, surrounded by low walls, shaded by clumps of trees, were pleasant little places, not at all macabre. We took our tone from the Chinese in respect to them, and if our visit did not fall at the same time as *Ch'ing Ming*, we used, when we were children, to hide and hunt our Easter eggs in these very sites.

An unpleasant feature of the Chinese village then, every Chinese village, was the presence of "wonks" or pi dogs—mongrels and scavengers, watchdogs, hostile and dangerous to strangers. You always had to be on your guard against them, for, though cowardly, they would on occasion attack a passerby.

Once we were at Ch'ang Ch'o at the time of the Dragon Boat Festival, the fifth day of the fifth moon, an important holiday. On that afternoon we hired a boat and went outside the water-gate of the town to watch the races. The First Families of Ch'ang Ch'o were lined up in handsome houseboats, and the water was everywhere astir with small craft, while the footpaths and housetops were thronged with spectators.

About twenty boats were racing, each with its double line of rowers, fifty to a boat. Decorated with banners and flags, with a scarlet and gold figurehead of a dragon, and a dragon's tail over the stern (made of carved wood), these made a fine show. Amid-ships was a red-canopied cabin, holding drummers, to whose furious beat the crew plied their paddles. They were very expert, turning, wheeling in their own length, and almost flying over the water in a fine spirited display.

The festival is to commemorate Ch'u Yüan, the third century statesman who, greatly disturbed by the corruption he saw about him, and falsely accused by his prince, drowned himself. His friends could never find his body; all they could do was to sacrifice to his spirit, when they presented his shade with a special sort of rice-cake. These are still made on this holiday, a part of the ritual.

Soochow's gardens have often been described: the Shih Tzu Lin, or Lion Grove, with its curious leonine rocks; the Hsi Yüan, destroyed by the T'ai-p'ings, and being restored in my time; the very old Wang Shih Yüan, renowned for its peonies. There was a garden which had many times changed its name, which had even been a *yamen*, and was particularly loved for its wisteria, its moongate in an undulating wall and the zig-zag bridge over its pond. This was the Cho Chêng Yuan, laid out at the beginning of the sixteenth century by the Wang family on the site of an old temple, and where the artist Wên Chêng-ming had lived. In the seventeenth century it was taken over by the local administration and given the name of the Garden of Inefficient Government (or the Garden of the Stupid Officials). Later a Manchu officer used it as his headquarters calling it the Eight Banners, the Pa Ch'i; once the T'ai-p'ings occupied it. But it's no good starting to describe gardens, one is never finished.

There was one outside Soochow near the hills, called the Prince's Garden, which I once visited. It was part of the villa of a rich family, which had fallen on hard times and moved away. An old *k'ai-men'ti* was taking care of it, and would let you in, proud of his neatly swept empty courts, the trim pebbled paths laid out in geometric patterns.

It was one of those romantic places you find as the *mise-en-scène* of an old Chinese novel, an affair of many courts, with long whitewashed walls and moon doorways; with the beautiful latticed windows of old China, when every frame was a work of art, particularly appropriate to its own district; where everything lent itself to the play of light and shadow; where it was all artless, suitable for a country villa, yet conceived with the greatest finesse.

Once candles burned behind the paper which covered the windows, casting their mild glow onto the paving of the courtyards, once wisteria and peonies had made the courtyards fragrant, and the sharp silhouettes of the bamboos, falling on the long white walls, had delighted the occupants—but now it was only a shell, charming still under the bright sky of a spring morning, but melancholy, deserted.

The Ningpo Lakes

THE TIME we went houseboating on the Ningpo Lakes was a very different thing from the Ch'ang Ch'o expeditions. We had to take a coaster from the Bund, which reached Ningpo in the morning. This old town is in Chekiang, and was once a Treaty Port, but as Shanghai grew it declined in importance for the foreigners and they gave up their status there.

In the Shanghai area Ningpo was considered the back of beyond. If a man's creditors were pressing him, if a thief were on the run, he was always supposed to have gone to "Ningpo more far." It was also famous for a strong varnish produced there, much used on furniture all over the country, and it exported mats, tea, fans, all sorts of articles to the Shanghai market.

We disembarked on the Ningpo Bund, with all our complicated gear piled up around us on the quay, and proceeded to hire three narrow country boats, each about twenty feet long, and with a matting cabin amidships. This trip took a lot of arranging, but my mother, always the guiding spirit in these affairs, pressed on undaunted. She wanted to go through the locks between the river and the lakes, and see the enchanted country beyond.

The horribly filthy river which runs beside the city, and the lakes which are farther out, are on different levels. This permitted the lake water to be comparatively pure, but entailed disadvantages. There had to be locks. The Chinese, superlatively ingenious in making do with almost nothing, had solved this problem within the same framework. How so brilliantly intelligent a people managed *not* to devise machinery is one of those mysteries. Here were the sons of Han, with all their talents, using locks which would have been feasible for savages. They had simply paved ramps between the river and the lakes with large flat stones, which they greased with wet mud whenever a boat wanted to make a passage between them. The vessel would be drawn up at the foot of a ramp, ropes arranged round it and attached to capstans, which were then wound up by straining coolies, till the ship (everything in her falling about) had reached the knife-edge at the top of the ramp. Then the ropes were loosened, and whoosh! She plunged downward, sliding into the water.

With our small fleet we watched this process six times, before we could let Ningpo fall away behind us and begin our progress over the sweet blue waters of the first lake, toward a causeway and a far shore where there was a particular temple to visit. Fishing boats scudded away before us under a light breeze; it was peaceful and silent; when we reached our anchorage we found the ground blue with violets.

The temple lay some distance away, in the hills. It had once been a great place, and even now was properly maintained by an active community of monks. As we approached it we came to a long, tree-lined avenue, paved with large stones, every ninth stone carved with a lotus. This led to a rectangular pool—a big pool, green as jade, within a stone embankment and overhung with peach trees, in full bloom, mirrored in the water, at that moment when we were there. Above this rose the tiered roofs and wide courts of the temple, hushed and calm.

Our cook, a big urbane man and a Buddhist, had been very pleased that we were going to the Ningpo Lakes, and was delighted that we were going to the temple. However, he did not know what lay ahead of him that morning, when he set off well before we did, attended by a little boy carrying his baskets. He had made himself look very smart, in a long gown and a fedora hat, with European shoes. In this setting he looked like a VIP. Once at the temple he made his devotions and paid his respects to the monks, asking if he might use their kitchens to prepare our lunch. They agreed at once, on one stipulation: that we ate neither fish, meat, nor even eggs. The temple and its precincts were included in this ban. The cook was quite put out—he had planned it otherwise. We would have done better to have shared the monks' delicious fare, they being so knowing with bean curd, lotus roots, and such things.

Shanghai Underground

THE USUAL VISITOR to Shanghai would be impressed by its bustling exterior, its lively evidence of commerce and trade, its
cosmopolitan flavor. He would admire the social services which the
city maintained, while enjoying the hospitality of the comfortably-
situated, with their hosts of excellent servants. He could hardly
fail to note the great poverty of the poor. But many of the people
who came to Shanghai were visitors of a particular sort: members
of the communist movement. They saw the city in another light.

Close under the surface of the city there were volcanic forces at
work, which in the twenties burst forth with almost titanic energy. These stemmed from the desperate conditions of labor, the
mounting tide of nationalism, and the subterranean operations of
the trained agents of international communism.

Labor conditions around Shanghai resembled those of the Industrial Revolution era in England. There were no laws to protect
the workman from his factory employer in an effectual way. The
Chinese themselves had no tradition, no regulations of this sort.
Their guilds had built up a system which the workmen tolerated,
in a patriarchal society, but which could not be carried over into
the mill. The foreigners in the industrial field were in general
better to their workmen than the Chinese, but with an inexhausti-
ble supply of labor and no real control—for what authority did
the Council have to enforce such rules?—greed and exploitation

were largely prevalent. Most of the factory workers had a seven-day week, and might be at their jobs even fourteen hours a day. Women and children were largely employed in the silk and cotton mills, under appalling conditions. The Japanese mills were harsh to their work force, though indeed no worse than they were in Japan. Enlightened working conditions had not yet reached the Far East, though the occasional employer was exemplary.

It was not easy for the individual to remedy these evils. For instance, my mother, who had a highly developed social conscience, once decided that it was iniquitous that our servants, of whom we had then about a dozen, had no free time, and that they must have a day off a week. This was an unheard-of arrangement in the city. The custom was that the servants were free only on one day, Chinese New Year. If anyone needed a few days off at any particular time, such a request was always granted, at least in homes like ours, but this was a favor, not a right. Our Number One Boy, an honest, stalwart, sensible man from Shantung, who was with us for many years, would have none of it. He said he could not work with any such arrangement, and insisted that our staff neither wanted nor expected such a thing. If they had a free day, said he, how would they employ it? They had no extra money, no place to go. We could not pay them more, unless they had been willing to double up on their work, which they were unwilling to do. So nothing came of it. The servants appeared contented, and we did not want to lose the Boy. It was an indication of the state of mind of the untrained poor Chinese worker. None of their peers had holidays. Sunday was a holiday only when the foreigners came in, anyway—if a country were not Christian, the seventh day was no different from any other. Probably the Chinese Jews took Saturdays as a day of rest, but there were scarcely any of them in the land.

This is no plea for such conditions, but indicates that in my time domestics in China were not fretting for better ones, as far as their employers were aware. Ours were always eager to stay with us, and we felt them friends. Most of the Westerners were on good terms with their servants, who came to them more readily than to the Chinese—as a rule the Westerners were kinder and paid better.

Shanghai, being open to the whole world, became a refuge not only to straightforward refugees, homeless people with no place else to go, like the White Russians, but also to international anarchists and communists, who might or might not have been declared persona non grata at home. These radicals of all nationalities used to settle down and intrigue together, publishing journals like *Peace and Liberty*, while they talked to the budding communists and dissatisfied students of the city. This was only to be expected. They published also propaganda leaflets for the factory workers. Shanghai had then 5,500 plants, with 600,000 workers, and the ideas in these leaflets very naturally fell on receptive ears. What hope had these poor people for better conditions as things were? Perhaps this would help them, they must have thought.

The formation of the Communist Party in the Rue Boppe led to further political action, though the leaders were obliged to disperse. Russian money came to their aid, and with some of this they bought Shanghai University, a modest establishment off the Bubbling Well Road, which had for a long time had a left-wing bias. The communist-oriented portion of the Kuomintang (this was several years before the party split), using Russian grants, turned the school into a center for training revolutionary cadres. Almost every faculty member was a communist. They and their students became the leaders of the Party in later years.

At Shanghai University, both the Russian language and Russian history were taught, the latter interpreted in terms of communist theory. The atmosphere of the institution was strongly anti-foreign (with the exception of their pro-Russian sentiments), and anti-Christian. They were intensely anti-Japanese in a rather special sense, this enemy being so near their gates. They learned here the methods and techniques of communist agitation and tactics. A bookstall provided the eager, enthusiastic students with plenty of communist literature. The university was crowded with young men, who afterward were considered by the Party to have been drawn too much from the bourgeois strata of society—it was not a place for workers. At that time, however, the laboring class could hardly have come forward, being too occupied in earning their existence, and the university presumably was glad to accept the youth who could apply and who were ready for this sort of curriculum. They did not deal with illiterates.

In the early twenties a figure appeared in Shanghai who was to win great renown in communist circles. This was Li Li-san, who had recently returned to China from France, where he had studied Marxism in Paris. During World War I, when the Chinese had sent a labor force of 140,000 to help the Allies, behind the lines, some of these men had organized themselves into unions and had learned from the French, particularly in Paris, a certain amount about the potentialities of federated labor. Students and advisors who had gone overseas with them, as interpreters and directors, had often stayed in Paris, which they found was not difficult, as they could easily find work and study at the same time. Some young Chinese, hearing of this, went to Paris after the war to avail themselves of these opportunities and, more especially perhaps, to study the theory of revolution. Li Li-san was one of these youths; in Paris he knew Chou En-lai and Chen Yi, other future stars of the Chinese Communist Party. On returning to China he found the stage set for him, with labor conditions in the great ports so terrible that a spark might set off a conflagration. China was now to receive the impact of a dedicated, very gifted, ardent group of trained young communists; of these Li Li-san was one of the most outstanding.

Li Li-san found Shanghai University too intellectual, too bourgeois, for him. He worked for a time in Hankow, among the miners of the region, opening a school for them and organizing their first strike. He too was backed with Russian money. In 1924 he came back to Shanghai and began to rouse the proletariat, using the students he encountered to help him. Not long before, the Third International had convened at Irkutsk and the Chinese Manifesto had been worked out. These people saw China as exploited in a unique way—not only by her own capitalists, but by the world in general, which was, to be fair, largely true. Their two enemies they felt to be capitalism and imperialism, and they were determined to convince the urban proletariat that the communist road was the one which would lead to their salvation.

In the spring of 1925 there was some trouble at a Japanese cotton mill on the outskirts of Shanghai, in which the Japanese guards killed a Chinese worker. This, deservedly, aroused the students of Shanghai (not only those of Shanghai University), and a parade was held on May 30 down the Nanking Road, protesting on behalf of the workers and those arrested at the mill. In front of the police station which was called Lousa, they halted and refused to disperse, crying out that the prisoners be released, that they had been unjustly detained. A Shanghai mob was an ugly one, and the men in charge of the station were not sensitive enough to deal with the situation. The head of the police had underestimated the seriousness of the protest, and was not even there. A young British officer was in charge and eventually, as the crowd refused to withdraw, he ordered his policemen to fire. Four students were killed, and a number of people wounded. The effect of this rash act was immediate and lasting—the "May 30 Incident" was really the beginning of the end as far as old Shanghai was concerned. Even though there was then scarcely the shadow of a real government in China, the whole country was roused at once. A general strike commenced and for a whole year thereafter there was a boycott of both Japanese and British goods. For the rest of 1925 Shanghai was strike-bound, a condition which soon spread to many of the other ports. Funds poured in, both from the country itself and from Russia, and a fever of anti-foreign feeling, nationalism, and general fury broke out.

The Shanghai Muncipal Council behaved blindly, not recognizing how serious this tragedy at the mill and on Nanking Road was. The Shanghai Chinese Chamber of Commerce came to see them the next day, very politely and correctly, to discuss the issue, but the foreign authorities brushed them off with considerable rudeness. This resulted in turning that would-be conciliatory body into enemies, ready to support the strikers.

Li Li-san engineered the general strike, with his knowledge of the technique of putting communism into an active role, his quickness in making the incident a symbol of foreign domination. He was the leading figure among the Chinese at this crucial hour. A natural orator, he could whip up a crowd of rather apathetic, stolid persons, into a frenzy, working on their emotions, channeling their thought as he wished. This was not really difficult in such a place—the foreign interests in Shanghai, their local power, were obvious. No one paused really to examine what lay behind extraterritoriality, no one cared about that sort of complicated history. Nationalism was an intoxicating theme, and the Marxist slogans seemed irresistible.

As is always true, communism could not have gained support if its alternative, the capitalist system in its "colonial" form, had not so lamentably failed in justice and humanity. Labor laws, so painfully fought through in Western legislatures, had no parallel among the rich firms in the East, and the Chinese had never even dreamed of such regulations.

We had a good friend in Shanghai, who came from South Carolina and was working for a tobacco company, a very large firm. He spoke such fluent Chinese, and was of so genial and approach-

able a nature, that he became their chief negotiator in labor dis-
putes. This post he filled willingly because he longed to help the
workmen and coolies, but he was sickened by the terms within
which he could operate. A commission had been set up to deter-
mine wage scales, the members arriving at the conclusion that the
minimum wage in Shanghai was simply the lowest figure a worker
would accept. A starving man will take very little. Our friend was
so dismayed by this awful statement, and with what it implied,
that he was tempted to throw up his job. The verdict had proceeded from rich men, who were living in the greatest comfort,
whose eyes were closed to the suffering all around them, who
were heartless. He protested, but in vain; men at his level in the
firm had no real authority.

Before this there had been a great number of small strikes in
Shanghai, but they never really came to anything, because the
strikers had practically no funds to fall back on. If they stayed out
they literally starved. The general strike had no such problems.
Money came from the Peking government, such as it was, and
from the warlords, elements which were generally at each other's
throats, but now found common cause in their rage against the
West. Chang Tso-lin, the ruler of Manchuria, sent funds, as did
his mortal enemy Wu Pei-fu, who had himself shot strikers when
they held up the operation of the Peking-Hankow Railway, which
was part of his empire. The "Christian General" Feng Yu-hsiang
contributed with the rest, his church affiliations not deterring him
from cooperating with the communists. Li Li-san took charge of
everything, including the money. All the unions came to heel at
his bidding, except one, the Seaman's Union, which continued to
manage its own affairs, though it also struck and was in sympathy
with the others. In all this, nine times out of ten, the labor leaders
and their poor followers had no notion that they were casting
their lot in with a movement which was communist inspired and
organized, which was part of a great Russian plan. Shanghai was
inundated with propaganda posters, leaflets, and the usual para-
phernalia of influence. The port of Canton was also rendered
immobile, and for some months Hong Kong as well. Incidents
took place all over the country: in Hankow, Chungking, Canton,
Nanking.

Something had to give. At last the Shanghai Municipal Council
saw the writing on the wall and backed down. Their members
were facing ruin if the strike continued. In December the British

Inspector of Police and his junior who was in charge that fatal afternoon were dismissed, and Ch. $75,000 idemnity was paid to the families of the dead and wounded. Eventually wages went up, and a few years later more Chinese were given membership on the Council.

While all these evils convulsed the foreign enclaves, those parts of Shanghai which were wholly Chinese, like Nantao and Chapei, were in a state approaching bedlam. They were, in the last analysis, controlled by the warlords, and on the ground by racketeers. The warlords, as predatory, ruthless, and cruel a class as ever existed, needed money, and here it was to be found, the proceeds of gun-running, kidnapping, opium deals, and every possible form of slavery. As the Red influence in the country increased, first Li Li-san and later Chou En-lai moved into the area, assuming partial control, initiating strikes, breeding more confusion. This condition continued while the two branches of the Kuomintang, that under the sway of Chiang Kai-shek, and the other, Sun Yat-sen's Moscow-oriented party, were still in harness together. When the split in the party came, Chiang Kai-shek was determined to wrest the control of Chinese Shanghai from communist control, which was accomplished in 1927 through the most bitter fighting and a series of captures, assassinations, and vendettas.

The longing for revenge the communists felt, when the Kuomintang proved at this stage to be the stronger faction, is still reflected in their feeling toward the Generalissimo and his government. Personal debts of this kind have never been forgotten or forgiven; when the communists took the country in 1949, they exacted the last drop of blood from every individual they could find who had taken part in chasing them out of Shanghai twenty years earlier.

While these struggles went on in 1925, 1926, and 1927, the foreign enclaves could only patrol their own borders, and not interfere. It was a purely Chinese battle, and to the death. Had the communists won then, Shanghai would have become a Red city.

After the Nationalist victory, and the consequent communist setback, the labor unions in Shanghai were for a period quiescent, but gradually they came back, most of them welded into one organization, which was thoroughly infiltrated by communist agents who managed to evade government supervision. This federation was organized by Liu Shao-chi. It will be seen how much talent was lavished on the city from the communist angle—all these men being of the top echelon.

Liu Shao-chi had then had several years of training in Sun Yat-sen University in Moscow, and had returned to devote himself to fomenting unrest in the cities of China. He was particularly interested in the urban scene, and this preference remained with him, causing friction in later years in his relationship with Mao Tze-tung, who believed the revolution should rest chiefly on the agricultural workers. Liu Shao-chi in this crisis went to Shanghai, and started planting cells and organizing a communication network between the various branches of his field of action, which he called the General Labor Union. He divided the city into districts, groups, and occupations which were remarkably inclusive. Since time immemorial China has been used to the strong, unseen hand of the secret societies, but they were never more powerful than this huge organization, which embraced nearly every Shanghai worker in one way or another.

The Comintern, which was very active and successful during this period, was fully aware of what was going on in Shanghai, and under its aegis many important communists came to the city from all over the world. Shanghai was even described as the "Red GHQ for Asia," and with justice. Among these persons were Thomas Mann, Manabendra Nath Roy, Earl Browder, Jacques Doriot. And not only were they in Shanghai, Canton was also a lodestone. André Malraux worked there organizing their giant strikes, and later even bore arms against the Kuomintang. Long afterward he would become de Gaulle's Minister of Youth, Culture, and Sports, and redecorate the Opéra in Paris. He would talk with President Nixon, certainly speaking favorably of Red China.

A man who became notorious locally was Hilaire Noulens; he and his wife were eventually arrested by the Kuomintang, tried, and sentenced to death as communist spies. They had a variety of names and passports, homes, bank accounts and postbox addresses. They were caught in 1931, through the information which was unearthed in Singapore by the British Special Branch Police on their capture of another agent, Joseph Ducroux. The trial of the Noulenses was important, not only to the situation in China, but to the whole network of communist underground activity in the Far East, laying bare the plans of the Comintern. Most of the other spies disappeared, fearful lest they share their fate. However, the Noulenses' sentence was changed to life imprisonment; they spent five years in jail in Nanking, and when the Japanese took the city in 1937 they were let out. Their capture and the damage their documents had done to the communist cause meant that they were discredited in the eyes of their former employers; they disappeared in the greater issues and troubles of that year.

Hankow, six hundred miles up-river, chief city of the Wuhan complex, where the Yangtze and the Han rivers meet, was the scene of most extraordinary events during the power struggle within the Kuomintang of 1926–27.

It was here that not only the Chinese communists but also many senior Kuomintang personalities of the Right came from Canton, at the moment before the whole alignment of the Party was broken up and reformed. Madame Sun Yat-sen, the widow of the man still revered in China as the Founder of the Republic, was there, clinging to her Moscow-oriented platform, and reinforced by such strange figures as Eugene Chen, a Chinese who had been born in Trinidad and who was ardent in his wish to make China Red. Borodin, the Russian advisor, was with them, as was General Galen, the military advisor later known as General Blucher. All were united in their anti-foreign stance and socialistic aims. While Chiang Kai-shek was down in Nanking, consolidating his position, they created in this town, which is sometimes called the Chicago of China (from its position in the heart of the country and its importance as a place of transshipment), an ephemeral region, a communist urban enclave, all on its own.

When they first arrived from the south, they had with them men who were close to Chiang Kai-shek, and who after the split were to become high officials of the Kuomintang, men like T. V. Soong and H. H. Kung, the first a brother of Madame Chiang (and also, of course, of Madame Sun), the second his brother-in-law. The marriages of the three Soong sisters to these dominant persons remains one of the peculiar features of the Kuomintang-Communist confrontation of those years, but is more easily understood when it is realized that at one time their husbands were in the same camp.

During the crisis in Shanghai, England had sent in a considerable number of troops to guard the Settlement (it was the first time the Coldstream Guards had ever been dispatched east of Suez), but these men remained there. There was no question of their being deployed all over the country. When mobs seized the foreign settlements in Kiukiang (four hundred miles upriver) and Hankow, the Conservative government in England concluded it would not attempt to reclaim them. They were not of paramount importance to the British—Kiukiang was not important at all—and at that point when (soon after the general strike in England) the strength of the communist push was becoming somewhat understood, it evidently seemed best in Whitehall not to make an issue of these Treaty Ports while China was in such a situation.

The communist part of the Kuomintang was acting in accord with Trotsky's aims for world revolution, and his followers were correspondingly delighted. Important figures of the communist world came to Hankow to rejoice in its establishment as a communist enclave, in a state of euphoria which endured for the few months the city went through this strange dream. Strikes started, the same strikes which were raging all over the country from Canton to Tientsin, and the peasants of the Wuhan area were organized. For a few days everyone enjoyed the exhaltation of "liberation," but no one had any money. There were no concrete plans, and though Trotsky was pleased, Stalin was not, and Moscow had no intention of financing Hankow. The new government of the city began to print paper money, which resulted in a devastating inflation. The experiment soon collapsed of its own ineptitude, and in the summer of 1927 Chiang Kai-shek was able to take it over without any difficulty. The Hankow chapter of this part of China's history seems improbable, and indeed it was, but on the other hand it did actually occur. In a country where for decades there had scarcely been stable government it was not so outlandish as one would think.

Chiang Kai-shek then broke with all this segment of the old party—with Borodin and with his sister-in-law, Madame Sun, which was a painful rupture within a Chinese family. The rest of his clan and that of the Soongs rallied round him, as he set himself on a course in which he wanted no more alliances with Russia. He now would ally himself with the West. The struggle between these factions was hardly scotched, though he had now at least a chance to build up the country. The communists bided their time and, as we know, would eventually drive him out of the country.

The non-Communist world, enormously relieved, prepared to help the Generalissimo. People who had thought they must pull up their stakes and leave China decided to stay after all. This included many thousands of missionaries who had decided they could no longer work in their parishes. But they still had a full decade with the new Kuomintang, and after that the years of the

Japanese War, in which they could be actively associated with a land most of them loved.

As for the loss of Hankow, some of the foreigners felt bitter about it. They were then of an imperial cast of thought. In line with this attitude, a notice appeared in the *North China Daily News* of May 13, 1927, which aptly illustrated their disapproval:

British Concession
Hankow

TO BE SOLD

This magnificent freehold property, occupying a river frontage of half-a-mile on the upper Yangtze, together with all its public buildings, banks, offices, private houses, leases, sub-leases, moveables, immoveables, appurtenances, etc., to be disposed of to the highest bidder without reserve.

This property, formerly belonging to the British Empire, was sold five months ago to Messrs. Chen, Borodin & Co., of Moscow, but owing to the sudden failure of that Firm it again comes into the market, the original vendors having decided not to exercise their right to take it back. *Must be disposed of. No Reasonable offer will be refused.*

Applications from any Political Group, War Lord, or Tuchun* of a Province, should be accompanied by a stamped envelope stating clearly name and address to which reply can be forwarded. To avoid confusion prospective bidders are particularly requested to notify vendors of any sudden change in address or alteration in status of applicant.

Sole Agents:
AUSTIN CHAMBERLAIN & CO.
FOREIGN OFFICE LONDON
To whom all applications should be addressed.

In those few years which the Kuomintang had to form their government in Nanking and to set about putting the country in order, their struggle with the communists continued unabated. So much else was going on, and we were so used to the interminable civil wars between this faction or that in every part of the land,

---

* *Tuchun*: a self-constituted provincial governor-warlord, the military governor of a province.

that the desperate importance, the long-term possibilities of this strife, was not taken sufficiently seriously by most of us at the time. As Chiang appeared to have achieved the near-miracle of unifying China and maintaining it in a state of equilibrium with progress in so many departments, we assumed he would in time rout these foes also. In those years world opinion was horrified by the Moscow trials and the Stalinist purges—many of the early advocates of communism, disillusioned, fell away from it.

Chiang Kai-shek between 1930 and 1934 launched campaign after campaign—five in all—to eradicate this enemy, which he well understood constituted his greatest danger. The first and second attempts were Nationalist failures; the third, which stood a fair chance of success, was scotched because just as it started in 1931 the Japanese seized Manchuria, diverting Nanking's attention from its armies. Two years later Chiang tried again and failed. These campaigns took place in the Kiangsi and Hunan countryside, and on the borders of Fukien.

The communists, in spite of their successes here vis-à-vis the Nationalists, were themselves in disarray, yet they were very active, fomenting strikes, rousing urban workers. They established soviets and, always helped by money and advice from Moscow, went steadily forward with the schemes employed by this system everywhere as it proceeds to take over a country. Nanchang and Changsha had notable risings; Shanghai never lost its formidable underground, and down in the south Mao Tze-tung was putting into practice his ideas about rousing the peasants. There was a great deal of personal rivalry between many of the leaders and the various cliques. One in particular, called the Twenty-Eight Bolsheviks, had serious differences with Mao and his supporters. The split between Stalin and Trotsky was also reflected in these Chinese organizations.

In the early part of this period the rural communists were obliged to take refuge in the mountains, living in the ranges between Kiangsi and Hunan, in the now famous Ching Kang Shan. Mao was then sometimes so unpopular with his peers that he was not even allowed membership in the Politburo. Less bigoted than he became later in life, he would divide up land between rich and poor peasants alike, which was thought by the more rigid and doctrinaire comrades to be ideologically incorrect. Mao was, in fact, in such disfavor that he was under arrest from July, 1934, until the Long March began in October of that year.

It was all very complicated and confused, and it was no wonder that most people could not follow from month to month the stories of personal quarrels, fighting, and disruptions which attended this stage of the communist development, though certainly every nuance was known to the Nanking government. To us it seemed like the old familiar Chinese power-struggle, warlordism under a new guise. But the Kuomintang we did not think of as warlords, we felt them a government, and respected them for it. They were working hard to improve their army under the tutorship of German advisors, and were determined to get the communist menace out of the way—Japan permitting. That reads sadly enough now.

The peasants were not necessarily as delighted with the communist design as one is given to believe in such books as Edgar Snow's *Red Star over China* (certainly one of the most influential works of our times), and Jan Myrdal's Potemkin village studies. The communists claimed that they lived among the peasants as fish swim in the sea, but to their often reluctant hosts they seemed to be, if fish, then predatory fish. There was not enough to eat; the newcomers could not raise all they needed up there in the hills; they had to have the cooperation of the farmers. Those who did not cooperate suffered the direct consequences, often fatal. Certainly the peasants were wronged, poor, and dissatisfied, and naturally they hoped for a new dispensation, which might give them their own land and free them from the moneylenders. Some thought they had found this, and took to the new dogma with hope and even elation. But, there were also stories brought back by missionaries who had long labored in the area, and could relate the stories of what had happened to their converts who didn't want the communist type of salvation. These people generally lost everything, including their lives. To some the communists, occupying and abandoning villages as military necessity dictated, constituted a sort of Terror.

As the years passed it became clear that the communists were not receiving the physical and psychological support they needed and claimed from the regions they dominated. The Reds from the first exploited the underlying hostility to Japan as a primary motive to win them adherents, but this was not enough. "The Politburo's ruthless drive for the land revolution and class struggle . . . drove nearly all classes of peasants—rich, middle, and poor—into desperation and apathy. They endeavored to avoid the Red army and the party to such a degree that the former was rendered incapable of recruitment, expansion, and proper mobilization."*

In 1934 Chiang Kai-shek launched his fifth campaign against the Reds, inflicting such losses upon them that they realized they had to run for it. It was in that October that they began their fabled Long March, which took them northward and westward for 6,000 miles to the loess caves of Yenan. A hundred thousand started, perhaps a quarter finally endured to the end. Suffering cruelly themselves, they were harsh, also, on the countryside, driven on as they were by the government troops. Ardently did the towns and cities that lay in their path hope that they would pass them by. It is from this time that the leadership of Mao Tze-tung and Chu Te was established.

But most of the Europeans and Americans in the Treaty Ports could have told you far more about the dangers inherent in the European situation than of those taking place on the continent to which they were assigned. Hitler was rising to power, the Spanish situation was full of danger, France was torn by strikes and disruptions, Russia was going through the Stalinist purges. The Generalissimo had naturally not been very anxious to publicize his many defeats on the field; and we were all hoping that the new government, with its immense problems in every field, would somehow be able to survive and pull the country out of its miseries.

No one had illusions. We knew that the people in Nanking were inexperienced, though often highly educated, and that the combination of the warlords and the communists within, and the Japanese without, was a fearful hindrance to the solving of the urgent problems of mass education, health, welfare, transport, and a thousand other necessities.

Yet under our eyes some of this made notable progress. For instance, roads. Until the Kuomintang came in there were hardly any modern roads outside the foreign enclaves—there were cobbled streets in the old walled cities, and dirt lanes for wheelbarrows in the country, there were paths by the creeks, but almost nothing a truck could drive on. In 1921 there were about a thousand kilometers of modern roads in the whole country. By 1936 the highways were reported to have come to almost 120,000 kilometers. This one activity alone was of primary importance. Be-

*C. Y. Hsü, *The Rise of Modern China*, Oxford University Press, 1970.

sides facilitating business enterprises and moving cargo faster, it helped open the minds of the country people, giving them a hint of the world beyond the horizon.

Aside from the actual building of the roads, and concurrently with their construction, the problem of the local bandit had to be dealt with. Bandits flourished everywhere, and no one was going to venture on roads which would be beset by highwaymen, wretched creatures who were desperate with poverty and could find no employment. Some of them must actually have been given work on the roads themselves. We had only a few months to enjoy these highways before the Japanese took the coast, yet by that time they were safe to travel on.

The Kuomintang launched all sorts of campaigns to improve the morals, morale, hygiene, patriotism, and general conduct of the citizens. The most obvious was the "New Life Movement," with its big wall posters, exhorting people to observe admirable standards of conduct. They also made a great attack on illiteracy. The need to instill new ideas, the need for basic reform, was as obvious to the Nanking government as it was to the communists—and to everyone else concerned with China's progress. They were very fortunate in that there was then in China probably the most expert man in the world in teaching characters. This was James Yen, whose Thousand-Character scheme was taking root, and fast. He had become deeply interested in and fond of the Chinese coolies with whom he went, in some supervisory capacity, to France in World War I. This was his first real contact with the Chinese poor; he was touched by their patient gallantry, their great need of and longing for education. They *had* to learn to read, and he made it the aim of his life to put this skill within their grasp.

But there was one terrible flaw the government failed to attack —the old, fatal weakness for corruption of most officials, indeed of most Chinese who had authority, position, and education. It was a legacy of the custom that an administrator was only paid a pittance with the understanding that he would make it up with perquisites. This venal trait was to be their undoing. Even during the Japanese War, when morale was for so long so high, this dreadful weakness in the national character lost the country and the government much of the respect it had earned in other directions. Many were honest, but the others attracted attention.

Another disastrous mistake on the part of the Kuomintang lay in their reluctance seriously to undertake the issue of land reform.

Basically a soldier, Chiang Kai-shek saw his struggle with the communists in martial terms, neglecting to probe the underlying causes on which his enemies built. The Kuomintang did not face up to the first overwhelming necessity of any government in power in China: poverty, and particularly rural poverty. Efforts were made to ameliorate the situation, but only in a limited way: rural cooperatives were set up, agricultural banks established, and a few areas in the country reorganized, but all this was only a drop in the bucket.

The communists had attempted, and were still attempting, to gain the cities, but their efforts among the urban proletariat were not as rewarding or decisive as they had hoped. Recognizing this, they turned to their advantage the undeniably terrible condition of the farmer, who passed his whole life in crushing debt, over half his crop (or more) pledged to the moneylender or to an absentee landlord before it was even sown.

Had Chiang from the first recognized that the question of land distribution, of putting the farmers in a position where they could be free of debt, keep their own crops, borrow at equitable rates of interest, was paramount, it is very possible that the communists would hardly have had a hearing in the countryside, except through the tactics of fear and terrorization.

But Chiang delayed. Neither he nor the Party saw how vitally important this was, and as most of his support came from moneyed interests, to espouse such a cause would not have been easy. Vast sums were expended on the anti-communist campaigns—that seemed to the government justifiable—but part of those funds should have been dispersed in another way. How sorely the farmers needed rural credit! Where were they to turn?

Part III
PEKING

Peking Generally

PEKING, GLORIOUS PEKING, was the great magnet of the country. It has been a capital many times—for the Liaos in the eleventh century and on into the twelfth, for the Chins (the Golden Tatars) after that, for the Mongols from 1280–1368, and again under the Ming when that house decided to leave Nanking. The Manchus had it as theirs for the whole of that long dynasty, right up to 1911, and sometimes the republic has installed itself there since. When it was not officially the capital (for romantically, sentimentally, it seemed to continue to have this eminence) it had to be renamed, as P'ei Ching means Northern Capital. On these occasions it would be called P'ei P'ing, or Northern Peace.

Ever since the earliest times when the reins of government had first lain there, since the days when it was called Yen Ching, the Swallow Capital, it exerted a potent charm. As it developed and then became the choice of the Ming, it captured fully the hearts and minds of the people of the whole country. It was so beautiful! Many cities had been built in China on the grand design which was here at last pefected—this became the epitome of what the Sons of Han wanted for a capital. The traces of Yen Ching, and Khanbalak, the city of the Khans which Marco Polo saw, were swallowed up in this miraculous town, low, peaceful, yet vibrant, the center of hundreds of arts, lying so near the Gobi. The majestic ceremonies of the imperial court, the splendor of the architecture of the Forbidden and Imperial cities, were framed by the simplicities of the long grey winding lanes, or *hutungs*, preserving their own secrecy, high-walled, mysterious. The wit of the capital, and its rich speech, interlarded with its characteristic *"erh,"** the accomplishments of its citizens, combined to make it the sort of place in which everyone wants to live.

When you thought of Peking, you thought of the amber roofs, the bastioned walls of the Tatar City, of the flights of pigeons, whose whistles, eleven-toned, sounded such wild and haunting notes as the birds flew suddenly up into the light, dry, pale blue air. You thought of the ice-lanterns of the Spring Festival, of the temples in the Western Hills, of the Sea Palaces and their winding, scarlet-columned galleries beside the water. The vast courts of the Forbidden City, its white marble balustrades, flights of steps and bridges, the spirit screens, would spring into mind, whenever the city was spoken of.

It was all so lovely that in spite of centuries of inept government it possessed a superb self-confidence. People felt it so ravishingly beautiful, so captivating in its sunny charms, its glinting colored roofs, that it didn't seem to matter what it actually did as a seat of power. It would, after Lu Kou Chiao, capitulate to the Japanese without firing a shot—yet everyone excused it, no one really condemned it—while Nanking, which went down heroically, contesting all the way, still could command no comparable aura of affection. The beautiful cities, like their human counterparts, seem to have an extraordinary invulnerability to public censure. One has only to think of Italy, as war came. The important thing, to most people, was that Florence, Venice, Rome, should not be hurt—the world couldn't lose them, no matter what they harbored in the way of plots, treason, intrigue. These crimes would pass, the beauty must be allowed to endure.

The train from Tientsin ran in under the Tatar wall, stopping near the Ch'ien Men, the huge gate which leads to the Forbidden City, at the heart of the town. I was once so overjoyed to see those walls again as I came in from Peitaiho that I burst into tears, to my own amazement. No other city ever did this to me, before or since—there was some magic about it.

The Mongols, uneasy if they were far from their deserts, felt that a city ought to look like an encampment, and laid out Khan-

---

* A suffix added to nouns and much in use in Peking.

balak like a camp, four-square, their great halls lying one behind the other, the heavy roofs bringing to mind the lines of a tent. But the city we know was created by Yung Lo of the Ming, the third emperor, who early in the fifteenth century turned his back on the first capital his dynasty had chosen—Nanking—and went north, to devote his passion for building and the wealth he could drain from the country to the creation of this vast imperial city.

In Peking the sun shines long and often; the air is dry, crisp, and when the wind blows from the Gobi, dusty. It is very cold in winter though little snow falls, intensely hot in summer, and has a beautiful mild autumn. When a real dust storm was in progress people wrapped their heads in veils, fending off as they could the thick, choking, yellow dust. When I knew it few of the streets were paved, the *hutungs* generated their own dust in dry weather and when it rained were deep in mud. These conditions did not depress the inhabitants; the Chinese used to be ready to laugh, everywhere, but never so much as in Peking, the sun made people cheerful, and the native humor did the rest. Peking was a really cheerful city. People rejoiced in the sunlight glinting on the glazed roof tiles, bringing out so many variants of their gold, turquoise, amethyst. The colors were so strong, the tiles so heavy and thickly glazed, that they lent brilliance to much of the city. The street booths contributed to this in their several ways, for instance in their heaps of crystallized fruit, a local specialty, possible because of the extreme dryness of the air. North China produces an abundance of fruit, and the vendors went about selling baskets heaped high with grapes, pears, and red-orange persimmons, small and delicious, which ripened in profusion on many high, shabby trees.

What an immense change this must have entailed for the Mings —to leave the soft Yangtze Valley terrain, the rains, the willows, the wide river, the green rice fields, for these northern plains, the wheat and *kaoliang* country, to come so near the Great Wall (the Nan K'o Pass is only forty miles away) and the deserts. To the west of Peking there is for a few miles a gentle countryside— beyond this stretch the fierce eroded mountains leading to the north. The Western Hills are a low circlet, where temples, monasteries, pagodas, and parks have been built since antiquity. Not far from this favored region the Mings placed those huge marble creatures (which also distinguished their tombs outside Nanking) on the long avenue leading to their later sepulchers.

Peking itself, as everyone knows, is laid out on an exact north-south axis, with one walled city enclosing another. At the center is the Forbidden City, once the imperial residence; outside its moat is the Imperial City, which has a rose-colored wall with amber tiles lying along the top—more pictorial perhaps than the Forbidden City wall. Next is the old Tatar City, much larger than the other two, with a magnificent wall of many huge gates, ramparts, and bastions. The Chinese were made to live in an area to the south of this section. Their quarter was undistinguished compared to the others, they being the occupied people, but it held still the Temples of Heaven and Earth, one with a round, the other with a square altar. Yung Lo's city of course had no district for the Tatars, that arrangement came with the Tatar conquest and continued after them, in name.

The old Legation Quarter was at the edge of the Tatar City, enclosing an area of about three-quarters of a square mile, housing the ministers and their staffs, about a dozen countries, besides a few other places; not everyone in the Quarter belonged to a legation. The chief envoys did not become ambassadors till on into the thirties. Next to the Quarter were the hotels the Westerners used—the Hôtel de Pékin, the Wagons Lits. The French bookshop of Henri Vetch was also there.

This enclave stretched almost from the Hata Men to the Ch'ien Men, and included the old Water Gate, through which an insalubrious stream made its way, joining the moat outside the wall (this has long since disappeared). The water came from the Jade Fountain, which springs up in the Western Hills, at Yü Ch'üan Shan. At its source it is as pure as jade, but after irrigating the fields in its eastward course to the city, it began to lose its freshness. It fed the lakes of the Sea Palaces and then, going on to the Legation Quarter, became at last a sorry, miserable trickle.

The Water Gate played an historic role during the Boxer, as through it the first troops of the rescuing forces entered Peking, and realized to their immense relief that they were not too late.

The Boxer Rebellion was a very complicated affair, and cannot fairly be assessed simply as a nationalistic movement, though it is true that at its inception the Society of Harmonious Fists was primarily interested in the desire to be free of the Manchus. The Chinese were naturally very dissatisfied with what mismanagement and corruption at the top had done to their country, and were expressing their feelings, to some extent, in the usual way—through their secret societies. The Empress Dowager, recognizing that this new group constituted a real threat to the government, cleverly diverted their emotions into anti-foreign channels, and more particularly into anti-Christian propaganda and acts, so that instead of plotting to attack the throne and the alien dynasty, they turned upon the Westerners, especially the missionaries and their converts.

In a short time the Boxers killed some thirty thousand converts, and a number of Western missioners, men, women, and children, attacking those who were working in isolated stations during the earlier part of their ferocious and indeed senseless campaign. Their technique was first to arouse local support, partly from malcontents and rabble, persons who often had little notion of what they were doing, but who were easily moved to cruelty (that all-too-often-used cry of "*sha!*" "*sha!*" which means "kill"), and who actually accepted in good faith the Boxers' assurance of their personal magical invulnerability to reprisals.

At the siege of Peking, the final phase, sixty-six foreigners were killed, more than one hundred fifty were wounded, and ten died as a direct result of the conditions of confinement. The casualty figures were very much larger at the French Cathedral, the Pei-tang, where there were many Chinese converts besides Frenchmen, both priests and defenders. The mystery of it all was why anyone survived, given the circumstances in this strangest of all sieges.

An article published in 1900 in *The Open Court*, written by the Reverend George T. Candlin, who was in China at the time, throws a good deal of light on the motives of the Boxers and the way they conducted their campaign. He was well able to make such an assessment, having been in China for thirty years as a Methodist missionary, and having become a sinologue as well as a keen student of the national scene. In this article, "The Associated Fists," Dr. Candlin writes, in part:

> This Society has been wrongly named the "Boxer Society." Though pugilism and wrestling are to some extent practised, "boxing" is entirely unknown in China. It is therefore inadmissable to call them "Boxers." The word employed by themselves, ch'üen, means literally "the fist," and the phrase *ta ch'üen t'ou* means to practise pugilism. But the exercises they engage in, now notorious to residents in China, and which have been named "Boxer Drill," bear little or no resemblance either to pugilism or to boxing. They consist of the repetition of words supposed to act as charms, violent contortions of the body, which appear to induce a state of

trance, during which the subject is supposed to deliver to the by-standers occult messages respecting the movement. On resuming his normal state he is said to be quite unconscious of anything he has said during his peculiar ecstacy. . . .

The Society aims at nothing less than the expulsion of all foreigners and all things foreign from China and the restoration of the Empire to its former position of exclusion and self-sufficiency. Its animus is peculiarly strong against foreign religions, not only because the missionary pervades the whole interior of the country, nor yet because his converts are now, for the first time, becoming a body respectable by its numbers and thoroughly imbued with sentiments earnestly desirous of foreign intercourse and innovation, but also because its leaders, by a true instinct, divine that religion is the great transforming force which, once permitted to permeate the very springs and secret spiritual forces of the nation's life, will "make all things new." This animus reaches its most extreme point of intensity in its opposition to the Roman Catholic missions, these being the longest established and the most numerous, and having, so far as we can learn, done more to protect and assist their converts in cases of litigation than the Protestant missions.

But these distinctions are trivial. In the significant phrase often employed in their literature everything foreign is to be driven off,—merchant hongs, machine shops, railways, telegraphs, guns, rifles: they propose to "make a clean sweep." The Society has been spoken of as patriotic, and it is for this reason, so it is said, that it is protected by the Empress Dowager. This, however, does not hinder it from assailing the government as it stands, and the Emperor himself with all the highest officials in the Empire is fiercely assailed in its publications. We are therefore justified in regarding it as a rebellion. Its manifesto seems rather against individual rulers than against the dynasty itself. Its aim differs from that of former rebellions and all other secret societies known to us, inasmuch as it is not a crusade of Ming against Ching. It is favored by the Manchu, and a prince of the blood is said to be a member of its secret conclave. . . .

Altogether the most singular feature of the strange movement is the peculiar relation to it of young children. In every district and in every town it has visited it has commenced its work among young people ranging between the ages of ten and twenty. The "drill" is always commenced by them. We have ourselves seen them practising it, and have received scores of reports of its exercise in town and village, but always when the question has been put what kind of people are they, the reply has been *hsiao hai tzü*, small children. Until actual rioting commenced we had never heard of grown men appearing in the movement. This has been the principal reason why it has been treated lightly by foreign observers, and perhaps has had something to do with the inactivity of the Chinese officials in dealing with it. Mandarins would not arrest and foreigners could not take seriously the doings of very young boys and even girls, until the sudden outburst of murderous and incendiary attacks proved that after all it was no mere child's play.

Of course when the rebels actually appear in arms it is men and not children who do the destructive work, but until that stage is reached, it appears for the most part an affair of children. It is not simply the case that children are aping in public the secret doings of their elders. They are an essential factor in the growth of the Society, in every place where it makes its appearance. It is they who most readily induce the strange trance characteristic of the "drill." To them the mystic messages of the impending advent of their leaders are given. They are its plastic and docile mediums.

The Society's method of procedure as it appears to the outside observer is as follows: In any particular place which has been so far undisturbed by their operations, the rumors become more persistent and wonderful as to their doings in other districts, placards of the character which we print below begin to appear, sometimes mysteriously posted on the walls of buildings by night, sometimes handed to individuals in a crowded market. A general state of mingled excitement, fear, and expectation is created, and especially the idea of the advent of invincible swordsmen, armed with supernatural power, and teachers and leaders, is instilled into the mind of a populace superstitious in the extreme, and a large portion of whom are ripe for any mischief and supremely covetous of loot. Then children, varying in age from ten to twenty, are seen in vacant spaces and on the corners of the streets "drilling." In addition to the revelations considered to be connected with these strange exercises, they are supposed to render those who engage in them invulnerable, alike to sword thrusts and rifle bullets. Gradually their numbers increase, older people take part, and then for the first time definite organisation is proposed. Leaders are appointed, adherents are formed into what are called *lu*, "hearths." These "hearths" are equivalent to camps. They number five hundred each, and every member is sworn in to obey the leaders, to sleep and take food together, and to have the grain and meal necessary for their support sent from home. The next step is to commence work by setting fire to some foreign house, railway station, mission chapel, or other obnoxious building, putting to the sword all native Christians they can find, and any hapless "foreign devil" who may fall into their hands. In the performance of this part of the programme it is impossible to distinguish the rebels from the populace. Swarming in thousands, they murder, destroy, and loot till there is little left behind.

In this way, though on a comparatively small scale, the work of the Society was commenced more than a year ago, and large numbers of Chinese Christians in the interior of Shantung were harried out of house and home, taking refuge in the foreign quarters of their mission. The murder of the Rev. Sydney Brooke, a member of the Society for the Propagation of the Gospel, near Ping-yin, was an incident in their campaign of ravage.

The movement has grown to enormous proportions during the year. It is much to be feared the court itself and the higher officials have connived at its destructive work; at any rate every Chinese official, civil and military, has been paralysed before it. Within hardly more than a month, starting with the massacre of some hundreds of Roman Catholic Christians in the villages round Paotingfu, it has swept down the Lu Han railway line, driving the Belgian Engineers before it, and though they made a brave stand again and again, killing four of them,—the rest of the party arriving wounded and almost naked in Tientsin,—it has burnt and looted every station on the line, wrecked the railway, demolished the shops at Fengtai, invested Pekin, poured down on the port of Tientsin, it has shut up all the foreign ministers in Pekin, the Japanese Secretary of Legation has been murdered, the advance of the British Admiral with a mixed body of three thousand foreign troops has been driven back on Tientsin, the Settlement there has been sacked, and at the moment of writing we do not know how many of the foreign residents of Pekin or Tientsin are alive, or what is the fate of the railway from Taku to Tangshan, and of the large railway works and mines there, which foreigners have been compelled to abandon.

Though very little information of a conclusive character is to be had, and there is, therefore, no absolute proof of its existence, everything points to the existence of a very powerful inner council or conclave, which, working in profound secret, matures the plans by which the Society works. It has been hatched in Buddhist monasteries and the purlieus of the yamens. Priests of the Buddhist faith are among the leaders, Governor Yü of Shantung and one of the princes of the blood, Tung Fu Hsiang, a much trusted Chinese general, and even the Empress Dowager herself, have been boldly mentioned as members of it. This council concocts the mysterious placards, sends forerunners who work up the bands in various districts, and has men in it of sufficient influence to bring over to its side the gentry of each district and above all to *silence* the officials.

Those nearly forty years between the Boxer and the final Japanese attack in 1937 brought to an end the era the Boxer had attempted to forestall, but, had instead, by their excesses and unreason, strengthened. To those of us who were born and brought up on the Coast during this span, the individual experiences and exploits of those who had endured the siege, who had taken part in raising it, or whose lives had been marked by it in one way or another, became legendary. Many of the older people on the Coast would talk of it—we knew with easy familiarity names like Morrison, the *Times* correspondent, and von Ketteler, the German Minister who was killed; we heard of the bravery of the Chamots, and of the heroic Henry at the Peitang.

An excellent account of it is to be found in Peter Fleming's *Siege at Peking*, based as it is not only on a thorough knowledge of the political, international, and military forces involved, as well as on the diaries and journals of those who waited out that hot summer under the wall, hoping for relief, so cut off from the world. Aside from this, due to the author's wit and lucidity of style, it is in spite of its grim theme extremely amusing. At such a time peoples' foibles and idiosyncrasies show up sharply, as well as the great qualities of the "superior men" (in the Confucian sense).

The Boxer was one of those events by which people come to date the circumstances of their lives: "That was before the Boxer . . ." they would say, or "That was after the Boxer . . ." "I was in such-and-such a place during the Boxer."

Long afterward, when as a child I was in California, we happened to go to a resort north of San Francisco. This region had been very much damaged by the San Francisco earthquake, which had somehow covered the fine sandy bottom of the bay with mud, greatly injuring Inverness's (for that was its name) prospects as a holiday town. There, in the now rather deserted little place, inhabited by many poor Italians who sent crabs, lobsters, abalones, and mushrooms down to the city, there was what had been a grandiose estate, a large piece of property, enclosed with a fence with tiled globes, surprising in that context. This, we found, had been the home of the Swiss hotelier, Chamot, who had done so much during the siege both for defense and to bring in food. He and his wife had been loaded with honors, and had finally come to live in California. The simplicity and quiet of Inverness had, however, according to local report, been too much for M. Chamot, who finally came to a tragic end. He had, alas, previously been divorced from his gallant wife of the Peking adventures.

There were at the time of the Boxer only some five hundred foreign residents in Peking: the Legation people, missionaries, men in the Customs, and a few businessmen, trade being still officially prohibited. But as the tension heightened, more and more Westerners flocked to the city, till when hostilities began there were actually nine hundred persons sheltering in the compound of the British Legation (which, being farthest from the wall, seemed the safest), an area of about three acres. In the Quarter were about three thousand Chinese, besides nationals of the other eleven countries involved. (As they began to order their disposition, some of these people took refuge in nearby compounds and buildings, but the overcrowding was extreme.)

Throughout the whole siege there was enough to eat; there were tons of grain laid up in a nearby shop under their aegis, they had meat from the great number of ponies which were already stabled in the quarter, and from some cattle the Chamots rounded up and brought in, and there were enough sweet wells within their defense perimeter to ensure that everyone could both drink and wash. That these necessities were so fully provided was a source of wonder to many, the missionaries feeling it a sign of Divine Protection.

Monsieur and Madame Auguste Chamot (the lady being an American), had run the Hôtel de Pékin. They stayed in it during the siege; it was on the perimeter of the Legation Quarter and a part of the defense. Madame Chamot remained at the barricades and never joined the other women in the shelter of the Legation— poor though that was, and often under a hail of bullets—but with her husband took an active part in actually repulsing the enemy. They worked together when they captured the cattle; according to legend, Chamot went ahead, a pistol in each hand, and she, close behind him, reloaded and passed the weapons to him. On May 29 they both rode out into the country, augmenting a small escorting force, helping to bring in twenty-nine Europeans who had been left in isolated posts. Later they repeated this feat, saving some Catholic missionaries from the South Cathedral shortly before it went up in flames.

Herbert Squiers, First Secretary at the American Legation, left an admirable record of leadership, courage, and calm resource; Dr. Morrison was a pillar of strength and intelligence. At the Peitang, the gallant Breton naval officer Paul Henry performed prodigies of valor, a selfless figure, till he was killed.

From first to last, and including the present, there was an almost complete lack of comprehension by the foreigners as to what the Manchu government intended to do once they had allowed the Boxers to get so entirely out of hand. They probably came to realize soon enough that they could not indefinitely take on the whole diplomatic world, as represented in Peking. The nation seemed, as far as their government went, almost rudderless—but at the same time very dangerous to their captives. Their behavior was quixotic—they could, had they so wished, have destroyed the whole foreign contingent, yet they continued to play with them as a cat does a mouse, now firing, now holding their fire. What had they to gain by such a course? Many analyses have been made, before and since, but none appears to account for the utter lack of rationality of the Manchu Court—probably it can never be explained. China was benighted in those hands, and with the strong passions let loose over the country.

After it was all over, the amazing thing was, really, that the country was not partitioned by the powers. John Hay's Open Door Policy won the day, and the reparations and exactions were not vindictive, considering what might have been.

The Empress Dowager—dominating, cruel, egotistic—had long closed her mind to the realities of what was passing. Her flight from the capital, as told in Wu Yung's touching document, shows her in a rare shaken mood. This confused loyal official, trying in his simplicity to give her every honor, indicates the bewilderment of many of the administrators, their complete inadequacy for the task in hand.

These events naturally left a strong imprint on the minds of all the foreigners, Western and Japanese alike, and colored their views of the country till, and even after, it had itself changed course. In a dozen years the Manchu dynasty had fallen, and the Republic was proclaimed. A new era began, of high hopes and bitter disappointments.

The Quarter still had, in the thirties, a very special atmosphere —privileged, quiet, cosmopolitan, sophisticated. After the siege the powers stipulated that they be able to control the wall running between the two gates, so that never again might they run the risk of being fired upon from it. This resulted in this section, high over the legations, being at that time the best maintained of any in its entire circumference—the weeds were pulled out from between the bricks, the road along the top kept free. It made a marvelous walk, giving a fine view of the city, reached by wide ramps from below, patroled unobtrusively by sentries from the different legations.

If you walked eastward, beyond the Hata Men to the southeast corner of the Tatar wall you would, after about a mile, come to the old observatory where, on a high buttress in the open, stood a number of huge, imposing, bronze instruments. Now, I understand, these have been put under shelter, which is no doubt what should have been done, but then it was a great pleasure to be able to study them in the sunshine, from a vantage point even higher than the wall itself. Kublai Khan had placed his observatory here on this very site, though before this wall was raised, under the guidance of his Persian astronomers, who had made the instruments—the Mongols were very interested in astronomy. The Chinese, though they too were interested, were too proud to learn this art from their conquerors; when the Jesuits came to China centuries later, they showed them the old instruments, but had no idea at all as to how to use them. This was an opportunity which exactly fitted in with the Jesuits' plans—they were prepared, by the relatively uncontroversial sciences of mathematics and astronomy, to become friendly with the Chinese scholars and, they hoped, ultimately to convert them to their religion.

In 1685 Louis XIV sent the Ch'ing Emperor, K'ang Hsi, a great bronze azimuth and a celestial globe as presents; these treasures became the responsibility of Father Verbiest, who was then in charge of the Board of Astronomy, so much were his powers admired by the dynasty. Teaching, observing, foretelling eclipses, he was himself designing instruments to replace the rather crude ones the Mongols had left behind. His designs were cast in bronze by the brilliantly endowed Chinese craftsmen, and the wonderful ancient implements they made were the ones we could see lying out under the sun on the wall.

The gates of the wall—the Hata Men, the Ch'ien Men, and all the rest, were surmounted by towers ninety-nine feet high, a proper height for beneficent spirits, according to the geomancers, roofed with heavy tiles, massive, imposing. The archways of the gates were of granite, the actual gates of thick wood studded with huge nails, and the surrounding bastions created inner enclosed courts, which were generally thronged with Peking carts, camels, pedestrians, rickshaws, all the vigorous types of Peking traffic which were so enthralling to watch, particularly when you were standing well above them, above the gates.

Exactly on the southeast corner of the wall was the Fox Tower, whose high, window-pitted, wide-eaved silhouette stood out above the battlements. The wall, being only about forty feet high, makes a fine foil to structures like this and the gate towers. The Fox Tower had a sort of ghostly prominence, foxes in China having all sorts of special mythological associations and supposed capabilities. To call a deserted, ruined fort like this a Fox Tower gave it a romantic, eerie aura.

If you were walking on the wall, having come up, say, by the ramp near the old Wagons Lits Hôtel, you would see easily, far and wide, over the city, as it was low, and spacious, and its innumerable monuments were not too difficult to place, amidst the maze of *hutungs*, the strong lines of the inner walls, everything oriented to the axis of the Forbidden City. If you were facing west (and in Peking people were always relating everything to the compass) you would see down on your left the low, poor section which was the old Chinese city, lying outside the Tatar wall, the district which was honored by possessing within its boundaries both the Temple of Heaven and the Temple of Earth. The splendid blue triple roofs of the Temple of Heaven are visible for miles, drawing the eye. Below, beside the wall, ran the railway line which led to Tientsin, but it was so modest an affair, and the wall so massive a fortress, that it could not mar the scene.

Passing above the green legation gardens, with their pleasant European houses, you would come to the Ch'ien Men itself, and would walk round it at this height to the north, so that standing under its great eaves you could look directly in front of you, downward along that tremendous line of the roofs of the Forbidden City, gold sweep upon gold sweep, each with its finial crowning the ridge, stretching out one after the other all the way to Coal Hill.

The roofs (whether of colored tile or not) and the walls were among the most notable points of old Peking—this was true to a degree of all the Chinese cities of the past, and more particularly so of the capital, it being in every way superlative. The traditional Chinese roof has a long, massive, horizontal ridge, held up by two converging concave surfaces; the wide eaves project far out and are turned upward to allow as much light as possible to enter the building and to divert the rain.

In Peking, because the whole of the Forbidden City (and many other areas of the town) had roofs tiled in these almost miraculously beautiful colors—the imperial yellow which, depending on the light, could look like gold or amber; the green which was neither dark nor light; the deep blue and the pale; the amethyst and the turquoise—and as these were set off by the lively vermilions and greens of the pillars and the coffered ceilings, the effect was almost overwhelming. In the brilliant climate of the province, where the sun shone so long and so often, where the air was so dry, nothing of this was lost. Beside the splendor, there was always a comic touch, some note of fantasy, like the nine creatures which sit side by side on the upturned eave (the hen, the *chi-lin*, and all the others). And the finish was so perfect: the end of every tile, as you saw it looking up from the ground, was molded.

Though the main halls followed one axis, in other respects the roofs were so arranged that they rose one against the other, one below the other, making a hundred different designs. Some of the lesser buildings had many-tiered roofs, layer on layer, rather like the gaudy *pailous*, the fantastic arches which used to be placed over wide streets. No people could ever have lavished more genius and artistry on this one feature of their building in the history of the world.

Immensely heavy and costly, the roofs were also, in my time, neglected. Grass grew long between the gleaming tiles, dislodging many of them, and thieves would steal the figures perched on the eaves. Swallows nested under the elaborate roofs, and flew up under the coffered ceilings, bats flew in and out of the towers. The secret of the tiles and the mysteries of the glaze were being lost; tile-making was a dying art, something which worried us all. When the Peking Union Medical College decided to roof its modern buildings with green tiles it not only enhanced their appearance (at great expense) but it brought back many of the old workers to their traditional skills (as was being done in Nanking also, for some of the new buildings). This sort of roof had obviously always been very expensive, and was only possible, on a vast scale, under a tyranny. Labor was impressed by the Mings when they built the city—it was either miserably paid, or a *corvée*.

The Forbidden City and Imperial City walls are decorative, but slight; the Tatar wall was of strategic importance, as well as being extremely handsome. It was forty feet high, and of an equal thickness, reinforced by citadels, bastions, archery towers, and with a moat. Its wide ramps were for the use of the cavalry, and at the top there was enough room for four carts to pass at the gallop, according to specifications. The Peking cart is a narrow vehicle— perhaps this could have been done.

Seen from the wall, the city was surprisingly green—when you were passing through the bare *hutungs* in your rickshaw you would never have suspected there could have been so many great trees behind those high walls and in the courtyards. Looking to the west, in that dry air, you could see the low half-moon of the Western Hills, blue in the distance. Except for their parks and pleasances, they were barren, like nearly all the Chinese ranges— everything cut down and burned during the long hard winters by the shivering peasantry.

Descending from the wall at the Ch'ien Men, by the ramp, you came down into a vast open space, from which you could walk directly into the Forbidden City, only a short distance away. Strings of camels often passed by here, led by their attendants, who, in the spring during the molting season, carried a bag to catch every scrap of fur that might fall. Camel wool brought a good price. To see these high and haughty creatures stalking under the Tatar wall, passing through its deep arched gates, was almost beyond the dreams of romance, it was the essence of the past, Marco Polo, Central Asia, the great silences of the Gobi.

With this introduction, the background of the wall, you came into the first great square of the Forbidden City somewhat accustomed to the grand plan of the buildings themselves—what was surprising then was the expanse of white, carved marble.

Every column of the balustrades is carved, with a dragon, a phoenix, the waves of the sea, the cloud pattern, or other traditional designs. The wide low flights of stairs are separated by spirit ramps, also carved in relief, over which the Emperor's sedan chair used to be carried. Otherwise these slopes were only for the convenience of spirits, and today for tourists.

There was so much space, so much glorious empty room, you wanted to fling your arms wide and start the echoes ringing, as you could well have done, as there were few people about and no one cared if you were a little odd—Peking was then tolerant of eccentrics. The pigeons would have been wheeling up aloft, making your accompaniment.

In the thirties all these places were open, anyone could go in, and there were generally people about but they were never thronged. Under the Kuomintang they didn't go in for mass demonstrations—that sort of thing was then going on in Nuremberg, in Moscow, and in Rome—but not in China. The Forbidden City seemed almost deserted and very calm.

The winding stream within the first court, banked and bridged by more carved white marble, led to the stairways; then you entered the first great hall, walked through it, and came out on the other side to the next court. In spite of their lavish décor these halls were so vast, and in basic plan so plain, with the colors following one range, that their ornamentation never seemed overdone. In some of them there were scrolls and vases to be seen. As you went north the courts grew smaller, and became subdivided and intimate, while pavilions and follies began to appear. At that period you could still see the last apartments occupied by poor Henry Pu Yi in the palace—small, narrow rooms, expensively ill-furnished, full of clocks. Then at last you came out through the North Gate of the Forbidden City wall, and found yourself facing Coal Hill, which lay exactly behind it. To the west lie the Sea Palaces, the most northerly of which has a hill crowned with a huge white *dagoba*—a hill matching Coal Hill in height. These low peaks are artificial, made of the earth excavated to form the lakes.

It was at this North Gate of the Forbidden City that the officials and courtiers who waited upon the Emperor used to muster, long before dawn, to await their summons of entry. In the dark, often in cold and windy weather, this was a trial to them, frequently remarked upon by writers and poets. Po Chü-i speaks of such an occasion in "An Early Levée," which was, in his day at Ch'ang-an, then the capital of the T'ang. Nothing had changed in the way of protocol and etiquette, however, right into our century in Peking. Poor Po Chü-i speaks of there being a foot of snow on the ground, and his having to attend a dawn levée to congratulate the Emperor for some reason. His horse slips on the causeway, his lantern blows out, and he has to ride facing north the whole way, his ears freezing, his hair and beard covered with icicles—how he envies his friend, who can stay warm under the covers, sleeping, at home!

We had an artistic friend, Billy Dunn, who lived in Peking quite early in the century, and in spite of bad weather, he used sometimes to go himself to that North Gate, in the dark, to watch the spectacle of the courtiers assembling, coming up in sedan chairs or on horseback, in their ceremonial clothes, their mandarin buttons and long feathers, with their files of servants, and having to wait for a long time before they were admitted. No one ever dared to be late—there was no shelter—it was an example of the imperial power, which could command even its senior administrators to undergo such an unnecessary trial. This continued right up to the fall of the dynasty; ceremonies have such endurance. The Emperor or Empress had of course also to rise before dawn to meet the officials, but they at least did not have to endure the storms at the outer gate. However, it was a fine show, and Billy used to wonder that he never met anyone else there watching—no one ever hindered him.

Coal Hill with its five peaks and their intervening miniature ravines was like a large model for the traditional brush-rest. Each of these hills was, however, crowned with a pavilion—in one the last of the Mings, seeing that all was lost, hanged himself, deserted by all his court except for one faithful servant. These peaks are within a small enclosure just across the road from the Forbidden City. The whole was considered, from the geomancer's point of view, as a vast spirit screen which could ward off those malignant spirits which descended so often from the north. But it was a small place, nothing compared to the Sea Palaces which it overlooks to the west, and which like Coal Hill are part of the Imperial City.

The Sea Palaces (the Pei Hai, the Chung Hai, and the Nan Hai, or the Northern, Central, and Southern Seas) are three large lakes, round which are artificial hills, with pavilions, bridges, and long galleries running by the water. Each sea has its own particular charms: the Nan Hai has a very remarkable long spirit screen, the Chung Hai is most obviously devoted to the water, and the Pei Hai has its high crowning hill with the great white *dagoba* on the summit, framed in tall trees.

This Buddhistic symbol, so familiar throughout China, and from which the pagoda was evc'ved, was seldom so large or so predominantly placed as this one within the city, a city, moreover, traditionally dominated by the Confucian mode—since the Mongols were driven out. This *dagoba* is not really old, having been erected early in the Ch'ing dynasty (in the middle of the seventeenth century) in honor of the first Tibetan Dalai Lama to visit Peking. It is rather startling to see it there, high among the green branches, something in the way the Eiffel Tower seems both essential to Paris and yet very foreign to it. The site of the Pai T'a (as it is locally known) was one long given over to temples and monasteries. This was true even before it was Khanbalak—it would always, I suppose, have been natural to have had some sort of a shrine there on the hill beside the water. Genghiz Khan is credited with having installed Taoists here, rather surprisingly, for though the Mongols were interested in Taoist mysteries and magic, they had, by some quirk of contrariness in so militant and bloodthirsty a race, by the time they settled in China, become enamored of Buddhism. This had been true also, from the fourth to the sixth centuries, of the Toba Wei, who created the great stone cave-temples in north and west China—they too loved Buddhism and honored it, rough nomadic Tatars though they were.

The lakes were frozen in winter; in summer they were full of lotus (as were all the moats of the city), and they formed a magical prospect which was everywhere exploited to the full. The long galleries, with their coffered ceilings and fretted balustrades, allowed you to saunter by the water protected from the sun, and the pavilions, the *t'ing-tze*, were placed with some particularly captivating view in mind. The Sea Palaces were rich in these pavilions, with their brilliant and extravagant roofs, like so many follies, each a fantasy of color. Those tiled roofs are heavy, but so marvelously balanced on their supporting woodwork that they appear delicate, like exotic parasols, capricious, gay, humorous, glinting with opalescent light. No two were alike except through deliberate plan—they were round, square, hexagonal, octagonal. Their lattices, eaves, ceilings, balustrades, and the benches which ran round their interiors were of a perfection of design and carving, all of wood, predominantly vermilion in color. Being rather neglected in the years when I saw them, these tones had softened to colors which were less brilliant, more evocative. Sitting on a low bench, you would look out upon the smooth waters of the seas, up to the coffered ceiling over you, out to the trees and the boats, while munching sunflower seeds and bracing yourself for a walk down to the fish tubs of the Nan Hai.

Here there used to stand hundreds of huge earthenware tubs, of the kind we associated with Soochow—ribbed brown, with a yellow pattern outside and glazed turquoise within, inhabited by exquisite, precious, and highly-bred goldfish. Keeping fish like this was an old Peking pleasure—there are records of the kilns of Ch'ing-tê-chen sending 40,000 fish bowls a year to the capital in the days of imperial splendor. The Chinese were deeply devoted to goldfish, and had through careful breeding produced a creature very unlike the narrow streamlined inhabitant of the Western glass bowl. The Nan Hai goldfish—perhaps the most remarkable in the country—came in several colors, from filmy white to black, as well as gold. Their bulbous eyes, sticking out sidewise, seemed immense in comparison with their short plump bodies, and their fins and tails were marvelous to behold, a miracle of wavy, tenuous, diaphanous fronds, delicate and translucent. Their tails were longer than their bodies, their movements very graceful. It is this type of fish the Chinese artist loved to paint, or sculpt, and I once had myself a pair of them in pale amber, which were very beautiful and almost weightless.

On a fine autumnal afternoon of mild sunshine, with an unflecked sky, it was a calm and agreeable pursuit to stand over these tubs, watching their noble occupants sculling lightly about in the turquoise waters. In among these bowls were pots of chrysanthemums, each fine stem with its bronzed or yellow flower supported by a bamboo rod. It was the very dream of a peaceful Oriental garden. Gardeners moved quietly about, watering the flowers, plucking off a leaf, stirring the soil. The wide arch of the sky would be interrupted, as it neared the earth, by the golden lines of the roofs of the Forbidden City, which the sun would be turning to liquid fire. Peking seemed almost silent, its low murmurs muted by the trees and water of the sea; in this stillness the voices of the crickets rang out almost loudly.

These parks took up a good deal of the area of the Imperial City, which in the old days was otherwise occupied by members of the court and important officials all behind the pink wall. It was not a very large place. When the Ch'ing fell, and the Republic was proclaimed, all these divisions became meaningless. The Tatar City became that only in name, Chinese moved into it and the Imperial City. The whole machinery of empire disappeared—the court, the ceremonies, the preference it had to offer. The Manchus had been the occupying power for centuries—they had reduced China to a woeful pass, and though in the last decades they had at last delegated some authority to Chinese administrators in senior posts, they were, naturally enough, blamed for everything that was wrong. Revenge, nationalism, cruelty, resulted in their being hunted, dispossessed, beggared, massacred. . . . To all intents and purposes, as a people in China they disappeared.

Compared to the misery and death which attended the fall of the Manchus, the Boxer fatalities and casualties seem small; the disruption and looting in its train not so considerable. It is the consequence which is striking. The foreigners remained, more numerous, more secure, more important. Christianity continued to be preached and more converts were gained. But the Manchus vanished.

In some places—like Sian—they were massacred in great numbers. In Peking their downfall, though complete, was bloodless. Their problems here were that they lost their jobs and their property. Some probably went back to Manchuria, but most had lost any intimate ties with that region, and would have been almost as helpless there as they became in China. Many lingered on in Peking, managing as they could, selling their houses and gardens, disposing of their jewelry, accepting humble posts if they were lucky enough to be offered any. As they could, they melted into the country, becoming sinicized in a way which they had always avoided. The dynasty was over, they had lost their status, and they endured as they could—no more was heard of them as a people.

Sometimes, as late as the thirties, one recognized Manchus in the streets—they were bigger, broader, taller than the Chinese, with broader faces, which were lighter in color and could flush. Their women always wore a robe, never trousers, and as they had never bound their feet, walked naturally (then you still saw very many Chinese women hobbling about on bound feet). The Manchus had their own peculiarity of gait, though, because the heel of their shoe was placed under the sole of the foot.

Peking is so rich in monuments that it would take years to explore them all, but two temples are of such significance that they must be mentioned in any discussion of the city. One of these is the Ta Cheng Miao, the Confucian temple which had the honor of sheltering the Stone Drums, great national treasures. It was austere and in good order, shaded by ancient cypresses, surrounded by an aura of calm. Near the entrance were stone tablets, commemorating distinguished scholars, and going back to the fourteenth century. A famous courtyard of the establishment contained several yellow-tiled pavilions, housing tablets mounted on turtles, and dedicated to military victories of the Ching during the K'ang Hsi, Yung Cheng, and Ch'ien Lung reigns—victories which took place far afield, in Sungaria, Tibet, Mongolia, and the Miao country in Yünnan. Then came the great hall of the temple, approached by steps and a spirit ramp. This was one of the finest halls in the city—of beautiful proportions, noble, calm, and dignified.

The drums, when I saw them, were kept in the long entrance gateway, five on either side. They are about three feet high, black and rough, and date from about 1000 B.C. Their gold inscriptions were long since dug out by impious hands, and in their tumultuous past they were taken to different parts of the land, and even put to use for the pounding of rice. Sometimes they were all lost—once only one was missing, which was terribly disconcerting for the Northern Sung, at which time only nine could be accounted for. The tenth, however, showed up in 1052, and since the twelfth century, when the Golden Tatars took North China, they have been in Peking.

They are inscribed with odes, in ancient seal characters, and have been blackened by the rubbings which have been made from them. They are a truly national monument, and every vicissitude of their history is known by, and important to, the Chinese.

Han Yü, the great T'ang official, scholar, and poet, was so distressed about them that he wrote a long poem on their plight, which became a classic. He was a man of strong and independent character, very anti-Buddhistic, a Confucian and a stylist.

He begins his poem by explaining that he had been presented with a rubbing from the drums, and was asked to write about them. He feels himself inadequate, but as the two great poets of the T'ang—Li Po and Tu Fu—are now dead, he will do what he can. He goes on to say that these drums are lying in the country, abandoned and neglected, overgrown with moss and dirty. Cows rub their horns on them, herd boys strike flints on their surfaces. This is dreadful. He urges someone in authority—a college president, for instance—to help him arrange for these precious relics to be wrapped in rugs, packed up, loaded on camels, and taken to a place of safety, like the Imperial Temple at the capital (then at Ch'ang-an). He thought perhaps the Emperor might even give them to the university, where they could be set up under a "massive building with wide eaves." He praises the calligraphy, remarks on the interest of the odes:

> The meaning deep, the phrases cryptic, difficult to read . . .
> Time has not yet vanquished the beauty of these letters—
> Looking like sharp daggers . . .
> Like phoenix-mates dancing . . .

Before Han Yü died the drums actually were taken out of the fields and to a Confucian temple, only to be once more dislodged during the confusion of the Five Dynasties which followed the T'ang. But in the end they did come, almost intact, to Peking, to a temple of great distinction and dignity. Han Yü would have rejoiced to have known it.

The Temple of Heaven was a very different sort of place— there was nothing stereotyped about Peking.

To reach it you had to go through Ch'ien Men down into the southern part of the city, till you came to a tangled, deserted, unkempt park. The temple, instead of extending over a wide area, court after court, is a high three-tiered building, roofed in blue. The altar stands alone, under the sky—three tiers of pure marble, on the highest of which (a great white circle) the Emperor alone made his devotions. The three tiers of the altar were of the same design and inspiration as the three which support the temple, everything here being based on the number nine, which was considered the most auspicious.

The steps leading from one tier to another are in three flights of nine, the marble blocks of the altar are laid in nine concentric circles, the entrances to the tiers are at the nine points of the compass, and the central stone of the whole was supposed to be at the center of the universe. The Chinese imagined that the heavens were composed of nine parts, hence this elaboration, but the beholder is chiefly struck by the concept of man being finally left alone with his thought, under the arc of the sky.

Out in the park were large open-work iron baskets, where offerings used to be burned—bullocks and rolls of silk, and there were special buildings where the Emperor had been robed, and where sacred tablets were preserved, but in my time most of this was in disarray. Troops were occasionally stationed here, different offices set themselves up, and young people came to play games. But they did not hurt either the temple or the altar.

Over on one side of the park were some beautiful long galleries, open on the side, tiled in green, with scarlet-painted pillars and fretted balustrades. These extended a great distance, but when I saw them were in the process of collapsing—it was a tragic thing to see how the pillars were rotting away, the heavy tiles bringing the posts down. At that period, no one seemed to have any responsibility for the repair, but now surely this has been remedied, though whether the galleries were saved I do not know. But even with these reminders of decay, it was so still and lovely out there, with the high grass and the crickets singing, so deserted that you could see the altar and look up at the azure tiles of the temple without any tourist or official distractions, that you finally left the temple enclosure with fewer feelings of dismay than you probably should have had.

On the other side of the road which brings you from Ch'ien Men to the Temple of Heaven is the enclosure of the Temple of Earth. This was extremely important to the Chinese, their whole world being based on agriculture, and it was here that the Emperor would symbolically plow a furrow, on behalf of all farmers. It was altogether a much humbler place than its heavenly neighbor; its tiles were of yellow, and there were for decoration rather homely objects—mountains and rivers, all as for the service of man. My husband remembers often coming here as a small child, to play in the care of his much loved Manchu *amah*, Wang Nai Nai.

How rich, how varied, was the life of Peking, the everyday life of the road and the market place! These places rang with street cries, each as distinctive as those of Elizabethan England, with vendors clacking bamboo clappers, ringing bells, twanging cymbals. The barber, who shaved his clients on the sidewalk, the man selling mare's milk and leading his source of supply with him, the artisan who sat in a corner of the street mending dishes so cleverly that you could never see the seams, all formed part of a play, in which everyone had his role.

Sweet water, for drinking, was sold from carts which men pushed through the lanes, carts which squeaked loudly, especially in winter. The chestnut vendors cooked their hot, dark, sugary wares in deep braziers, and had their own particular cry; the noodle men offered also squares of fried bean curd; on the sidewalks in some sections of the town—notably those where Moham-medans lived—brass trays three feet in diameter were set out, laden with mutton chops, hot and sizzling.

Different trades had their own quarters, often amounting to many streets: the lantern *hutungs,* the artificial flower area, the glass district. Peking glass was thick, strongly colored, and beauti-ful. In China, as a rule, glass was never very highly regarded—the country had cast its weight on the side of porcelain. In Peking, however, this was an important manufacture. Using the same methods they had employed for centuries, the glass blowers pro-duced amber glass, matching the imperial roofs, dark blue glass, and a lighter, very ethereal shade, dark red, green, and the beloved amethyst. They made wide, low, shallow bowls, with wide mar-gins where fruit could be heaped up, and for the foreign trade glass fruit plates and finger bowls. These they would pack up for you in tightly woven baskets, so that nothing was ever broken, no matter how far away you traveled with them, and the basket itself would serve you for years.

These establishments used up every scrap of molten glass, by turning these oddments into fantasies—frogs, cicadas, anything that came to the blower's mind, which they would toss in with your purchases for good measure. They had a lavish, fertile in-vention—waste was unknown to them and every morsel of mate-rial an opportunity to express an idea.

There were streets for the jewelers, where the shops were full of silver rings set with semi-precious stones—carnelian, amber, coral, turquoise, lapis lazuli, rose quartz. They made necklaces of these stones and of glass too—glass which was cut as though it were a fine substance, as indeed in their hands it was. They made filigree necklaces and brooches. Here they sold jade trees, and silver hair ornaments, and amidst all these was a treasury of pre-cious jade, with rings, bracelets, and pins made wholly from this cool, mysterious, lustrous substance, which the Chinese value above all other jewels.

Peking was a place for furs—sables from Siberia, flying fox from Yünnan, white fox, yellow fox, stone marten, squirrel. The rich Chinese used to line their winter gowns with them. There were leopard skins and seal skins, which the foreigners liked to buy, and there were fur-lined hats with ear flaps, part of the Russian trade. An ordinary fur coat was much cheaper than a good wool coat, but padded cotton, though unwieldy, was as warm as either and cost only a fraction as much.

Beautiful furniture was made, and beautiful old pieces sold also: high tables, sideboards, cupboards, the graceful uncomfortable chairs, the shining carved stools.

Then there were all the miscellaneous occupations: the jugglers, the letter writers, the people who specialized in making landscapes of colored ice, the fire-cracker manufacturers (a big business), and the itinerant dentists. Near the entrance to one of the fairs (the Lung Fo Ssu) was a sign in English, reading "Insertion false teeth and eyes, latest Methodists." Flights into English enhanced many an odd corner, like one in a temple, reading: "Altar for Sacrificing Forefathers," and down a blackwood lane, "The Artful Furnitures Shop."

And there were the restaurants, an important feature of the city whose cuisine was renowned all over the country. One of the most famous was the one outside Ch'ien Men, whose specialty was Peking duck, but there were many, many others, known all over China to gourmets. Being in the north, more flour was used than in the rice-growing south—people liked to eat sweet steamed dumplings, *chiao-tzu* filled with meat, vegetables, or crab, and *mien*, which are noodles.

The dish foreigners call "chicken velvet," which is the smooth paste made from the meat, is really "chicken mimosa," as it supposedly is like the white mimosa to look at. The Pekingese were very clever with cooking duck, not only the famous Peking duck (which is roasted and cut into small sections which are eaten on pancakes with a special dark sauce), and they made "spun-silk" potatoes, and roasted the winter bamboo shoots. They made wonderful dishes with carp and with shrimp, with cauliflower and cabbage, with mushrooms—with every ingredient imaginable, from sharks' fins to bean sprouts. They made sweet dishes of almonds and lotus seeds and honey balls, and served wines made from *kaoliang* and millet, scented with rose petals and Buddha fingers.

In ways like this Peking made you think of Paris. Food was a serious matter, though you laughed a lot over it.

Fairs took place on stated traditional days of the month, many in temple grounds, like the Lung Fo Ssu. There was an old-clothes market where you could buy for very little old Chinese coats of fine silk and brocade, thick luscious silk, with the cash pattern, or floral motives woven into it, pitiful reminders of fallen fortunes. In the fairs you found snuff bottles, jades, seals, ceramics, and a myriad other things, including foreign books. I found my Epictetus and an old edition of *Alice in Wonderland* at the Tung An Chieh Ch'ang. People came to buy and sell, to watch the world go by, to be amused, pick pockets, and air their birds.

The Chinese have always had a great affection for birds as pets, and used to take them out, in their cages, for walks. When they came to an agreeable open area, they would set the cages on a fence or some other convenient place, and let their mynah, or whatever it was, enjoy a social hour. Sometimes they would release their pet, to fly out among the trees, a long string tied to its claw, so that it would not go too far. The cages were generally of bamboo, and equipped with dark blue cotton covers, to be put on if the occupant became tired or nervous. This habit of taking your bird out was to be seen all over the country. In Shanghai a favorite place for them was along the Race Course, where in the late afternoon you could see cage after cage set out, the owners conversing, the birds twittering and hopping about.

Other regular visitors to the fairs were the beggars, the professionals, who were members of the Beggars' Guild, and whose attentions could not be avoided—they followed you about, till you had bought them off. But there were so many persons thronging the fairs that no one class absorbed your thoughts, for good or ill. People went through with high bamboo scaffoldings, hung with sweetmeats: pink and white cocks and hens, camels, pagodas, fish, and geese. When they had sold enough they would put down their stand, and taking out a reserve of fondant, make more figures, watched by a delighted crowd. This was true, as well, of other makers of ill-considered trifles—the old men who made bamboo frogs and crickets, the artist with his impromptu sketches, who, sitting on the ground, patiently turned out one drawing after another of bamboos, orchids, walled towns, lakes, and fishing boats.

Fairs exist as a livelihood, but also for pleasure. There was in those old fair grounds in Peking, in the courts of the temples and monasteries, so much liveliness, so much smiling and talk and eager interest, that you entered there, literally, into that mood called "the fun of the fair."

As everywhere in the country the year was marked by special festivals, but, it being Peking, these were managed here with a more traditional panache. Early in the spring the children, stuffed into bright padded cotton robes, with the most fanciful hats, quivering with wire antennae and pompons, with tiger shoes and silver bangles, came out at dusk pulling behind them the unbelievably fascinating paper rabbits, with fluffy paper fur. These were for some reason the favorite model but there were also dragons and lotuses, each with its candle. Sometimes these fantasies were made of ice. Such joys were not only for rich children, but were truly a part of the general scene. Though the disparity of income was great, and a burden on the conscience, though there was always this great spectre of poverty lurking behind you, the Chinese were, in themselves, relatively classless. They had a true comprehension of democracy in the social sense, though very little in the political. When it came to that most of them threw up their hands in cynical despair, and went about their own affairs.

Billy Dunn, the artist-architect, who used to watch at the North Gate of the Forbidden City, once decided while in Peking to call in a Chinese doctor of the old school. Billy had been troubled for a long time by a persistent cold, and was tired of trying the usual Western remedies, which he found quite ineffectual.

The doctor was a person in a long gown, attended by a young boy assistant, who had brought along the equivalent of the "black bag"—in this case a brazier, some charcoal, and a number of herbs. He asked Billy a few questions, and then drew out some mysterious tables which he consulted, before beginning to concoct a brew over his brazier in the courtyard. In a couple of hours the broth was ready and presented to our friend, who drank it off at once. He said that it tasted like a strange sort of bean soup; in any event, he was soon perfectly recovered. Delighted, he asked the medico if he might have the recipe, but the doctor replied that it would be useless to him, as it would never be the same again. Such remedies, he explained, varied every time according to the state of the patient, his horoscope, the time of the year, and other factors. Billy then asked him his fee, to be told that a Chinese doctor expected to be paid when the patient was well, not when he was ill. Then the doctor bore the cost.

Few foreigners ever followed this course. The Chinese in the ports used the foreign clinics, and up-country went to mission hospitals, but often with reluctance—they were rather afraid of them. The most common remedy in the country was acupuncture, and you constantly saw people going about with reddish bruises on their necks and arms from these needles—it seemed to the patients quite effectual, it was cheap, it demanded no watching of the clock, they had no fear of it.

There were all sorts of quack remedies of which we became aware. For instance, we were fond of cats, and often had kittens about the house—it was not uncommon for one of these to turn up with its whiskers mysteriously clipped because these were salable and could be made up into an eye lotion. There was still in the country a strong legendary feeling about tigers, and it was believed that a certain ointment, helpful for rheumatism, was made partly with their bones; there were many fantastic remedies like this which still had their adherents. The apothecaries' shops harbored strange and romantic ingredients, mostly herbs, some of compounded bones, even of minerals.

Some of the Westerners liked Shanghai, liked its modernity, comforts, and racy flavor; but others loved Peking, and would, like myself, have given anything to have lived there. But it wasn't easy to do so, unless you were independent—and even then, a girl at that time could not properly have struck out alone in Peking, or indeed in most Chinese cities. In Peking there were hardly any jobs to be had—it was no place for business, having been traditionally opposed to foreign trade on any large scale. There were a few banks—but only small branches—a few firms, but again the employees were not generally left there long. It was too hard to leave Peking once you were used to it, if you had fallen in love with it—you couldn't bear the tempo of other towns after it. The quiet, the subdued magnificence, the artistic wealth—where would you find that again, in company with so few harsh modern tones?

The great exception to this was the *corps diplomatique*, who did indeed live a charmed life—but that was a closed circle. The diplomats lived in a sort of rarefied state, everything had come true, they had achieved bliss (as far as surroundings went). They were so contented that they could for long not endure the very idea of moving away to Nanking, when the Kuomintang made it the capital, and resisted going for years. Everyone understood their position exactly. Then there were some fortunate missionaries, the people at Yen Ching, at the Peking Union Medical College, at the Language School—but again these institutions were not large enough to take in anyone but their own. And there were artists.

It was so cheap, if you were living in a Chinese house, and so comfortable and amusing with your jolly servants—but even these artists had to have some income. This was long before the days of hippy indigence, consuls wouldn't put up with waif-and-stray nationals; if you couldn't take care of yourself you were generally sent home. The artists in Peking were those who rested on some sure supplies, and it was fortunate that this could be, else men like Thomas Handforth, for example, could not have accomplished what he did there. There was a rather irritating assumption that if you were sensitive to beauty you would live in Peking, but it had to be a supported sensitivity, and most people in China had to earn their living. There was almost no market for people's paintings and drawings—there weren't enough Europeans to support an artists' colony—anyway this is seldom possible anywhere. And if you bought pictures, you bought Chinese pictures, or oils by some of the gifted Russians, or you brought back pictures from your leaves at home.

There were people who had managed to find a way to live there—General Munthe, for instance, who had long before commanded Chinese troops, and then taken part in lifting the siege during the Boxer. He lived in a big Chinese house, full of treasures. Some individuals had found niches for themselves in one way or another—but they were few. The old Austrian Legation, which its country had long given up, was in my time the home of a number of White Russians, who lived there in spacious, opulent flats, charmingly disorderly, round the great staircase. But to most of us it remained a dream city, afar off, separated from us by bandit-infested country, warlords, Japanese, money barriers.

The Western Hills

. . . and descending the hill, [Ch'en] turned into a
copse where there was a building which he thought
would in all probability be a monastery. On getting
nearer, he saw that the place was surrounded by a wall,
and between him and a half-open red door was a brook
spanned by a stone bridge leading up to it. Pulling back
the door, he beheld within a number of ornamental
buildings circling in the air like so many clouds, and for
all the world resembling the Imperial pleasure-grounds;
and thinking it must be the park of some official personage, he walked quietly in, enjoying the delicious fragrance of the flowers as he pushed aside the thick
vegetation which obstructed his way. After traversing a
winding path fenced in by balustrades, Ch'en reached a
second enclosure, wherein were a quantity of tall willow-
trees which swept the red eaves of the buildings with
their branches. The note of some bird would set the
petals of the flowers fluttering in the air, and the least
wind would bring the seed-vessels down from the elm-
trees above; and the effect upon the eye and heart of the
beholder was something quite unknown in the world of
mortals.

(P'u Sung-ling, *Strange Stories from a Chinese Studio*,
trans. by H. A. Giles)

THE HSI MEN, the West Gate of the Tatar city, brings you out
onto the plain facing the Western Hills. Here once lay the
fabled Yüan Ming Yuan of the Ch'ing Emperors, who caused it to
be built when the Jesuits were in favor, and it amused the sovereigns
to experiment with semi-Europeanized architecture. It was of a
rococo splendor, designed by men who had Versailles at the back
of their minds, as did all such Europeans in the eighteenth century. In 1860 during the second phase of the Opium Wars it was
totally destroyed, razed to the ground, looted—by the Chinese as
well as the foreign soldiery, who were maddened by the refusal of

the authorities to give up the prisoners they had taken and were torturing. In my time there was nothing left here to see except a vast expanse of pitted ground, with here and there a few arches left standing, or a florid .pillar resting on the earth, broken and discolored.

Not very long afterward the Empress Dowager, Tzu Hsi, the "Old Buddha," decided that she would put up her own Summer Palace near this abandoned site. This comparatively modern, not wholly attractive place is now a popular excursion for the citizens of Peking. Here is the fabled and infamous marble boat she financed by misappropriating funds which had been put aside for the navy, here is a wide lake, and on the other side, the quite striking, even startling palace, which ascends in a high sheer stone wall, rather like a Tibetan structure. The best part of the palace is by the water—the long painted galleries, shady and cool in summer, and the sight of the marble camel-backed bridge.

Behind the Summer Palace is the tomb of Yeh Lü Ch'u Ts'ai, the wise and temperate councillor of Genghiz Khan, and one of the most admirable and interesting figures of his age. He was born in 1190, a Liao prince, whose father had held office under the Golden Tatars, somehow accommodating himself to the reigning power without being scorned as a collaborator, a faculty the son shared. Yeh Lü Ch'u Ts'ai was brought up by his mother to become a highly cultivated man (his father died early), and when still very young was made governor of Peking. When Genghiz Khan took the city he was so impressed by his obvious qualities that he took him into his own personal service, making him his scribe, administrator, and advisor—as much as anyone could ever advise Genghiz. Undoubtedly Yeh Lü Ch'u Ts'ai did temper the wind for many peoples in those terrible years, averting massacres, introducing monetary reforms, making the great Khan understand that though he had conquered his empire on horseback he could not govern it in that way.

People used to be able to rent courts in many of the Buddhist temples and monasteries in the Western Hills—these were beautiful places, and much cooler than the city. You had to take your camp bed, wash basin, food, lights, and servants with you, establishing a base for yourself in the hills, from which you could explore the region. In these silent and remote buildings, lying in the folds of the hills, you were able partially to enter another way of life which was very delightful, very calm, very beautiful to the eye. Out there nothing seemed to have changed for centuries; there were still no roads.

(I have been told, on good authority, that this area is now the preserve of high government and party officials, and closed to the public. If so, it is a great pity.)

In the first circle of the hills lies Wo Fo Ssu, the Temple of the Sleeping Buddha. I stayed here several times—it was easy to arrange to rent a courtyard with a hall. Once we found ourselves under a low rocky cliff, over which clambered two white goats, giving us unexpected companionship. From Wo Fo Ssu there are many excursions to be made by donkey to other places of the Pa Ta Chu group—to the Hunting Park, where the Ch'ing noblemen enjoyed the chase, and to the Jade Fountain Hills. On the way home in the evenings, it was an enchanted hour as we rode past the little delicate porcelain pagoda of the Yü Ch'üan on its eminence, and the small Moorish tower with its onion dome, which confronted it on an adjacent hill, the sunset behind them.

The two finest monasteries lie farther to the west: Chieh T'ai Ssu and T'an Cheh Ssu, very old places, very large, and in the thirties still active with many monks in residence. They lie on well-wooded slopes and have fine halls, with beautiful roofs of colored tile and painted eaves, with paved courts and pavilions—the wonders of the capital transposed to monastic splendor. The first is renowned for its white pines, the second for its gingkoes. In the spring, these monasteries, and the countryside about them, are lovely with flowering almond, apricot, peach, and pear.

Chieh T'ai Ssu has a dramatic situation, well up a mountain slope, on a cliff, enclosing within its many retaining walls a valley. Built on terraces, of which the most astonishing is four hundred feet long by twenty wide, it commands a fine view over the plain, and down into the temple. Thousands of stone steps, lichened with age, lead up to its heights, from the great entrance *pailou* at the forecourt. It was a place of immense importance in the Buddhistic world, because here priests were ordained, the ordinands coming from as far as the Yangtze. To become an abbot, you had to have been ordained at Chieh T'ai Ssu.

The ceremonies took place in an immense ordination hall, high on the hill, containing a huge square marble altar. During these the ordinands would pass all the way from the lowest entrance up to the top of the altar, while on their shaven heads nine sticks of incense burned right down into their skulls, marking them as priests for life. In the thirties Alan Priest, an American art historian who became a Buddhist priest, was ordained here. At his expense (most people could not have afforded it) candles burned on every step all the way from the *pailou* and along the balustrades of the terraces, a wonderful sight.

Out from the terraces lean the white pines, the most famous being the Sleeping Dragon and the Nine-Dragon. Near them is a small octagonal column with bas-reliefs of girl musicians, sweet and smiling, a type of Buddhistic sprite. High on the mountain above the monastery are the monks' burial grounds, glades and hillsides of tombs, hundreds of crumbling grey stupas. On these heights are a few stone tables with round stone seats, one table with a chessboard cut in it. The view from here, avoiding the temple, is more aloof, less terrestrial—this is a relief, I have been told (for I never saw Chieh T'ai Ssu); the monastery was a place of great pride, great ecclesiastical authority and dominance.

T'an Cheh Ssu was quite different—everyone loved it, the Temple of the Oak Pool, where stone channels led down hill past the courts, with pure sweet water freely flowing from the springs above. It is a place associated with dragons, which finally became snakes, and in modern times, seemed to be only one snake, which hibernated but came out in the spring to its pool.

The trees here sometimes met overhead—it was a place of artful interplay of light and shade. The oaks were of a special species—Mathew defines "Cheh" as "Thorny tree about fifteen feet high, the leaves are used for feeding silkworms before the mulberry leaves are ready or when they are scarce. Bark produces a yellow dye." Behind a courtyard where the leaves almost made a covered canopy, the beautifully colored tiles of the roofs made a striking effect.

Our friend Li, of the rickshaw, believed in the occult powers of the T'an Cheh Ssu snake, though he told us he had for a long time scoffed at any such ideas. One day, however, when he was visiting the monastery, he happened to say openly that it was nonsense to think that this snake could affect anyone. Soon afterward he got up to go, and found that having raised his foot to take a step, he was unable to lower it to the ground. He was thoroughly frightened, apparently without a suspicion that the priests there would be versed in hypnotism and ready to employ it against persons like himself. When he admitted that the snake was holding him in thrall, the spell ended, and he could put his foot down. After that, he said, "I b'lieve."

T'an Cheh Ssu, with its long pink enclosing wall, its trees, its position on the hill, its glorious roofs, is of the stuff of dreams—and so too is the whole plain which stretches out before you from the height—tawny, mauve, with a glint of gold shining through an amethystine haze—it is almost beyond belief. I think I never saw, before or since, so beautiful an expanse as that which lies on the far side of the Western Hills, with its subtle colors, its sense of mystery, of unreality.

T'an Cheh Ssu has a famous guest courtyard, called the Bamboo Court, where the Emperor Ch'ien Lung used to stay when he visited the monastery. The grove itself lies up the hill from the court, and is extremely beautiful—the gleaming trunks of the trees, with their sharply marked joints, the incisive lines of the sharp leaves, their movement when the wind blows, always a delight to see.

The courtyard is simple, the buildings tiled in grey, as it was a country retreat and intended to be austere. The eaves and rafters were brilliantly painted, however, and within the courtyard a yellow roofed pavilion protected an important spring. The water flowed out through a stone channel, which had been formed with grooves into the likeness of a dragon's head, which seemed to come alive as water passed over it. Then the stream flowed down through runnels, to supply the monastery.

The Emperor's room was built so that he could observe the bamboo grove from a slight height, giving him an enchanting prospect of the whole. Beyond this lies a very ancient stupa, the oldest part of T'an Cheh Ssu, and somewhat apart from the monastery itself. It was so old that it formed no part of the present enclave; it was a precious monument, its spire adorned by a golden crown, and once encircled by golden bells.

This temple and monastery was, I believe, the finest flower of all these beautiful places in the Western Hills, and the one which had the most peaceful and noble atmosphere attending it. Those who loved it used to speak of T'an Cheh Ssu in a very special way, as though it were a secret treasure in their hearts.

Part IV

MOUNTAINS AND LAKES

The Lushan

THE LUSHAN, the high ranges lying south of the Yangtze above Kiukiang, are beautiful and spectacular, rich in monuments and temples, and give splendid views of the Poyang Lake, which extends blue and shimmering far below. They were greatly loved by both Li Po and Po Chü-i, who left poems about them which have made them even more significant to the Chinese—they are traditionally a great part of the Chinese inheritance of natural wonders.

Chiang Kai-shek was fond of going to the Lushan; when the government was in Nanking, he would sometimes come here in the summer, to spend several weeks at a time in the cool air. He stayed, like almost everyone else, in or near the ugly foreignized town of Kuling, which was also much frequented by missionaries escaping from the heat of the plains. It was quite a big place, with room for conferences and meetings.

In the summer of 1937, when the Japanese attacked at Lu Kou Chiao, there was an important conference held here in the mountains, attended by the leaders of the Kuomintang, after which the Generalissimo issued the statement which declared that this time China would resist to the hilt, and asked that the Japanese recall their soldiers. This was promulgated about a week after the "incident" took place, that is, about July 16, and confirmed that there would now be a major war. In this he told the country what sacrifices would be necessary, and how terrible the struggle would inevitably be.

We once went to Kuling when I was a young girl, taking a river steamer to Kiukiang, a couple of days' sailing from Shanghai, a pleasant journey, giving one time to watch the wide river. We passed the famous Gold and Silver Islands, which were green and lovely with their high trees, partly hiding the monasteries which crowded all the way to the top of each of them, their grey curved roofs fitting into the contours of the rocks. Both of these islands were then popular goals for pilgrimages, undertaken partly from a sense of piety, partly just to have a summer excursion. That year we went up-stream was, however, a sad one; the Yangtze had flooded badly, and hundreds of farmhouses were isolated in the midst of the muddy waters, even within our range of vision. The river was depositing rich silt on the fields, but ruining that year's crops and taking a heavy toll of life.

Kiukiang was flooded, too. We took a sampan through the streets from the ship to Duff's Farm, the only possible hostelry, except that it was impossible. But there was no alternative. It was a filthy caravanserai, built round a courtyard, and we were over-joyed to leave it early the next morning. At the foot of the mountains we were met by great numbers of chair-coolies, seeking fares. It was a long way up, and people generally walked part of it and rode the rest. The climb was the harder because the paths were mostly composed of thousands of steep stone steps. The ravines were deep, the precipices high, and the way narrow—it was a little frightening at certain places. But the coolies were used to it, and moved fast and fearlessly, changing the carriers when they were tired. After the intense, damp heat of the valley the air was wonderfully sweet and pure. Flowers grew richly on the hillsides, tall tiger lilies and the little white fringed parnassia.

The Lushan is a region subject to sudden dangerous storms, which turn its streams into raging torrents in a few moments, and fill its icy pools to overflowing. People were always being warned to be on guard against this, as they set off on the long expeditions which were so much a part of the life of Kuling. We swam in the Dragon's Pool, deep and cold and dark, with its high slippery stone walls, and we walked far out to Lion's Leap, which gave a wide view over the plains. There were many sites which were famous because hermits had lived there long ago, existing simply on stones, water, flowers, and grass, as good Taoists should.

Po Chü-i was stationed in Kiukiang as an official during his career (in the T'ang), and made many excursions up the mountains. He liked to visit the twin Forest Monasteries which had been founded in the fourth century, and were renowned in the Buddhistic world: the Western Forest Monastery (which lay to the north), and the Eastern Forest Monastery. He found Incense-Burner Peak so lovely that he built himself a cottage there, near a stream and a waterfall. In those times the hills were full of monkeys, whose melancholy cries were strangely inspiring to poets.

Li Po, in the course of his difficult life, was several times a widower; the fourth wife is spoken of in connection with the Lushan, as at one time she became a Taoist nun, living in a convent in these mountains. There is a record, too, of an occasion when Li Po went up to the Eastern Forest Monastery to say farewell to his friends among the monks there. He wrote a number of poems on places he loved in these hills—two to the cataract of the Lushan, in which he ascends Incense-Burner Peak and looks south to this waterfall with awe and joy, and the famous *Song of Lushan*, full of allusions to historical and mythical subjects, making plain his own great love of the ranges.

On Hearing a Buddhist Priest from Shu Play the Lute with Great Power

Taking the western path,
His lute well-wrapped,
  In a fine silk sheath of figured green,
A priest made his way down Mt. Omei.

He swept his hand over the strings,
  And I (a stranger, and alone)
Heard a myriad pines sough,
I was calmed by flowing water.

Then came notes like bells, crystal-clear,
I neither saw that dusk was darkening the jade green hills
Nor marked the lowering clouds of Fall.

                                                Li Po

. . .

At the moment of parting
  Far over the river, the moon was reflected
Suddenly we heard over the water the sound of a lute—

The Breach in the Wall

The host forgot that he was taking his leave,
  The guest that he was starting a journey.

She struck one note on all four strings,
  Like ripping silk.
The boats,
  One on the east, one on the west,
Were still—no one said a word—
Watching, at the river's heart,
The white path of the autumn moon.
            From *The Song of the Lute*, Po Chü-i

Hangchow

To the Chinese, Hangchow is one of those idyllic places—beautiful, rich in history, enshrined in memories. The Southern Sung made it their capital in the twelfth century, after the dynasty had been driven south of the Yangtze, surviving only as half a country. Because of this catastrophe, the provincial city attained imperial rank, and had for over a century great painters, academicians, statesmen, and a court in its midst. It was then that Ch'an Buddhism (which the Japanese call Zen) was highlighted through so many great artists embracing its interpretations, men like Mu Ch'i, Liang K'ai, and Ying Yü-chien. In Mongol times, when the Chinese had once more been defeated by the Tatars, the city continued to be important and handsome—it was in this era that it was visited by Marco Polo. He admired it (calling it Kinsai, as the Tatars did) and made it known to the West.

Set about with low hills, resting on a lake, near the pictorial Ch'ien T'ang River, it is pleasant, mild, pretty, though lacking the strong artistic impact we have come to expect of famous Chinese cities. It has no wall—it is almost a spa. Green willows hang over the water, and the many temples in the hills are shaded with great trees, set about with fine clumps of bamboo. It was for a time a center for orthodox Buddhism. The Ch'an painters of the Sung first worked at the court, resting on its lavish artistic patronage; when they decided to break with this tradition they went off to a monastery by the water, seeking sudden inspiration, individual understanding—a sort of rebirth. This was a manifestation of great vigor, something rather alien to this mild town.

Aside from its quiet, gentle ambiance, Hangchow was distinguished, before the Court came to it, because of its association with two of the most famous men of Chinese history: Po Chü-i, the poet, and Su T'ung-p'o.

Po Chü-i was once in residence here as the governor, and had a causeway laid down across the lake, a great help to the pedestrians, the poor, shortening their long walk around the shore. The very fact that one of China's foremost poets lived and wrote here was something for the local people to be proud of, even apart from this important public work.

Su T'ung-p'o, who lived during the Northern Sung, was a universal genius—poet, artist, administrator, philosopher, scholar. He was also a profoundly good and moral man, full of kindness, cheerful, urbane. He came first to Hangchow at the beginning of his official career, in 1071, a young deputy magistrate, and at once fell in love with the soft charm of the place, its birds and bamboos, the river and the hills. He visited the monasteries, and wrote a good deal of poetry, but he was in considerable distress most of the time. He chafed at the restrictions his position placed upon him, being opposed to many of the government's edicts, which were harsh and unjust. He could do nothing to ameliorate these policies that he could see—he had to carry them out. But then, as always, he felt intensely for the poor, the helpless downtrodden victims of the state.

Eighteen years later, as governor of the province, he came back. Then he was able to bring about many important changes. He worked on the canals, which were choked with silt, purifying them by an ingenious system of locks extending to the river; he improved the reservoirs, enabling the town to have good drinking water; and he had the weeds, which were choking West Lake, the heart of Hangchow, its pleasure and its pride, pulled out. With the vegetable matter and mud which were cleared out of the water he built another causeway, fifty feet wide, edged by willows, and cut by graceful bridges.

The Northern Sung court was torn by factions, and a man of such evident genius made powerful enemies by his very successes. Su was disgraced (if such a man could be disgraced by such a government), exiled, subjected to endless indignities and sufferings. Everyone who helped him was punished for it. But he never lost his breadth of outlook, his talents, nor his real friends; as he died before the dynasty was attacked by the Golden Tatars, he never had to take part in the flight of the government to the south, and never knew of the loss of all the northern provinces. The diminished state, finally settling down in Hangchow, ironically enough, was to find itself the beneficiary of the man it had tormented and spurned.

Hangchow people like to go down to the lake and hire a boat; looking out from the water they take pleasure in the hills, the pagodas, the islands. In the thirties a few missionaries labored in the town, and not far away was an American flying school, where General Claire Chennault taught the "Flying Tigers"—but there was little evidence of the West, it was a really Chinese place.

Mokanshan

MOKANSHAN WAS another mountain resort which was popular with the missionaries; it was near Shanghai, much lower than Kuling, less romantic in every way, though when it was under snow it had its moments. My father once went up there for a few days in midwinter; the party with him agreed that it was like Switzerland. I was only there for a few grey November days, and remember its chilly mists more than anything else. But of course, it was a *summer* resort; anyone going in November knew what to expect.

Just at that time I was preparing for my first examination in Chinese, which would be given at the British Consulate, and was absorbed in going over and over the few (only five hundred) characters this test covered. Added to this was the fact that I had just ridden in my first hunt (we only chased paper round Shanghai, but it was very arduous), in which my pony, in spite of considerable hindrance from me, had come in among the first twenty in a field of well over a hundred. I was still dazed and exhausted from that long hard gallop and the many jumps of this demanding ride, and what with this and the characters I was almost oblivious to my surroundings. It was just as well that Mokanshan offered no inducements to tempt me out to explore it—I wouldn't have seen it anyway.

Colonel Hayley Bell had loaned my mother and myself his

bungalow and his boy for a few days; there we went and there we stayed, shivering in front of the fireplaces, while the fog pressed in on the dripping November windowpanes. It was a little stone house, the walls hung with photographs of his children, very angelic in their white embroidered dresses and sailor suits. Colonel Hayley Bell (whose granddaughters are famous actresses, Hayley and Juliet Mills) was a man of parts: a great rider, a wit, musical, and a keen Chinese scholar. He gave me my first dictionary (Soothill's), a small black book of very fine print holding thousands of characters—I took it with me everywhere, poring over it. It looked like a prayerbook, from the outside; anyone else studying Chinese would recognize it at a glance, it was like a badge.

I asked Hayley once how many characters he knew. "How many are there?" was his answer. A tall, thin, romantic figure, even as the years passed, he never lost his zest for living. People said of him that as a young man he had fluttered every heart in the drawing rooms on the coast.

Part V
NANKING

Nanking Generally

Everyone always says that south of the river
  It's wonderful, wonderful.
There you should live till you're old.
In spring the water's as green as the sky
And you fall asleep in your painted boat
To the sound of beating rain.
The wineshop girls are as fair as the moon
Their white wrists like driven snow.
Don't ever go back to your village—
  Not till you're old—
If you do, you know, you'll break your heart.
                 Wei Chuang, c. 836–910

A POEM like this struck a responsive chord during the T'ang, but it's an immense time since anyone has felt romantic about Nanking—except possibly Chiang Kai-shek. In my day everyone disparaged it, chiefly because it wasn't Peking—one of those insuperable arguments. Of course it wasn't.

It could neither sustain its periods of brilliance, nor decline with grace. Long ago it had a great reputation for art, splendor, wit. When that epoch passed, though the green willows still trailed their branches in the mist along the dikes, they could no longer touch peoples' hearts as they had, they didn't seem so important. Once the very thought of Nanking evoked images of youth, beauty, warmth (even though, then as now, it had a hard, chill, damp winter). But it had so many bad times that they came to overbalance the good ones.

It was so often razed to the ground, and so much cruelty was enacted there, that something essential went out of it. It couldn't give an iota of the pleasure that Peking, for instance, can afford, with its palaces and parks still intact, though many times rebuilt and restored. Yet it was a Ming emperor who built the Peking we know today, giving it the opportunities he denied Nanking, the city his own house had chosen—even then there must have been something untoward about it. Peking has known terrible occasions, but happily no one let it fade away—Nanking couldn't inspire that devotion. It was a tragic place, which, almost worse, had become dull. But most people didn't think of it as pitiful, they just ran it down. They weren't curious as to what might lie under the low, broken mounds of the town, all those uneven, empty places, standing within the wide embrace of the massive wall.

In the T'ang, Nanking was considered as the south. Canton, though already a great commercial port, large enough to contain a colony of a hundred thousand Arabs, was too far away from the center of the world (Ch'ang-an and Lo-yang) to be taken seriously by a civilized man. Whereas Nanking, though still far away from the T'ang capitals up there by the Lo River (haunted by its beautiful fairy), was still within the bounds of sentiment. That was true both before and after that dynasty—it fared better in antiquity than it ever did afterwards as far as the bubble reputation went.

In the turbulent centuries after the fall of the Han and the rise of the Sui, and again after the fall of the T'ang, smaller kingdoms sprang up, flourished for a season, and perished. It was then that Nanking became several times a rich prize, the capital of ephemeral states, whose artistic achievements, religious fervor, and eccentricities have lived on in history. These briefly flowering principalities were not small in the European sense—China herself was too vast for that—but comparatively they were not large, and the number of persons who made their names in them was not great. Yet the southern dynasty people, who lived under the early Sung, Ch'i, Liang, Ch'en, Southern T'ang, were extraordinarily gifted. Countless inspired artisans living there could weave, make pottery and lacquer, carve wood, cast bronze, with consummate skill. The names of the writers, artists, poets, are still extolled. Right here, on this barren, wasted ground, on these miles which lie between the Yangtze and Purple Mountain, great pictures were painted, philosophy and religion argued, the art of conversation deeply valued, plots were laid for conquest, vast hopes raised. Again and again, after a military disaster Nanking had picked itself up, and become once more renowned for its artists, its music, gaiety, wit, the elegance of its court, its panache. Where had it all vanished?

Perhaps in its light, genial, southern way it had given itself too much to the luxuries (or necessities) of the spirit to be able to survive in those harsh times. In the period of the Warring States, this region was close to that part of the country called Ch'u, which stretched westward from it, and was known for its love songs and fantasies, for the soft, artistic nature of its people. Ch'u was mown down in the third century B.C. by the brutal and spartan state of Ch'in, from which China takes its name, the state which built the Wall.

The thing that seems rather uncanny, as you read of Ch'in today, is that the Emperor was guided in his statecraft by a small book, just that book which crops up periodically throughout history in one form or another. Like the others of its sort, it was so wholly infamous, so explicit in the evils it planned to consummate, that people didn't take it seriously—that is, in the other states. The wretched people of Ch'in, who were the first to be victimized by it, might have told them to take note of it, but as usual, enlightenment came very late.

This little bamboo volume, called *The Book of Lord Shang* (after its author) is a serious textbook for a dictatorship. Lord Shang himself, a man of towering ambition, finally fell into his own trap, but his influence lived on within the governing circle of Ch'in long after he had been pulled apart by chariots, one of the more unpleasant forms of execution in old China. Its authoritarian message is contrary to the basic constituents of Chinese thought: the reforming, considered ways of the Confucians, the individualism of the Taoists, the compassion and the worldly complaisance of the Buddhists (which influence had not yet entered China). These two antagonistic streams: that of the legalists, the rule of law as interpreted by Lord Shang, and the rule of reason, inspiration, custom, manners, have pulled the Chinese from one side to the other ever since.

In *The Book of Lord Shang* the doctrine of the supreme state is expounded. The state controlled every individual, war was extolled, and the Six Maggots despised. This was the curious term used for what the rest of the world considers virtues: the cultivation of moral culture, and of beauty, the love of music, the pursuit of "benevolence and integrity, sophistry and intelligence."

The people of Ch'u, south of the river, were deeply attached to the Six Maggots, so they were an easy prey on the field of battle to Ch'in, whose miserable populace had either been brought in line with the thoughts of Lord Shang, or had perished. The Ch'u characteristics were, however, so strong and inbred, that even under the yoke of the Ch'in, they persisted. Their soft and senti-mental ideas, their weakness for comfortable living, their levity, were contagious, and their aura extended eastward towards Nan-king. This town was probably then called Shih-tou, or Chien-k'ang, Chin-ling, Chi-ch'ing. It has had many names; Nanking is actually not much of a *name*, per se, meaning simply "southern capital."

Some time after this, but when the city was still comparatively young—anyway youngish—say about the end of the fourth cen-tury, it was especially wedded to amusements and bravura. Stabil-ity still eluded it, but it made its mark in other perhaps more important ways. In that century it was the home of its most fa-mous son, Ku K'ai-chih, the greatest artist of antiquity, and, be-sides, a writer, critic, musician, and the best company in the world. As a guest his worth was incomparable, and his *bons mots* are still treasured and repeated. Nanking could hardly have been a dull hole then.

It seems, alas, that even then people used to play foolish games to pass the time after dinner; but as sometimes happens, in the hands of sparkling people, these pastimes do not turn out to be so trivial. With Ku, it was nothing to deplore. Once he took part in a contest which sought to define in a few words the idea of absolute finality. Ku said, "A flat plain burnt by a great fire, when the last spark has smoldered out." For a sentence evocative of great dan-ger, he suggested, "A new-born child asleep upon the cross-bar of a well." It is reassuring to realize what acclaim this man had in his own generation and ever afterward—and how modern he remains, so that we would be at ease with him, I feel, at a dinner party ourselves. Wit is timeless.

An often-quoted conversation took place here in the sixth cen-tury, between the then Emperor and an Indian missionary, Prince Bodhidharma, who had called at the palace. Their discussion touched upon the nature of reality, on merit, and on identity, issues still of burning interest today. (Old Nanking in fact seems nearer to many of us now than did its twentieth-century manifes-tation.) The Emperor, talking with the priest, naïvely admitted that he thought he had stacked up merit for himself through his alms-giving and temple-building; he was disabused of any such illusions by his ascetic visitor, who told him that matter must be obliterated through the knowledge of the Absolute; that he had achieved no success through these gestures. The interview seems not to have been a success on either side. Bodhidharma stopped seeing emperors; he went to no more kingdoms, but crossing the Yangtze on a single reed, settled himself in a cave, where, motionless, he passed the next nine years in meditation.

Such an interchange is a proud possession for any town, even though it seems clear that the Nanking people were much too worldly really to grasp the Absolute, except perhaps on rare occasions. However, as Buddhists they made enthusiastic converts, put up plenty of temples, and commissioned their artists to paint an impressive number of frescoes and scrolls illustrative of the religion—Buddhas and *bodhisattvas*, lotuses, wheels of the law, and the lively legends with which the faith was all too soon embroidered. Nothing of this survived—it was all burned down in some devastation or other as the kingdoms fell. But the fame of the paintings endured, we still read of them.

Rather late, in our context—at the end of the tenth century—a famous picture was painted in Nanking, a documentary scroll, intended to incriminate a minister who was suspected, probably correctly, of venality. The artist, Ku Hung-chung, seems to have been loaned to the private intelligence service of the then Emperor, so that the sovereign could be exactly informed of what was going on.

Happily this scroll was copied a couple of hundred years later and the copy has survived, giving us a clear picture of the Beautiful People of Nanking, of the standard of living it was possible for the few to enjoy during the reign of Li Hou-chu, the last ruler of the Southern T'ang. This interesting and charmingly painted work, thought in its time extremely scandalous, is called *The Night Revels of Han Hsi-tsia*. It seems to our hardened eyes anything but shocking, but I believe it did bring about the downfall of the extravagant Minister Han. It shows a handsome palace, beautifully furnished with carved blackwood, of many halls and courts, in which a banquet is taking place, where there is music, and where there are a great number of exquisitely dressed ladies. Everyone is decorously clothed, and appears to the uninitiated eye to be behaving with extreme correctness, but in this we are no doubt wrong. At any rate no one could doubt that the whole establishment was most expensive, far beyond any ministerial salary. And all those ladies? Rumor had it that there were a hundred girls attached to the Minister's palace! Anyway, it ruined him.

Not long after this incident the Sung came down from the north and wiped out the Southern T'ang. Everyone should have known this was inevitable. The Sung had taken over most of the country in 960, and now in 975 after fifteen years of orderly mopping up, they had come to the Southern T'ang, which was still independent, still shamelessly going in for the Six Maggots, in fact a sitting duck. The Sung was a dynasty devoted to the Six Maggots also, but they were still fresh in the saddle, they still had an effective army. They took Emperor Li Hou-chu back to Pien Liang, their capital, with them, first having appropriated his splendid collections of art (which included, probably, the treasures recently in the possession of Minister Han). The ex-Emperor felt extremely bad about this, and being a poet was able to let the literary world know all about it. For instance:

> *In Constant Remembrance of*
> *My Kingdom South of the River*
> How much sorrow, how much anger
> Torments my soul, when,
> Waking from a dream, at midnight,
> I knew I had been wandering, as of old,
> In the palace gardens.
> My chariots glided like flowing water
> The horses very dragons.
> Under the moon, swayed by spring breezes,
> Bloomed the flowers.
>
> Beyond the barrier of the dream
> Lay my southern kingdom, in fragrant spring.
> I was in a boat,
> The music of pipe and strings
> Wafted over the green water.
> But the city seemed full of confusion—
>   Cotton flew in the light dust
>   Those who spun the cotton—
>   Ah! Tragically were they killed!
> Still beyond the barrier of the dream
> I saw my southern kingdom in the clear, pure fall
> The great expanse of the river, the cold hills,
>   the color of evening

Where the reeds flowered, there, in deep water,
   idled a solitary boat—
By a tower, under the bright moon, I heard a flute.

All this was certainly a far cry from the Nanking of my day.
The only comparable events I can remember—comparable in any
way—aside from dancing on the roof of the International Club in
the hot summer nights, were the ball given by the British Ambassador to celebrate the coronation of George VI, and perhaps a
reception given at the Soviet Embassy—I can't remember what
that was to mark. To the latter I was not asked—if you weren't in
an embassy you didn't generally know any of the Soviet citizens,
and never met them anywhere. But rumors of this party got
about, and we were told that if we signed the book at the Soviet
Chancery door we would receive invitations. I felt this would be a
shabby act, and didn't do it—but in a way I have regretted that.

People who went said afterwards that this affair had been like
those fabled receptions beyond the dreams of avarice, something
pre-World War I, that they had actually seen champagne flow in
fountains, black caviar heaped up in shining mountains, *zakouska*,
smoked salmon, huge stuffed fish, roast capons, ices in unimagin-
able profusion. Not what a purist would ask of a Soviet Socialist
Republic, but no doubt Minister Han would have understood this
very well—a Tatar Night Revel.

I went up to Nanking on a bitter, clouded January day in 1936,
and stayed there till mid-August, 1937, when the Japanese attack
on the Yangtze Valley theater began—a fateful period. But of
course we were hooded—we suspected it would come, but one
never is sure, one never knows when.

Having a good deal of luggage, I took the day train, something
over a six-hour journey, starting from North Station in Hongkew,
which had patched up its scars from the 1932 Japanese battle, and
turned itself back into an ordinary, crowded Chinese station. The
line soon ran out of the industrial suburbs on the northern edge of
Shanghai, and as the vigorous dynamic energy of the city was a
phenomenon quite peculiar to itself, once away from it the whole
atmosphere slipped away like a dream, and you found yourself at
once back in old China.

The train struck inland over the flat, frost-bound fields, but the
pace outside it was that of the walker, the wheelbarrow, the cart,

the sail. I loved it and it was a comfort to see it, it seemed to breathe the sturdy calm, the patience of the country—not just that wrong-headed kind of patience which puts up forever with suffering and intolerable conditions, but the endurance with which everyone really has to face necessary tasks—an endurance the Chinese peasant so often invested with a real mental grace.

The little fields, bounded with low mud paths, were uniformly brown, with stumps of old paddy sticking out—dry, frozen, and hard—from those plots which in a few months would be flooded and full of the brilliant green shoots of the early rice. The water-wheels were still, the buffaloes herded away under the shelter of the farmyards, and only the ducks still plied their active paths through the brown waters of the creeks. It was not as cold as it seemed—none of these were frozen, it was only the damp and the wind that made it seem so icy—even seen from the warm shelter of the train you could sense how hard it was to bear. The few peasants about seemed much stouter than they really were, in their bulging padded cotton clothes, the trousers tightly bound in at the ankles. The villages and hamlets with their low roofs, thatched, occasionally black-tiled, were silhouetted with that incomparable harmony every Chinese rural scene then seemed to bear, against the thin leafless arms of the willows, the trunks of the planes, the arched stone bridges by the waterways. Some of the farmyards lay behind low fences of pollarded willows, very dark at this season. Here nothing seemed to have changed since the Six Dynasty times, even the sleet, the willows, the dreamlike quality, the melancholy, were the same. And the extreme poverty. But now there was more hope—things were beginning to change.

Wei Chuang, who well knew that Nanking wasn't always luscious as far as weather went, that you couldn't spend all your time in that painted boat, that there was a lot more to it than snow-white wrists and a green sky, has another lyric about it that is more realistic:

> The river rain, the sleet, the sleet,
> The river reeds bent low!
> Like the cry of a bird, like an empty dream,
> The Six Dynasties went by—
> Yet still
>> Dim are the terraced willows down below the wall
>> Still mists enshroud the long paths of the dikes.

Millions of people must have been cold in Nanking, I remember its chill to this day—it is like London. People had stoves if they could, and most of the foreigners had central heating of a sort, but you still shivered. It was like Shanghai in this, with its penetrating damp cold.

Melancholy is a characteristic of Chinese poetry, and I felt deeply tinged with it myself the day I left Shanghai, as though partaking of the national outlook. It was hard to leave my family, the old garden, the quartette, my friends, my riding. This was the most absurd waste of feeling, as, though I didn't realize it, I would constantly return to Shanghai in the months to come: the work I was engaged to do would be carried on in both cities. However, the subtle influence of the old Chinese poets did perhaps render their admirers more susceptible to this weakness than they otherwise might have been, and particularly so over the matter of partings. One of their dominant themes was their grief over "life partings," not the parting brought about by death, which they took more calmly. It was very much a poetry of friendship, and the friends, nearly always officials of the civil service, were too often forced to live apart. They were sent as magistrates all over the country, and once they were appointed, seldom met. Also, so suspicious was the government, they ran a serious risk of exile to remote parts of the land, or even of banishment, if they wittingly or unwittingly offended someone of importance. Settled in lonely provincial towns, where there were few people with whom they could converse, they would endlessly lament their separation from their colleagues.

"Life partings" have largely disappeared with the age of flight; but the age of steam was not so long ago. The Westerners who served in India and China knew very well what these long absences entailed in a family, though they have written little verse on the subject; the Chinese obsession with the issue touched a responsive chord in the hearts of the few who knew anything about Chinese poetry. The sound of the gong beating "All ashore who's going ashore" had rung too many times in our ears, on shipboard as we grew up, for us ever to forget it.

Though I scarcely ever went again by daylight, I was to make this short passage between Shanghai and Nanking dozens of times until this stretch of country was abruptly closed by the Japanese. There was a slow night train, which I often took, and always enjoyed, in a comfortable wagons-lit. It used to leave Shanghai about nine or ten at night, and come in under the Nanking wall at a reasonable hour—after they had brought you your early glass of tea. But more often I would fly, which only took an hour in the air, and those early simple airports were almost deserted—it was an easy and peaceful way to go. There was even a hydroplane, which took off from the Whangpoo opposite the Bund, and landed on the Yangtze near Nanking. Then the few passengers had to balance their precarious way on slippery planks across yards of mud flats all the way to the bank, an incongruous ending to a flight which had often led through marvelous roseate cumulus clouds.

Near Nanking the train entered the hilly area which encircles the city on the east. The low hills, sere and rounded, which from the air looked like rumpled velvet, were dominated by Chung Shan, or as the foreigners called it, Purple Mountain, the peak which overlooks the city. This beautiful height changed color with every differentiation of light all day long, bringing out each note in that long scale which runs from deep blue to pale amethyst, from the color of the plum and that of Parma violets to a tone hardly deeper than that of an evening sky in summer. On the day I first arrived it was lightly dusted with snow, and seemed to stand out like a guardian, hanging over the town, brooding over it in the cold still air.

Low down on its approaches are a few monuments, the most visible being the new, ugly, ill-proportioned tomb for Sun Yat-sen, reached by a long flight of white steps. Lower down is a line of stone warriors and animals, legendary and real, leading the way to the Ming tombs. The founder of that dynasty was buried here, much more handsomely than the Father of the Republic. The city itself lies some eight miles away, on the banks of the river.

Dr. Buck, with whom I was to work, met me at the station and drove me to my first lodging. The impression Nanking gave me then was its immense emptiness inside its splendid wall—you sensed that fine houses and parks had once been here, that they had fallen away, and that all new building would always be on old sites. It was, in fact, a little like those bombed cities of Europe, with which ten years later I was to become so familiar—a strange, oblique glance into the mirror of the future.

We came into the center of the town, near the Drum Tower, and went through a small crossroads which rejoiced in the name of Shih Miao K'o, or Ten Temples Entry. The Ten Temples seemed to have disappeared, but I was glad of the name, that syllable *miao* (which means *temple*) never failing to give me a linguistic fillip. All about Shih Miao K'o were low black-tiled Chinese houses, and the roads were no more than narrow lanes, cobbled or unpaved. It was terribly cold and bleak; the skies were leaden, a real Nanking setting.

That evening someone called for me and I was taken to a party, mostly of people connected with the University of Nanking, where there was a good deal of singing and acting of charades. Many of the singers and actors have since made their names as authors, scholars, and advisors on the international scene.

Next morning was a Monday. Though there were stoves downstairs my room was icy cold; but there was a fireplace, and on that freezing January morning, before it was light, the door opened, and an old coolie came softly in on his cloth shoes, to lay a fire and kindle it—a big coal fire. He held a newspaper over the grate opening, opening his arms wide, to make it draw, and before he left, the room, though certainly still bitterly cold, was at least lit by a dancing, comforting glow. He never glanced in my direction. I lay in my warm bed, silent and full of compassion for this man, who had to get up so early, no doubt in total cold, for he was a house servant, and in their quarters there would have been no provision against the cold—any more than in most of the poor Nanking rooms. The peasants in the country still had brick *k'angs*, under which they lit fires if they could find the fuel, but city people had iron beds with thin mattresses. And coming from these chill rooms, his first task was to light the fire of the stranger.

> Früh, wann die Hähne krähn,
> Eh' die Sternlein verschwinden,
> Muss ich am Herde stehn,
> Muss Feuer zünden.
> Schön ist der Flammen Schein,
> Es springen die Funken:
> Ich schaue so drein,
> In Leid versunken.

However, he did not seem to be at all *in Leid versunken*, not sad nor discouraged, he just went on with his work. By Chinese standards this man was not poor: he had a living wage and good employers. He was not hungry, he was adequately clad in padded cotton. I was working, too, earning my living, and it would be hard work—but still there it was, though you could think it out in this way, the terrible disparity between us (that is, between those who were comfortable and those who were poor) was a constant torment to me. We were ourselves without reserves; there never seemed anything one could do except to be as generous and kind as possible to those who came our way.

Soon I got up; the room was still frigid, fireplaces being one of the poorer inventions, but by the fire it was glowingly hot, and it was luxurious to dress beside it. Then there was a knock on the door and a young girl came in, dressed in dark trousers and a short white jacket, her braid hanging down her back, to ask if she might make my bed, though it was a little early, and I had not yet gone downstairs. I wanted to ask her to fold my nightgown and put it under the pillow, but none of the words came to me. She knew at once what I was trying to say, and laughing and speaking in crystal-clear tones, said "*Kê ts'ai chên-t'o ti-hsia*," suiting her actions to these directions. She was so winning and sweet as she bent over the bed, slender and smiling, that it became one of those apparently inconsequential moments one never forgets.

While I was still at breakfast a young man called, who was to escort me to the office. He had his bicycle, and a rickshaw was called for me; we set off through the lane which led to Shih Miao K'o where, I saw now, there was a modest livery stable. Soon afterward we came to the T'ao Yüan, or the Hall of the Peach, where we were both employed. It lay behind the Ministry of Justice, in its own garden—a modern academic building with a lecture theater, offices, and a curling roof. This was the Department of Agricultural Economics of the University of Nanking, a place which harbored many activities.

Henry Morgenthau, then Secretary of the United States Treasury Department, had recently appointed Dr. J. Lossing Buck to be his personal representative in China, which was in a period of monetary change and adjustment, about which the Treasury wished to be constantly informed. Dr. Buck had long ago founded the Department of Agricultural Economics, and for many years had been its head. Now this office had passed to a Chinese scholar, but this did not mean that Dr. Buck was any less interested in the work there, or less productive. The department had, over a long period, trained students to go out all over China, and gather in statistics on the condition of Chinese agriculture—the land, the soil, the crops, the people, and everything else which might be relevant. These data had by 1936 been collected and brought back to the T'ao Yüan, where they were being assessed, and the findings incorporated into a great work called *Land Utilization in China*, the first book (it was a trilogy) of its kind ever made in the country. Once all these facts were clearly stated and put together, the basic agricultural problems of China could begin to be solved as a whole, it was hoped. Though very many people were engaged on it, *Land Utilization* was Dr. Buck's book and project, and he went on with it while working for the U.S. Treasury.

The first volume was a text, to which a number of eminent people were contributing. The students' findings were being built into a huge statistical volume which, when it was finished, came to some six hundred pages—great folio pages—with all the data presented both in Chinese and in English. Then there was an atlas, also very large. It was the cartographer who had brought me to work on my first morning. He was making over a hundred maps, showing rainfall, crops, population distribution, minerals—the sort of maps one used to take for granted in geography books.

All this cost a fabulous sum of money, which had been contributed by a number of institutions, from the Rockefeller Foundation to the Institute of Pacific Relations. The latter has now been exposed as an organization of dubious reputation and intent, but as far as the book went it was as honest as the day; it was ostensibly created to assist just this sort of writing and research.

The number of persons slaving away at this in one way or another was very great; meanwhile, as it had been a long time in the making—eight years at least—the sponsors and publishers kept on tormenting us to finish it, to get it down to Shanghai, where the Commercial Press and the presses of the *North China Daily News* were waiting to receive it. But it was one of those staggering Herculean labors, which seem too vast *ever* to finish.

In the center of the T'ao Yüan was a large lecture theater with unusually wide descending tiers, on which tables had been set out. Here worked slender girls in long dresses slit up on the sides, and earnest bespectacled young men, all ferreting away in huge forms, making up lists, the Chinese characters on one side, the English on the other. It had been going on for years, and made you think of a hive.

Their information lay about them in great bundles of papers, the questions and answers which had passed between the young regional investigators and the puzzled and wily farmers all over the country. "How many donkeys do you have? Pigs? Ducks? Children?" "Do you hibernate in winter?" "How much land in this region is given over to graves?" And so on. Statistics are always alarmingly elastic and open to interpretations of many sorts, but here there were even more factors than usual to be taken into account. Why should any sensible old peasant answer such queries from an unknown whipper-snapper from a semiforeign university often thousands of miles away? Did it in fact exist? The investigators explained that their replies would be printed in a book, which would be very helpful as from it knowledge would be gained to enable everyone to farm better and become prosperous. "Indeed?" mused the farmer. "A likely story!" Many of the peasants suspected it was a ruse, to get more taxes out of them. It would be ridiculous to admit the full amount of the harvest—perhaps unlucky . . . and as to vital statistics, children, that naturally would only mean the boys. All these peculiar questions could not possibly be what they appeared on the surface, everyone knew that.

But the investigators could not go back empty-handed. The forms had to be filled out. Some of the peasants actually did cooperate; in one way or another an enormous amount of figures came back. And besides these there were marvelous lists of crops, giving their ancient poetic names, and much wise lore about the fields. There was enough material to keep everyone busy for a lifetime, it seemed, sorting out, documenting, interpreting.

I was so delighted with some of the forms I came to see that I meant to copy out special names and comments when I had time—but I was always so occupied with Treasury work, that I never got to it, and then in the end the Japanese came so suddenly that it was too late—most were lost to me forever. For instance, I remember there was a certain millet, whose "favorable quality" was "escaping bird eating."

Land Utilization, a precomputer opus, was worked out person by person, under the watchful eyes of skilled and experienced statisticians and people highly trained in agricultural studies. The T'ao Yüan had then several young men from Cornell, and other schools in the States and elsewhere, who knew all about cooperatives, marketing, farm implements, soil—they were teaching in the department, and helping the book as well.

The manuscript finally got down to Shanghai in 1937, and was published as the Japanese were seizing the coast and the students fleeing inland. The three volumes made a set so huge, heavy, and expensive that hardly anyone could manage to take them—it was hard enough to get away at all. (Not one train ran from Nanking up into Szechwan—the railway net was only in the process of expansion. The West has been severely condemned for their predatory ways with railways, but at that juncture it would have been splendid to have had more, and those running westward.) However, *Land Utilization* proved a classic, survived this initial disaster, and has been reprinted.

One of the pleasures of living in Nanking, as in any of the up-country Chinese cities, was that it was a bilingual existence. We enjoyed speaking two languages, using special phrases from each of them, laughing at jokes peculiar to this muddled speech, laughing the hardest at our mistakes, which were generally untranslatable, but struck us as extremely hilarious. Most of the Westerners were taking Chinese lessons—even Dr. Buck, who had spoken Chinese for over twenty years, had a teacher who came every day and read the newspapers with him. I had a lesson every day myself —and in the middle of the morning! What a luxury! At the T'ao Yüan people were recognized as civilized beings; no one needed to be reminded that if you had an hour free you would make it up in your own time. We often worked late, but we weren't slaves of a machine. Looking back on it I realize how splendid it was that there was no computer dictating to us, that no army of serfs was transferring ciphers from blue cards to brown hour after hour day after day.

It was in Nanking that I was given my Chinese name of Sang Tê Tze, or, The Idea of a Virtuous Mulberry. This being rather long, I was actually called Sang Hsiao Chieh, or Miss Mulberry, by the Chinese in the office and at home. I liked the name enormously.

Foreigners in China were generally given Chinese names, if they lived up-country, and sometimes also in Shanghai—this made things easier for the Chinese. The foreign name would be considered by a Chinese scholar, and transliterated into Chinese monosyllables which to his ear sounded like the Western ones. Then he would choose suitable characters to fit the sounds, and draw the characters so that cards could be made. My first Nanking teacher thought that Saunders sounded like Sang Tê Tze. I forgot then that my father had gone through this process long years before, or

I would have used his name, which had been turned into Shan Tê Tze, or The Mountain Receives the Scholar, also an agreeable combination.

The Chinese loved playing with names and used to twist flowery syllables to have all sorts of meanings and innuendos, as when they called Lord Napier, a British envoy, Laboriously Vile—though the chosen sounds had been fitted to flattering characters, these could also be read into them. The nations had picked out fine translations for themselves—England was I Kuo, the Righteous Country, America May Kuo, the Beautiful Country, Germany Tê Kuo, the Virtuous Country, and so on. As everyone knows who has read Chinese stories or the lives of their famous men and artists, it was common practice for a Chinese to have a number of names aside from his formal name—there was a great deal of interest in the subject.

The Chinese, noticing that barbarians generally had *one* long surname, felt this confirmed their assumption that a civilized person had, as a rule, a three- or at any rate a two-syllable name. They were always willing to break up the names of most foreign nationals into three syllables, if at all possible, but with the Russians and the Mongols they proceeded on rather different lines. Though transliterating the sounds, they left their names as long as ever, so that they often included four or even five syllables, and thus never became to Chinese ears truly sinicized—an interesting angle on the mentalities involved.

Some of the Chinese in the department spoke very good English, some only a little—some, like the coolie, Lao Ta, who brought our tea, none at all. The regional investigators had large English vocabularies within their own field, but not much outside it—they had great demands made upon them linguistically—they had to size up complicated situations in a few words, and sometimes did this extraordinarily well. Their English would rise to an occasion, though sometimes in an unorthodox way.

A Mr. Hwa, who worked in the office and was not, I think, really an investigator, went off on a trip, and was asked to report on the currency situation for us. It was the time when the government, following British and American advice, was calling in the silver coinage and substituting a managed paper currency. The paramount question was, would the people comply? Mr. Hwa, observing the people in Chekiang, wrote in, "The people in this district are burying their silver very usually, very secretly, and also very widely." This struck me as a masterpiece of concise reportage.

Another report, one before which a computer ought to pale, was about Kiangsu:

> In the north, people are wilder than in the other parts. Bandits and robbers are quite common, and fighting is more favored than talking. In the central part they are quite cautious, and do not venture to do anything. They stay at home and starve and endure hardship rather than go out and search for a living. They are illiterate and superstitious and temples are numerous. On the south side of the river the nature of the people is quite different from those to the north. They like to talk and enjoy themselves. It is a richer part of the area, which makes the people very delicate. They are clever and smart but coward.

There were a number of persons in the T'ao Yüan who had been engaged to work on one or another of the many projects: either with the university, the Treasury, the book, or doing clerical work in all directions. Among them was a bewitching young lady with dimples in her pink cheeks, who came from Chungchow Island in the river near Shanghai. She was a very pretty girl, who dressed well—I still remember an apple-green gown she used to wear. She and I met in Nanking; later we found ourselves together once more in the Hong Kong office as refugees, when we cemented our relationship and became good friends. For some weeks we were the only two people from the T'ao Yüan working down there in the colony. It was a great bond, and more than that, we found we had much in common.

This charmer's name was then Lomay Chang—afterward it became Mrs. John Lossing Buck.

Minnie and the Computer

NANKING WAS in 1936 experiencing a brief moment of bloom, when all sorts of people were beginning to flock in, sensing that it might have a powerful destiny. Chinese and foreign, they came to be advisors to some important official, to a ministry, to offer a tempting project, to produce plans for the city or for the government. Minnie was attached to one of these projects.

She was lodging in the house in Shih Miao K'o at the same time I was, a place (I believe) belonging to the YMCA, and allotted to its local director. She arrived a few days after I did, and I was there only a few weeks—hardly a month, I think, in which time I was more than absorbed by my new post, the people I was meeting, and events in general, but even so my fellow lodger made a strong impression upon me. She didn't fit into any of the Nanking niches.

Minnie was seventeen, and had never before left her birthplace, Shanghai; she was terribly homesick for it, and for her Russian-Jewish family, very forlorn, pitifully unprepared for adventures of any kind. We met at the table, where I was continually surprised and moved by her extraordinary ignorance of the factors which had made up her life, by her vulnerability, by her tender trusting nature. She was a thin, waiflike little creature, upon whom hardship had left unmistakable marks.

A year later, when she was married in Shanghai, in the O-Hel Rachel Synagogue, she made a beautiful, radiant bride under the canopy. The only gentile guest, the only stranger at the wedding, I was delighted at her transformation. Probably I was the only person there who had known her in Nanking. By this time her experiences there, which had not continued for very long, seemed to have faded from her thoughts, but in the January when we met she was very exercised over the mysteries of her job, and with good reason.

She had been engaged, she told me, straight from her typing school, though she had not even finished the course, to come up to Nanking and push buttons on a huge machine, to feed it tickets— from this very machine would then come all the answers one could wish for to any questions. Her employers were Austrians, more she did not know. All the knowledge in the whole world, said Minnie, wondering, was contained in this enormous piece of machinery, which filled a whole room. How this could be, what it was, even what it was called, she had no idea. She was learning to feed it something like bus tickets.

This clearly must have been a very early computer, in the hands of some adventurous Austrian firm. Computers weren't known even by name to most people in 1936; I had never heard of one, and it all sounded of a piece with Minnie's other confused accounts of the world around her—straightforward herself, she looked out on a scene where everyone wore motley. It was curious that it was from her that I learned of this great invention.

She told me, among many other things, that her father, now a struggling Shanghai businessman, had been a corporal in the tzar's army. One night he was traveling by train, in the course of his duties in Russia, when strange events took place so that somehow in the morning (said Minnie, wondering) when the train stopped, he suddenly became a general. Lots of other people became generals too, she added. She couldn't explain, she just knew it had happened, her father had often told her about it. She vaguely knew of the Revolution, hardly of the revolt of the army.

She had learned English in a Shanghai school; they still spoke Russian at home—and she knew no Chinese. Her way of describing the computer, her family's fortunes, her own hopes, with her bushy hair pushed back, her large brown eyes filled with affection and a sort of habitual hopelessness of ever understanding what was passing round her, was so touching that I believe even Women's Lib would feel that the only place for her was a well-sheltered home.

As far as I know, no one ever suggested the wonders of this fabulous machine to the Agricultural Economics Department at the T'ao Yüan, that hotbed of statisticians. There was a *Looking Glass* quality about this whole encounter; as I look back on it I feel that some little time-cog must have slipped, somewhere, somehow.

The Mild-eyed Opium Eaters

I SOON LEFT the YMCA house for another in the same neighborhood, that is, East of the Drum Tower, our area. My relationship
with my hosts had been warm; afterwards they gave me a very
handsome present, a pair of jade sticks from Sian, eight inches
long, apple-green and white, straight as a die, translucent as water.

From them I went to live with the Mills family, also long in
China, at 65 Mo Ts'ou Lou, where I had the two rooms at the top
of the house. One Sunday afternoon that same winter, feeling at a
loose end, I went for a walk in the south city, not far away.
People didn't generally go for walks in Chinese cities, but I
wanted to see the Confucian Temple and it seemed a good time to
do it. It wasn't long before I caught sight of its sweeping dark
roofs, rising above the poor low houses of the district. The south
city was crowded, being the old, rather poor, section of the town,
untouched by modern modes. Still, I was surprised as I went
through the wide temple portals to find the whole enclave, with
its many courtyards, was absolutely full of people. They were not
there to perform their devotions, that much was clear.

Going from court to court, it seemed to me that each was fuller
than the last, and with a very strange assemblage—mostly men,
but with a fair proportion of women, all of whom were very thin,
indeed emaciated, very sallow and languid. They were sitting
about on the stone platforms and balustrades, or wandering slowly

into the patches of winter sunshine which had found their way into the temple past the heavy eaves. No one seemed to show any interest in anything, no one was speaking to anyone else, and I passed among them as though I had been invisible. I soon tired of this *Ancient Mariner* atmosphere and turned back. At the gate I asked the *k'ai-men-ti* who they were and what they were doing. "*Chih mêng yao*," he answered. I didn't know what he meant, except I thought "*mêng*" could mean "dream." I started back to Mo Ts'ou Lou, wondering. The streets were cobbled, the shops with their open fronts were busy selling paper, charcoal, tea, satin, *jao tzes*—it was as normal as possible. In those days, even in China, people weren't drug-conscious as they are today.

Once at the house, I was rapidly enlightened. These poor creatures were opium eaters, "eating dream medicine," just as the watchman had said. The government had launched a strong anti-opium drive, and had rounded up addicts, forcing them to take a cure of sorts. The medical facilities of the country could not have begun to handle the problem of taking in and treating the vast numbers of people needing rehabilitation—in lieu of that the modest attentions offered them in a temple like this one were probably of some avail. Millions of people took opium, just a little, with no particularly bad effects—they would smoke it as naturally as a cigarette, so it aroused no comment. To see hundreds of addicts in an advanced stage was an altogether new experience for me.

Penalties for hard-core opium smokers and the vendors were severe—the Kuomintang were wholly serious in their determination to fight this evil. But the money in it was so powerful that, as today, it was very hard to quench the sources, though undoubtedly a good deal was done and many people induced to give it up. The poppies were such a rich cash crop that some of the provinces couldn't bring themselves to abandon it; farmers could save themselves from ruin by it; it was a fearful temptation.

Men who traveled up-country for firms like the British American Tobacco Company, passing from one province to another, used to say that sometimes you could follow the boundaries by this crop, blowing in full beauty, with its range of subtle colors, on one side of the line, seductive as Circe herself, while on the other side grew the legitimate, ill-rewarded, unglamorous, honest fields of grain.

The people at Mo Ts'ou Lou could enlighten me about a great many things, having long experience in China and sharp eyes, but even they would on occasion be baffled by the Chinese mind. There was the time for instance, when the gardener pulled up all the forget-me-nots which Cornelia Mills had so tenderly and hopefully planted. She worked hard in her garden, and with great success. Her borders and her roses were a delight to everyone. Questioning the gardener as to his foul deed, he calmly replied, "*Mei yu i-ssu*"—that is, they had no meaning. In the long repertory of Chinese flowers, as far as he was concerned, they could not be found, and therefore they ought not to have a place in the garden.

East of the Drum Tower

MOST OF the old Chinese cities had drum and bell towers. Pierced with deep gates and high arches, their curling eaves rising over faded vermilion columns, they made fine silhouettes against the sky. Higher than the low houses clustered about them, they were visible from afar, and they were often half-fortified since they played a part in defense arrangements, warning and awakening the people in times of danger. The drums and bells they held were often very beautiful and could be extremely large. They were supported on handsome frames and kept in good order, as they were in constant use, marking the passing of the hours.

These towers were commonly set into city walls as part of their structure, where the drums and bells would boom out the hours when the gates must be opened or closed, but in large cities like Peking and Nanking they were located in the center where everyone could hear them. In the past, time was measured by the water-clock or clepsydra, a contraption like an hourglass, except that water dripped through it instead of sand. These had the most melancholy sound, and with their sad implications are often to be met with in Chinese poetry. People can't sleep, their gloom intensifies, life is running out, youth is gone, nothing has been accomplished, see my grey hairs, and all possible variations. In the Sung there was a popular melody called "The Air of the Water-clock"; many songs were set to it. These were not necessarily related to the clepsydra, however—it only meant that the rhythm of the tune would fit with the words of the poem. For instance, Wei Chuang's Nanking poem about the water and the wine shop girls was supposed to be set to the rather unlikely music of "Strangers in Buddhists' Cowls," an air everyone was singing during the years of Buddhistic expansion. (Many of these names for songs are very poetic: "The Willow Twig," "A Sprig of Plum," "Wave-Washed Sand," "The Fairy of the Lo River." A favorite melody in the tenth century was called "The Conquest of Tibet," a theme which has outlived water-clocks.)

I believe that it was not till 1930 that the old system of calling the hours after traditional animals was officially over. Up to that time old-fashioned persons and countrymen probably still thought of time as divided into the hour (or the year) of the rat, the tiger, the dragon, the pig, but on January 1, 1930, as I see from a Sapajou cartoon in the *North China Daily News*, Nanking did something about this. The cartoon was called "The Cycle of Distinguished Years Are Instructed in Calendar Reform," and depicts a Nanking official on a podium, holding up a modern calendar dated January 1, while stridently declaiming what this means to an indignant and dismayed circle of animals. The monkey, the ox, the dragon, and the goat look particularly upset—out of work through no fault of their own.

This area round the Drum and Bell Towers in Nanking was one where many a splendid building of antiquity once stood. The palace enclave of the Southern T'ang (which came before the Sung) had been in this very district, near Ku Lou; all this had been swept away, then rebuilt, again destroyed. Few people knew or were really interested in these old tales in modern China. The young Chinese educated in Western-oriented schools seldom even wanted to discuss their ancient writers; they were tired of the classics and the dynastic histories, angry and bored with their country's literature.

They thought the sentiment portrayed in the novels and poetry sickly—they found it dishonest to gild unpleasant realities with fantasy. And besides, so much of their rich cultural heritage, their imagination and elegance with the pen, had been sifted through such travesties as the Eight-Legged Essays of the examinations, till people's minds had been lulled into a sort of deadness, which in turn was partly responsible for the plight of the country, they claimed. And they had a case in saying this. Dr. Hu Shih was in the forefront of the movement which strongly denounced the fetish the Chinese had made of their old classical style, a vehicle which had so long resisted change that it had no meaning for the modern world. He was constantly urging the young writers to portray the world as they saw it themselves, with open eyes and in today's speech.

It was the foreigners (the relatively few who cared about such things) who were now disposed to hear old tales and songs—for us they carried no aftermath of decadence, defeat, ignominy. Resurgent nations tend to go through a phase of being disgusted with the honeyed literature of their past, particularly if they feel that has led to a dead end—there was nothing to be wondered at in this, but it did keep us from a full enjoyment of such places as Nanking.

Though the great majority of Chinese were still illiterate, this did not mean that they were uncultivated. On the contrary, you would find among those who were unschooled a sensitivity and an awareness often attributed only to the intellectually privileged. The country's legends, ballads, and history came to them through storytellers and singers, and these listeners had, very often, remarkable memories, the memories of highly intelligent persons who have never had the opportunity to study. If the script had not been so difficult and complicated, they would somehow have found a way to master it. Often they could read a considerable number of characters, but not enough—and you couldn't figure them out by yourself, as you can read a new word in our simple phonetic writing.

Most of the Westerners were very ignorant about Nanking's past, but it really was not our fault. By 1936 very little had been published in any Western language on the country as a whole, let alone on the history of particular cities. There still is not much. Arthur Waley was known, chiefly through his translations of poetry, but his *Yuan Mei*, which tells so much of eighteenth-century Nanking, would not be out for almost twenty years. Mai-Mai Tzu's translation of the *Mustard Seed Garden* was still years away in the womb of time, as was Mote's book on Kao Ch'i, the tragic poet of the early Ming.

Kao Ch'i, a good poet and a scholar-official, a Soochow man, had the misfortune to come to maturity in the middle of the fourteenth century, and to suffer from the political turmoil attendant on the new dynasty. He was already writing before the Ming

244

was established, when the country was falling away from the Mongol yoke, and into the hands of native adventurers, before it was clear who would succeed in seizing power. This was a great source of anxiety to the generation which under normal circumstances would have been taking up official appointments in the bureaucracy. They found themselves both out of work, and uncertain as to where their allegiance should rest. They rejoiced that the Tatars were going, but whom could they trust? Loyalty rested on a personal basis; it took time to form connections; these could prove temporary, and perhaps, afterwards, dangerous.

When Hung Wu, first emperor of the Ming, was firmly on the throne, Kao Ch'i's problems appeared at first to be solved. He was called to Nanking, and appointed to work on the official history of the recently overthrown Yüan dynasty. The new emperor, who had been a peasant, a bandit, a monk, and a warrior, retained an affection for the religion which had succored him in a dark hour; when he had taken Nanking and made it his capital, he appropriated the palace of a Mongol prince and gave it to the priests. They made of it the finest temple within the wall—the T'ien-chieh Miao, a great Buddhistic enclave. Some of its courts were set aside for the official historians, and it was here that Kao Ch'i worked on the Yüan records. At first, though homesick for Soochow and his family, he was elated with his position, its interest, promise, and prestige.

He wrote here, aside from his share of the history, a good deal of poetry, much of it necessarily after the dictates of the court. The beginning of the dynasty was a colorful epoch, a time of pomp and circumstance, of general pleasure that a native house once more held sway, that the kings of Korea, Annam, and Cambodia again came to pay tribute to the Chinese.

Soon, however, the climate of the capital was clouded over with fear and anxiety, as it became evident that the mind of the emperor was unbalanced. Kao Ch'i became nervous as he saw many of his peers capriciously handled and summarily disgraced; though he had recently been honored with a substantial promotion, both in rank and pay, he was afraid to accept it. He was also afraid to decline, lest this gesture should anger the emperor. In 1374, he found the way to do so, apparently without causing offense. He was too sanguine—misreading his poems, finding allusions in them which he fancied favored his enemies, Hung Wu persuaded himself that even this innocent poet constituted a danger to the throne. Kao Ch'i was sent for after he had returned to Soochow, and brought back to the capital in an open cart, in chains; there he was cut in half at the waist, his body thrown into a public square. This was a particularly terrible fate for a Chinese, proper burial being of prime importance in the Confucian system. He was not yet forty. Too late, the emperor seems to have realized that he had made a mistake, and Kao's family was able to recover the body and take it home for burial.

From Kao Ch'i's poems comes something of a picture of the capital, though his verses were not particularly descriptive of any given scene, as a rule. On his way to Nanking in 1369, a journey which took him about a week, mostly by boat through the canals, he spent a night in an old temple in Chinkiang, the Monastery of Sweet Dew, Kan-lu Ssu. Here, on "a clear and starlit night . . . he lingers in the temple courtyard . . . 'sitting idly talking about former dynasties.' "

That was the sort of poetry which was written through the centuries in China, but it touches the heart, even though hackneyed, and in the case of Kao Ch'i, is rendered pitiful because we know what would befall him in a few short years. There is an easy simplicity about it, a vitality.

The memory of these unhappy years was perhaps one factor in the decision of the third Ming emperor, Yung Lo, to leave Nanking, go north and rebuild Khanbalak (Peking), making it the new capital of the dynasty—the new-old capital, lavishing upon it, rather than on this southern city, all his passion for building.

The Ming dynasty never seemed very long ago to us in China—compared to the cherished eras of antiquity, what were the fourteenth, fifteenth, sixteenth centuries? Practically yesterday.

In recent times Ku Lou Tung, because of the many schools and universities in the district, was intellectually rather distinguished, but not sparkling, not much praised. "East of the Drum Tower" sounds romantic, but most of the girls didn't find it so; it was too strongly identified with the missionary world. It was a fine place in its way, all the same.

The city as a whole had yet to make its mark socially—few people were eager to be a part of it. The Chinese ladies whose husbands were posted to the new ministries there used to dig in their toes and do all they could to stay in Shanghai, where they found things both comfortable and amusing—they didn't want to pioneer. The foreigners found it too earnest, too dull, too limited.

When I went up my friends commiserated with me, some even trying to dissuade me from accepting what was clearly a splendid offer, on the grounds that it would be ghastly to live in Nanking. To many people, true enough, it seemed dull after the vivacity and glitter of Shanghai, the cosmopolitan flavor of that worldly city. Too large a proportion of the Westerners in Nanking were church-oriented, complained the business community; it had the feeling of the missionary convention, of a YMCA meeting. Other than that, there were the embassies, but they had so recently come from Peking, they weren't settled, they were small, they were snobbish. Just as for so long the *corps diplomatique* had deplored leaving Istanbul for Ankara, so did the same body feel now vis-à-vis Peking and Nanking. It shared that same sort of disparagement, along with many heavier burdens. It didn't have the bright spell which lures the artist, the adventurer, the eccentric, who so embellish their milieu. Perhaps they would have come, had there been time . . .

Like its predecessors, it was to perish there by the wide and curving river under the shadow of the opalescent mountain, silent spectator of interminable sorrows.

I didn't altogether believe what I heard, not being prejudiced in favor of Shanghai's meretricious lights. I bought myself a new evening dress, black taffeta, spangled in gold, to take with me. Colonel Hayley Bell told me that this dress was most unsuitable; for Nanking, he said, I should have found black on black, no gold, indeed no. I would never have a proper occasion on which to wear it. He was quite wrong, but it was a typical example of the low estate of the city in public opinion.

East of the Drum Tower there were many houses where the faculty of the University of Nanking lived—solid, comfortable places, very like those they had themselves lived in in their youth in the United States, houses you still see everywhere in New England and on college campuses in America. They were roomy and adequately kept, as most of the families had two or three servants—not nearly as many as non-missionary families employed, so that the style of living was simpler, but compared to today's servantless state they were very easy to run. The wives generally did something on behalf of their missions—they taught Chinese or their own young people in the small local school which had been set up, taking pupils too young to go down to Shanghai, or they did evangelical work.

And all these people were very hospitable, there was plenty of entertaining and good conversation. I remember a gathering of some sort where I. encountered Margaret Thompson, a good friend of mine and a wit. (Her son James is now an outstanding member of Harvard's faculty—then he was four.) I asked her how our cartographer, Brian Low, was getting on. He lived in the attic rooms of her house, and he had been away from the T'ao Yüan for some days, sick. "I don't know how he is," she answered, "perhaps he's dead, I haven't been up to the attic for three days, it's too hot." Dr. Buck was standing near us and heard this. "Oh, my poor atlas!" he cried.

I remember a dinner party where the conversation turned on languages. The gentleman on my left, who was Chinese, surprised me by attacking English. "One outstanding weakness of the English language," he said, "and indeed of most Western languages, is that it has almost no vocabulary for the supernatural." "We have *fairy*," I began, "and *troll* and *pixie*," but I knew as I spoke that these were weak terms. He waved these trifling entities away with contempt—they were, he implied, *silly*, compared to the personages of the richly populated world of Chinese studios and legends. No, he did not refer to what we call ghosts, either. He meant the—well, shall we say (admitting the poverty of our tongue) the *apparitions* which arise from wells, the lovely girls on the frescoed walls of temples, their maiden tresses flowing down their backs, who sometimes disappear to return with their hair done up in the matron's knot. What would we call them? Fairy? Bah!

Mr. Johnson, the American Ambassador, was sitting on my other side, and plunged into the conversation with zest. "I have been told," he said, "that on meeting a young lady who is fascinating and quick-witted one should look at the hem of her skirt to see if there is the tip of a red tail showing." "Yes," replied the Chinese gentleman, "naturally—but it is not exact to say that she is a *fox-fairy*, or a *fox-spirit*. Now we have a great many terms for such presentations." I felt that the language of the *Tempest* and *Midsummer Night's Dream* could not really be lacking in these words, but, it was true, none of them occurred to me.

People were very active in Nanking, aside from their ordinary duties. Dr. Smythe, a professor of sociology at the University of Nanking, for instance, had made an heroic effort to start a wool-weaving industry, on a small scale, among some of the near-destitute local craftsmen. Nanking had for centuries been a center for the weaving of silk, particularly brocades—now only a little of this had survived. You could still hear the sound of the shuttle as you went down certain lanes, and looking through a narrow door, see a few high heavy looms being worked—but machinery had essentially put an end to this old art.

The professor thought it would be a fine thing to get wool-weaving going. The Chinese had almost never done anything with wool, except in the way of rugs. Now the West had introduced them to the advantages of wool—many Chinese women had learned to knit and a sweater was no longer a rarity. The missionaries taught knitting (especially in the schools for the blind which they set up—these were a particular province of the German Lutheran Mission), but the industry as a whole was in its infancy. If the Chinese were really to start wearing wool on any considerable scale they would have to manufacture it themselves, not import it.

Dr. Smythe began at the beginning. He got hold of some sheep —rather rare animals in those parts (you never saw sheep grazing on the hills, for instance), and started his group of workers from scratch, shearing, washing, dyeing, carding. Now they were at the point where they were producing a coarse, tweedy material, which was much cheaper than any imported cloth, and quite useful. But it was an immense labor for him, and poor Dr. Smythe would groan when he spoke of it, though he lavished upon it and his workers the most earnest and kindly supervision. He felt he would never be free of it and its endless petty demands, somehow it didn't flow, it was alien.

Hardly anyone even had a radio. We entertained ourselves. If we wanted a play we put one on—as nearly everyone has histrionic talent, and loves to use it, this made for many lively evenings. We put on these performances in each other's houses, and as no one had time for rehearsals or learning lines, we read our words, after one or at the most two practices. It was astonishing how good some of these performances were, so great is the talent hidden away in most of us. The costuming was slight and easy. I wanted once, for Milne's *The Ivory Door*, which I had agreed to produce, three medieval swords. These we sketched, and a local artisan cut them from wood and painted them. His bill (for almost nothing) was written in flowing grass characters, so charming that it was worthy of a frame.

Sometimes visiting artists came to Nanking, but not often—the foreign contingent was so small. Once a young man, on some

Boxer scholarship arrangement, came to the university and read Shakespeare to a breathlessly still audience, almost entirely Chinese. He was English, and gave the students some idea of the marvels of sound contained in the plays; he read so well that he lifted his audience with him into glorious heights. "She hangs upon the cheek of night/Like a rich jewel in an Ethiope's ear," and "Not poppy nor mandragora,/Nor all the dulcet syrups of the time;/Shall ever medicine thee to that sweet sleep/Thou owst yesterday."

That same year there was a performance of *The Merchant of Venice* in Nanking, which ran for some time to crowded houses. It was acted by a Chinese company and in Chinese.

There was always Chinese opera to be seen, but that was something of an acquired taste for the Westerner. I saw Mei Lan-fang a number of times in Shanghai—whether you understood or enjoyed Chinese opera or not, you could not but be enchanted and astonished by the grace and genius of this amazing actor. He always played women's roles (as in the classical opera women never took part), and he epitomized the willow-waisted, swaying, slender, delicate, sweet, intelligent maiden of romance—universal romance. His every gesture—moving his long-fingered hands, turning his head, arranging his robes, opening a fan—seemed a revelation of what movement could be. He didn't walk, he glided, floated, lightness itself.

But if he wasn't on the boards, opera tended to drag for many of us. The shrill falsetto of the singers, the sawing away of the determined fiddles, the complexity of the plots (though our operas are as bad) were difficult for those who weren't accustomed to them, who didn't have favorite arias, didn't know the important moments of a drama, and how famous actors had played them. The Chinese audience was always amusing to watch, however, as they took their ease, ate oranges and drank tea, dandled their children and wiped their faces with hot towels. They listened attentively when they were interested, but most of the time they seemed simply to be enjoying their evening out. It was safer to bring the children—no one kidnapped anyone in an opera house.

A young German photographer whom I came to know in Nanking obtained permission to photograph the members of an operatic company as they were putting on their makeup. This was a long and traditional business, involving the painting on of the white mask that indicates an evil character, and such things. The night he did this, he took me with him. We entered the theater in the usual way; an opera was already in progress, and the hall was full. The operas started early and went on for many hours—it was customary for people to come and go as they liked. The important performance of the evening used to start late, about eleven.

We sat down; soon some attendants appeared, saying we were expected backstage, and an usher calmly led us to the front of the hall, up the steps to the stage, and across it between the singers to the dressing rooms in the rear. The Chinese stage discipline is such that you don't see anything that you are not supposed to see, and what you do see has many well-understood symbolic elements. This is gratifying to the audience, which participates in this way to an unusual degree in what everyone knows is an illusory situation, and makes scenery almost unnecessary.

Nanking, 1927

PEOPLE SELDOM SPOKE of the bad times they had gone through in Nanking in 1927, but they had affected too many persons too deeply to have been forgotten. Chiang Kai-shek, anticipating trouble in the city, knowing that if the troops ran amok he could not control the situation, being too completely occupied elsewhere in that fateful year, had advised the Westerners to leave till the situation was in hand.

How often did this sort of request come our way! You were first advised to go, then urged, then strongly urged. If disaster overtook a town, who could be responsible for you? It was so much easier for the authorities if the civilians, particularly those of foreign nationality, would decamp. But not everyone can do this.

Rumors fly about, perhaps you'd like to leave. What, then, happens to your house, your job, your family? Who will pay for the move? Where would you go? The big firms generally took care of their people, as did the consulates, though someone usually had to stay behind. If you were a missionary was not this the very time when you should stay and minister to your flock? The ordinary persons, especially after many alarms which proved false, tended to hang on and hope for the best.

One family of whom I became very fond in Nanking told me that they had decided to stay and weather the storm in 1927. They had three small children, and an aged grandmother in their household; the difficulties involved in flight seemed greater than those of chancing it.

In the several days of terror which befell the city their house was burned to the ground, with everything in it except themselves. The father of the family was lined up against a wall to be shot by some uniformed youths, on the sufficient ground that he was a foreigner, therefore obviously an imperialist and their enemy. That he was a missionary and a teacher made no difference. The young soldiers were so inept with their weapons that in trying to load their rifles, one of them dropped his cartridges. Their captive automatically picked them up and returned them, which took the soldiers so much aback that they let him go.

As the troops withdrew from the area East of the Drum Tower, the Americans there, praising God, assembled themselves, and with their native genius for organization, improvised shelter, found some food, succored those who had been badly hurt. In a few days they were taken down to Shanghai by gunboat.

Though they had lost all their possessions, my friends were far from stricken by this experience. They felt that they had been wonderfully protected, and they found an immense freedom in owning absolutely nothing. Nothing to pack, lift, carry, guard, wash! Later in Shanghai some officious person reproached my friend for exposing her children to this ordeal, assuring her that they would never forget it, but would be marked for life. Distressed but unconvinced, Margaret (for it was Margaret Thompson), on going back to their hostel, asked her seven-, six-, and five-year-olds what they best remembered of the previous week. "The monkey on the gunboat," they answered with one voice.

There were other reminders of that time which would crop up. When I wondered why we had so many clerks at the T'ao Yüan, who could perhaps usefully be transferred, and broached the matter to Dr. Buck he cried, "Get rid of Mr. Li? I can't ever do that! He saved my life in '27!"

Everyone's life was not saved, and some persons were very roughly handled, even if they did manage to survive. The consulates had been singled out as special areas for attack: the Japanese Consul, who was ill, was shot but happily not killed; the British port doctor, and the harbor master, who were at the British Consulate, were killed. The Vice-President of Nanking University also lost his life.

Down on the wall above the British Consulate stood the Standard Oil house, on what we called Socony Hill. This was a place of dramatic incidents, and a severe trial for those who had gathered there. The foreigners tried to buy off their attackers and the looters, by giving them all the valuables they could collect, but their tormentors were never satisfied. Finally the gunboats on the river opened fire, and with the first few shots most of the soldiery melted away from all those points where they had been killing, outraging, despoiling the Westerners. About fifty people managed to get outside the city, by lowering themselves down the wall below Socony Hill on knotted sheets. Once on the ground they had about a mile to walk to the river, where the gunboats picked them up. It was altogether a very ugly "incident," and a bad blot on the opening stages of the Nationalist campaign.

The basic reason for the command difficulties of the Nationalists was that at this time there existed within the army (as within the party) what was known as the "bloc within"—that is, many members of the Kuomintang also belonged to the Communist Party. In the inevitable conflict of loyalties, intensified after the two groups split apart, discipline was hard to maintain, and the leaders could not rely on their subordinates following orders. Those who had dual membership were then often only nominal KMT members, and actually owed their allegiance to the CCP.

A Spring Excursion

I WAS GLAD, really, that Mr. Li was a fixture, particularly after we went on a spring excursion together and became friends. There was considerable *esprit de corps* at the T'ao Yüan. It was a matter of concern to the authorities that most of the graduates from this very essential department did not, after their years of study, want to return to the land and work out in practice what they had been studying in theory. Still, the place itself was serious and conscientious, and ran extremely smoothly. This was due to the fact that a usually able young manager took care of the administration, a Mr. Ch'en, watching over every detail, helping everyone. His influence was felt throughout the building, so that when he announced one day in spring that he believed we would all be the better for a holiday outing, we agreed with enthusiasm, especially as he said he would make all the arrangements.

A Saturday was chosen, and a destination agreed upon. We were to take a very early train, for something over an hour, out to the hills by the river, and spend the day looking at temples and famous sites near the water. Everyone would bring his own provisions, but meals could be had at a temple. We were to meet at the T'ao Yüan at six in the morning. As there were no forecasts on the weather, no one foresaw that this particular Saturday would be a day of continuous rain.

I woke up that morning shortly after five to the sound of heavy drops bouncing on the roof, and looked out from my top-floor windows above Mo Ts'ou Lou upon low and leaden skies. It was too early to telephone anyone about the excursion—most of my colleagues had no telephones—no one had a private phone. Most of us lived in families, as I did. I had to make my decision myself, and following the rule "Nine times out of ten take the active course," I concluded I would go. The prospects seemed poor, but I felt it would be a great shame to miss the affair if it came off, and in any event my sleep was over. I dressed in my most rain-resistant clothes—I had a raincoat, but neither boots nor a rain hat, and my paper umbrella was so badly torn that it was only an encumbrance.

It was about a mile to the T'ao Yüan from Mo Ts'ou Lou, mostly through narrow *hutungs*, and generally I made this journey on my old Japanese bicycle, but this morning a rickshaw man appeared at the gate, hoping for a fare. Perhaps he had heard rumors of the excursion, and I was glad to think that at any rate he would gain a little from the adventure. Before I left, the old coolie at the house gave me some tea, an encouraging gesture. He evidently thought my sporting instincts deserved support. The day was already gaining momentum for me.

The rain splashed in through the apron of the rickshaw and leaked in at the top. I feared that I would find the T'ao Yüan deserted, and would only have to turn round when we got there, but no! Two persons were already there: Mr. Ch'en and Mr. Li, the one who had saved Dr. Buck in 1927. Before long three others showed up: a pretty student called Annie Lu, the secretary of the department, who was a young English woman, and the cartographer. We shook the rain out of the newcomers' coats, while we congratulated each other on our mutual enterprise and wondered if the clouds might lift.

After half an hour's waiting, more heavy rain, and no more arrivals, we decided that the expedition was definitely on, but would be confined to us six only and we got hold of some rickshaws and went to the station, where happily we soon caught a train. In it we dried ourselves off once more, while trying to see through the streaming windows, and Mr. Ch'en and Annie Lu had breakfast, huge plates of rice and egg. Annie Lu's waist, I thought, would measure about fifteen inches and I wondered what she did with it all. The rest of us watched them in a spirit of affection—already a strong bond of companionship was forming among us.

When we reached our wayside station it seemed to be raining harder than ever. Deep puddles had collected in the muddy, unpaved country roads. No one was afoot. We closed ranks and started to walk to the hills which, though hidden by mist, lay beyond the fields. Our destination lay high above a hamlet of a few little cottages, which lay beneath a spur. From it stone steps, hundreds upon hundreds of them, joined by paths, led to the old monastery which was our goal, and from which we were to have, said the sanguine Mr. Ch'en, such a splendid view.

By the time we reached the hills, the party had strung out in a thinner line. Annie Lu and I, it was obvious from the first, were by far the worst walkers of the six, so we stayed together. The others disappeared in clouds of mist and fog, while we splashed after them, rain soaking our head scarves, trickling down our necks, oozing into our rain-sodden shoes. Beyond speech, we plodded on like two dumb creatures, companions in a pleasurable misery of wetness and endeavor, united by a timeless mutual recognition of the worth of endurance for its own sake. We reached the hill and dragged ourselves upwards. But Annie and I never got to the top, nor saw the monastery veiled in those endless clouds, without its view, without anything around it but mud. Without any spoken agreement, suddenly we both simultaneously gave up. Side by side on a stone step we sank down and waited for the others, blissful that we could stop moving. A rivulet formed round us. Huddled together, we created a circle of relative warmth and ease—fortunately, as it was late spring, the rain held no hint of chill and the air was fresh and sweet. At last, from their vantage point the others strode down to us. One of them had taken note of our position, and made afterwards a sketch of us which I have to this day.

With them we made our way downward to the village, and past it by another route to the station. We never saw a living soul. All the country people had shut themselves inside their homes in silence. At one crossroads we came upon something I have never forgotten: an old traveling stage. Long ago theatricals must have been elaborately performed here on some auspicious occasion, and they had brought in a wheeled platform, with carved pillars and lattices, whose red paint had faded and peeled, but which still conveyed a sense of spectacle, vivacity, and life, even there under the falling rain.

This romantic glimpse of the distant past, the friendship which arose among the six indomitable excursionists of the department, and the sense of having spent the whole day in great floods, remain strongly with me, though now I am not even clear as to where we went, or what day we were commemorating. Only the old stage and the rain-washed faces of the stoical six, taking their pleasures sadly, have never faded into oblivion, and I know that given the choice I would do it again.

The Nanking Wall

COME WHAT MAY, Nanking has three great advantages: its position on the river, Purple Mountain, and the great Ming wall, one of the most glorious walls in the world, remarkable even in China, where splendid walls abounded.

Twenty-two miles in circumference, it embraces an area twenty miles long (running north and south) and fifteen miles across, and was pierced by thirteen fine gates, several of them water-gates—not many for such a structure. The Mings built it, incorporating into it ancient, earlier sections, some going back to the fifth century B.C. when the King of Yueh defeated the King of Wu, and promptly started fortifying his new territory with a wall, as well he might, this being in the period of the Warring States. The stone was brought from Shih T'ou Shan—for a time they called the place Shih T'ou, or Stone City. It became Nanking at the end of the Eastern, or Later, Han, in 211 A.D., when it was only a country place out on the edge of civilization. The world, to the Han, was centered far away in the northwest, in the loess country.

When I lived in Nanking, the city gates were still shut every night. If you had gone outside the wall, and lingered in the woods below Purple Mountain on some soft summer night, listening to the gongs booming in the temple, watching the moonlight, you might well find yourself shut out when you returned. That was a medieval note, indeed. Perhaps this ancient practice was continued as a security check of a kind, in that huge half-empty place. In its limited way the wall was really quite a barrier—it isn't possible for most people to scale fifty or sixty feet.

Lossing Buck did it once, starting out from the deck of a boat on the Lotus Lakes which come right up to the foot of the wall at one part. This was a legendary feat. His party was discussing the possibility of doing it at all when he sprang out, clutching at the low bushes and grasses which sometimes grew between the great stones, finding niches for his feet. His spectators were enormously relieved when he finally threw himself over the crenellations at the top. The lakes were very shallow, to have fallen would have been serious.

Very rarely, and then only in limited areas, was it possible to walk on the wall in my time—if you tried, a sentry generally popped up from somewhere and would politely escort you to the nearest ramp which led down into the city. That was a pity. There is no better place to walk than on a city wall. You look straight down between the crenellations to the moat and then far out over the land, on one side; on the other are the narrow streets, the tiled roofs of the houses, forming an intricate pattern. I was fortunate in that I didn't know, when I first came to Nanking, that it was forbidden to walk on the wall, and enjoyed several good long promenades before I had to give up this innocent pursuit. I used to walk on the Purple Mountain side, as there was a ramp not far from Shih Miao K'o. Far off across the city, on a clear day, you could see the opposing wall and in some places the glitter of the river. Then, down below, your eye would fall on the sere grass of the old moat.

Up there, above the town, there was a marvelous feeling of space, distance, and strength. The height of the structure was so commanding, and it was wide enough to let two big vehicles pass, the bricks and stones facing it were huge. The ramparts, bastions, watchtowers, and the heavy wooden doors which hung on the gates, studded with square-headed nails, were all splendid to see. Looking out over Hsiian Hu, or Lotus Lakes, and seeing the causeways planted with their long lines of willows, made you think of all the songs and poems about Nanking's willows, and tied you to the past.

It was on the Nanking wall that an incident took place which my father loved to relate, though it might have happened almost any place in China. A friend of ours was walking along it, when he discovered he had left his watch in his room. Wanting to know the time, he asked a Chinese, who was passing, what it was. Without an instant's hesitation the Chinese walked a few steps to where a cat was sunning itself, picked it up by the scruff of the neck, looked at the pupils of its eyes, and said calmly, "Twelve o'clock." Checking this by his timepiece a little later, it was found that this was, truly, the time. The Chinese were never at a loss, it seemed to us then. Of course, it's easily explained, because the pupils of a cat's eyes contract with the light, and the Chinese have been particularly aware of this. For this reason they liked to paint them with peonies, a flower which also marks the passing hours in its own way.

A wall like this gives a place something absolutely tremendous—it enables a town to hold up its head, in a way, no matter what happens. That was very true of Nanking—it might be torn to pieces inside the wall, but as long as the wall itself stood, the town existed.

Gardens and Painting

Gardens used to be a feature of Nanking. Here lived the authors of that famous painting manual, the *Mustard Seed Garden*, the book which swept the country like a high wind at the end of the seventeenth century. To be sure, the treatise isn't about gardens, but naming it after one is indicative of the affection felt there towards these walled, fanciful retreats. Some people say that the *Mustard Seed* crushed the spontaneity out of painting, as it showed everyone just how to sketch every plum petal, every bird's beak, the fold of a rock, the slant of a cricket's wing—it opened the art to the skilful but uninspired, too fully, too mechanically. But others feel that the more people who can paint the better, that it is, after all, partly manual in expression, and it's no more wrong to do it by rote than it is to learn scales and chords. Afterward the imagery, the individual feeling, will come, when the hand can obey the thought. Anyway, no lover of painting can be without the *Mustard Seed Garden;* it holds too much, its phraseology is too penetrating, too poetic, to push aside.

A Nanking poet who was also a passionate gardener, but who did not share the tragic destiny of Kao Ch'i (though he also lived in a time of literary persecution) was Yüan Mei. He was an outstanding eighteenth-century figure—a good poet, a great man for parties, and so interested in cooking that he is renowned not only for his verses but also for his cookbook. He had an enormous admiration for his cook, whom he rightly considered to have the soul of a true artist, able to make even a scrap of celery or a little salt cabbage into a *bonne bouche*, and who never deserted his master for a more opulent kitchen because he valued the poet's appreciation of his art. Yüan Mei's garden absorbed much of his affection, and no doubt helped him to endure the anxieties he and his fellow writers suffered through the literary inquisition which raged in their time under the tyrannical control of the Manchu Emperor Ch'ien Lung.

The Manchus were very jealous of their honor and reputation, and could not endure the slightest suggestion of what might be criticism, even fancied criticism, of their race. They would not tolerate the idea that their past was not as highly civilized and productive as that of the Chinese, whom they had conquered. Anyone who put out a line that the censors thought subversive, or who penned an allusion that was questionable, was at once in danger. Things hadn't really changed much since Kao Ch'i's day, though the genius of Ch'ien Lung overrides tenfold the abilities of the demented Hung Wu. Espionage and thought-control, the suppression of freedom, are nothing new in China. However, in spite of this, the old city seems to have been in Yüan Mei's time still a place much invigorated by the writers, critics, and artists who were there, to have had a lively theater and many sophisticated pleasures.

One of these artists, who was neither cramped by the rules of the *Mustard Seed Garden*, nor beguiled by the bonhomie of the hedonistic circles, was Kung Hsien. Many of his strange and somber landscapes, those dark scenes under heavy clouded skies, where hardly a living soul is to be seen, were painted in and about Nanking. I can well undertand him now, but when I was in Nanking I had not even heard his name.

All of us who loved pictures knew very well what was going on in the art world of Europe and America—what oils were changing hands, whose collection was being formed—but in China, where there were so few museums or galleries—where would pictures have been safe?—it was hard to know of the artists at all. The great Palace Collection was the one tremendous exception—but that was in Peking. To be exact, in that very year of 1936, these scrolls were for the first time making their unforgettable impact on the West; they were being sent to London for their epoch-making appearance in the great Chinese art exhibit in Burlington

House. When they came back they were shown to the public both in Nanking and Shanghai—marvelous occasions, not one moment of which has ever left me. But they were only on view for a very short time, and could only be seen in the company of great crowds, in Nanking, so thirsty were the people to view their heritage.

Long, Long Ago,
Long Ago, Long Ago ...

ONE MAY MORNING in 1936 three of us from the T'ao Yüan decided to go down to the famous cliff of Ts'ai Shih-chi, on the
Yangtze. Near it, after the fall of the Northern Sung, a riverine
engagement had been fought out; long before that time it had
been visited by Li Po. Perhaps it was from here that the poet set
out in a little boat, and attempting to embrace the reflection of the
moon, fell into water and was seen no more. It is one of those
famous places.

We engaged a wonderful old landau, with well-sprung seats,
and a deep-fringed, cream-colored silken awning. It was just like
the ones we see in royal processions except that it had fallen on
evil days—and therefore we were able to use it ourselves, not gaze
at it from afar. Whoever had brought it out from Europe, long
ago, had had to lose it, and now it belonged to a livery stable and
was let out by the day. The *mafoo* wore the shallow white conical
hat of his profession, over which lay the long red strands of a
silken tassel. The horse, it must be admitted, was rather a poor
creature, but we were not heavy, and he had been smartened up
for the occasion with a light straw hat trimmed with red pom-
poms.

It was a beautiful morning. The spring was at its most delicious
moment—warm, really warm, but not too hot. We were delighted
to see the landau, having expected an ordinary trap, and found

that from it we had an ideal view of everything around us. The third member of the party, the cartographer, scorned the feminine luxury of such an equipage, and rode his bicycle, from which he serenaded us throughout the expedition. It was one of those rare days—I think each of us instinctively sensed that this was to be a *fête champêtre* which would not come again. The sun shone, we forgot about *Land Utilization*, the Treasury, the Japanese, the threats of doom, and simply enjoyed ourselves.

Starting near the Drum Tower, at Mo Ts'ou Lou, we went down to the North Gate, another of those fine, massive, bastioned openings, particularly splendid from the vantage point of the landau. There were few cars; a carriage was in no way out of place in the diverse Nanking traffic, and we had the pleasure of seeing in slow, intimate detail the people on their way to market, the donkeys laden with panniers, the wheelbarrows loaded with cabbages, the wayside stalls, selling noodles and tea, and over on the right above the wall, the fine shoulder of Purple Mountain, today glowing with an added emphasis, as we thought, the color of Parma violets.

Once outside the wall we picked up speed, rushing on at perhaps six or seven miles an hour. The cartographer sang more loudly, mostly Hebridean songs, in a joyous tenor. Soon we found ourselves passing through the fields which were either green with the young rice, or butter-yellow with mustard. A few blue temple-of-heaven flowers were already in bloom in the ditches.

About noon we reached Ts'ai Shih-chi, the Promontory of the Rainbow Rocks, the scene of the defeat of the Ch'in navy. This had been an immensely significant battle—the Tatars, unable to pass the river, could not further pursue the Sung, and the onslaught of the tribes from without the Great Wall was deferred till the advent of Genghiz Khan. Happily he had not been present at Ts'ai Shih-chi, or the outcome might have been different—though the Mongols were never fortunate at sea. In any event, this was truly a national monument.

Quite apart from this (and no one had played it up with signs or guides—it was unspoiled), it was naturally a charming place, meant for pleasure. The cliffs rose above the brown river, on which sailed junks and sampans, fishing boats, ferries. The countryside spread out beside the water, the thatched cottages under the willows seemed particularly harmonious, the buffaloes stood majestically by the banks, the waterwheels turned in the distance.

We walked out to the end of the cliff, where there was a leap from which, according to legend, disappointed lovers and embittered students had jumped out into the eddies below—but all long-ago tales which could not mar our mood on that glorious day.

Before starting off on this mild climb we had ordered our lunch at one of the temple restaurants. A number of temples had been built in the ravines of the rocks, curving their roofs upward, in the extraordinarily natural way that architecture adapts itself to its background, their courts reached by winding stone stairs. There was, of course, only vegetarian fare to be had, and nothing could have been better, so succulent were the bamboo shoots, so delicious the water chestnuts, the mushrooms, so brilliant the green vegetables above the pearly rice and the lotus roots, fried to a turn. The restaurant overlooked the Yangtze, straight across to the Pukow side.

Then came the long drive home, seeing again the idyll of the countryside, and the mild bustle of the town within the North Gate. How we laughed that day! And at nothing! How we enjoyed our escort's singing, the clopping of the horse's hooves, the haze rising slowly up the flanks of Purple Mountain! Perhaps people didn't much like Nanking, or want to live there, but a day like this at Ts'ai Shih-chi would make you aware of Content itself.

The Government

THE KUOMINTANG had then had nearly a decade of power—their brief span of grace. In this period they had had to subdue the warlords, unify the country, try to put down the communists, build roads and railways, stimulate and expand education, put the finances of the nation on a sound basis, and somehow to learn how to govern, for which most of them had no experience. They also should have been espousing the cause of the farmer for all they were worth. But there was too much to do, and too many people were absorbed in their own interests. Long chaos had made the ordinary citizen predisposed to take care of himself first, to try and secure his own future. Even though a great many individuals honestly wanted this new government to thrive, and were not primarily self-seeking, they didn't have the ability, in the face of so many acute problems, to make their presence and opinions sufficiently felt.

For a long time people hoped, even believed, that now the foundations were being laid for an entirely new course in China—that the Kuomintang would endure, improve, and make the country a viable, flourishing state, not only for the few but for the many. In this struggling city, with the ruins of palaces below the soil, and chickens pecking away at anything they could find in the streets above, lived a great proportion of the important men of the hour—the Generalissimo himself, the heads of ministries, the leaders in education and finance. There were also a considerable number of not-insignificant Westerners—a great many of the names in Nanking's small telephone book already were, or would be, known throughout the world.

Chiang Kai-shek had only a modest house—he was never interested in display himself. His heart was in the survival of the country, in his dream for it, in the framework which seemed to him the most acceptable, and possible.

To an extent, what was going on in Nanking was that movement which used to be recommended in the nineteenth century by those Chinese who were eager for reform—Self-Strengthening. The early Self-Strengtheners had stressed education (particularly in the sciences, so long neglected), character, change. Something had already been done, more than a little, in these fields—in great part due to Western help—and now it was realized that character had to be developed, that the will to sacrifice, the rejection of corruption, must be built up.

The New Life Movement took up these goals. They painted huge characters on walls, recommending virtuous behavior, cleanliness, courtesy, like a sort of giant Boy Scout propaganda machine, which was easy to poke fun at, but probably did some good. There are always people who misuse such campaigns—in Canton a girl called Ann Tan was even sent to jail because she had cut off the sleeves of her dresses above the elbows, thus being immodest, said some officious busybody. But that wasn't at all typical. It would be very difficult to impose a New Life Movement on any society simply by persuasion—there is, I think, no precedent for it. The men at the top would have to have absolutely clean hands, in any event; there's your initial stumbling block.

In 1931, a year of disastrous floods, the Chinese under Nationalist leadership, rose to the occasion in a way that delighted (and astonished) us all. The Han, the Yellow, and the Yangtze rivers were all in flood, over 70,000 square miles being inundated. At Hankow the flood waters were over fifty feet above the dikes; even at Nanking, several hundred miles down river, they were twenty feet above normal. Over a quarter of a million people were drowned or physically injured, and twenty millions were affected in some way by the catastrophe. The financial loss was tremendous, and fell most heavily on the very poor. Starvation was imminent for millions of people.

Nanking acted at once, organizing relief on a vast scale, and undertaking flood-control measures. They built dikes, put the people to work, and paid in grain. Money and help arrived from all over the world, but it was the government which took charge. Their engineers employed over a million workers, following up the first part of the program with economic arrangements which were so timely that the next year there was a proper harvest. They inspired the people, who were enthusiastic, self-sacrificing, and tireless.

This was an example of what the Chinese are capable of, under certain conditions. Time and again throughout their history they have done this sort of thing—when they were fighting the Japanese they would repair roads, replace railway lines, carry huge burdens—whatever was asked of them. Sometimes this has occurred as a voluntary gesture, more often under tyrannies, tyrannies being a more common condition of life in their history. Lord Macartney, when he was proceeding by canal up to the environs of Peking in the eighteenth century, on his ill-fated mission, was immensely struck with the laborers he encountered. He saw them dredging the canals, digging, carrying earth, at the command of a harsh government, and for only the meanest remuneration (perhaps for none), and yet doing these tasks cheerfully, with a will, and with great skill. He even thought them the people of that Brave New World of which men have always dreamed.

The Nationalist government is often under fire for being, it is said, a police state, so that no one could speak out with impunity, but in point of fact, a great many people were speaking out, criticizing the regime fiercely, in that decade of the thirties. With all the new government had on its hands, and given the communist element already boring away so hard, and the Japanese collaborationists stoking the fires of their new ventures, coupled with the fact that democratic government (as the West understands it) was still untried in China, obviously there was going to be a great deal of surveillance in certain quarters. It could not knowingly allow itself to be pushed over right at the start, and from within.

Summer, 1936

IN THE SUMMER of 1936 there was another challenge to the Nationalist government, when the two rich southern provinces of Kwangtung and Kwangsi revolted, threatening to secede under the leadership of Li Tsung-jen and Pai Jung-hsi. They wanted to run their region for themselves as governors or warlords, they were tired of the overlordship of that distant area, the Yangtze valley. After some anxious weeks they were persuaded to stay within the fold, and the affair was patched up. There had been no fighting, and we all breathed more easily. The central government seemed firmer if it could come out of such an affair so well. A return to the old anarchy would have been a blow to everyone.

The communists were on the run, and the areas they had devastated on the Long March were being rebuilt. There were some successes within the New Life Movement, with education, roads, finance. The cooperatives were multiplying. In the midst of these encouraging signs, the Japanese issue continued to be extremely grave, however. Everyone, of every nation, was horrified by their incessant insolent smuggling. Flouting every regulation and tariff, ignoring the Customs, they poured their goods into the country. Who was going to stop them? There should have been some international action. The words "should have been" are among the most unbearable in the world. There were more and more "incidents," from the seizure of a few horses on a hillside (the *chi p'i* *ma shih**) to disturbances among marching soldiers, which created excuses for the Japanese to cordon off an area and then control it. What was to be expected, when they were overrunning the country with troops? What was to stop this?

There were other actions which were even more menacing. For at least a dozen years, particularly in North China, the Japanese had been conducting a deliberate campaign to subvert the Chinese by the use of drugs: opium and morphine, most of which they obtained from abroad. As the Kuomintang labored to put down the opium habit, and with some success, so did the Japanese reverse these attempts wherever they could. They understood very well what a social and political weapon drugs can be in the poisoning of the body politic, so they smuggled them in and distributed them as widely as possible, intending to corrupt the people to the point where they would be able to seize North China without having to fight for it. This activity was run by a special section of the Japanese army, with full official connivance, and the results were to justify their hopes.

Meanwhile Manchukuo was to all intents and purposes firmly held. We knew that only the railway belt and the big towns were actually under Japanese control, that the province was not really subdued, but it was beyond the powers of Nanking to free it. Aggression flourished there, and the League of Nations could only expostulate, mourn, harangue.

In fact, 1936 was a fairly bad year, a time of incessant trouble. Hitler moved into the Rhineland; no one did anything. There were Nazi demonstrations both in England and in France, aside from Germany. It was the year of the Ethiopian crisis, of Arab terror in Palestine. The complexities and miseries of Spain, where the Germans and the Russians used the unfortunate people as pawns in their own game, appalled the world. There were more difficulties in Czechoslovakia, where Hitler was pressing for the "rights" of the Sudeten Germans. The Soviet-French alliance squared off against the German Nazi-oriented sympathy with Japan. There were added anxieties as to the oil on the island of Saghalien and with the Japanese fisheries, making for increased tension between Russia and Japan. The presence of the Italian fleet in the Mediterranean, reflecting the wildly expansive ambitions of Mussolini, was something of a shock to those who still thought of

* The affair of a few horses.

it as a British preserve. Stalin continued his horrifying purges, on a scale which most of the world found unbelievable, and therefore did not believe.

On November 30, 1936, Sapajou drew an immortal cartoon in the *North China Daily News*, showing Mussolini galloping off with Ethiopia behind him, Japan riding beside them with Manchukuo pillion, while in the background, on his hands and knees, Hitler stealthily creeps up on a peasant maiden who is busy harvesting grain—the Ukraine herself. He called this "The New Rape of the Sabines."

The League of Nations continued to expostulate and reprimand, but did nothing. What could they do?

Sian

AT THE BEGINNING of December, 1936, the Sian incident stunned
the world. The news that the Generalissimo had been kidnapped in Sian, where he had gone to confer with the Young
Marshal, Chang Hsueh Liang, seemed too much to believe. The
old warlord days, we had come to accept, were past—people
wouldn't do this any more—not with so big a figure, in as respectable a country as modern China was becoming. It was too high-
handed even for the son of Chang Tso-lin, accustomed to the
lawless behavior of the Manchurian clique. But it was true. Chiang
was held up there, a captive. The remarkable thing was the reaction of the country. This misfortune made it glaringly apparent,
all at once, that the Chinese people as a whole did take Chiang Kai-
shek as their president, that he was truly the legitimate representative of many millions. Indignation and concern were everywhere
displayed: on the streets, in the buses, the restaurants, the firms.
The Chinese press was outraged. How was it to end? Being China
(even a rather modern China), it was arranged in a few days that
the Generalissimo should leave Sian, honorably, with his wife,
who had flown up to be with him, as had the Australian, Mr.
Donald. The explanations for this came out more slowly, and were
devious. People put it down to Oriental inscrutability. But really it
was not so inscrutable. It was just a novel way of patching up a
quarrel.

The menace of Japan was now so great that the whole of China was alarmed. The communists, who had completed their Long Marcl., were still hard-pressed by the Nationalists, up in their northwest corner—their position was vulnerable, and their numbers had been immensely reduced. Sincerely anti-Japanese as they were, they reasoned that if they could only unite with the Kuomintang in a common front against the island enemy, they would halt if not end the civil war, relieve their own position, and divert attention from their aims. This was in part a reflection of the position of world communism at that juncture, which had lately decided that it would be better if all the leftist movements were to join up, as much as possible, and together attack the right, the fascists.

From the beginning of the year a number of quasi-communist groups had been formed in China, many of whose members did not even realize that their new affiliation was under communist inspiration: the People's Anti-Japanese League, the National Liberation Anti-Japanese Association, and others. But the Nanking government, primarily led by a military mentality, felt strongly that now, as the communists were isolated up there in the northwest and only a remnant, it would be possible to destroy the movement once and for all in a decisive military defeat, and really end the civil war.

Chiang Kai-shek had therefore ordered the Northwestern Army, which was under the Young Marshal, to take the offensive against the communists. The latter's propaganda, helped involuntarily by the Japanese, made this campaign on the part of the government troops half-hearted. The result was that, contrary to Chiang's hopes and expectations, no progress was made, and therefore he flew north to rouse the men's morale. While on this mission he was kidnapped and presented with a number of demands, the chief of which were to stop the civil war, release political prisoners, and allow all parties to be included in the Nanking government.

While Chiang was still held captive, some of his Nanking supporters advocated sending up planes to bomb the Sian rebels. Meanwhile the communists themselves were discovering that they had been somewhat misinformed as to the temper of the troops under Chang Hsueh Liang: they realized that they were not really bitterly anti-Japanese, but had become opposed to the Generalissimo. Their propaganda machine, working in the midst of this ignorant and muddled army, had not had the exact effect they had anticipated. A war with Chiang Kai-shek—that is, a prolongation of the long struggle in which they had been engaged with him—would at that time have been very dangerous to the Yenan people. They needed time to recoup their losses, to recover; it was much more to their advantage to set Chiang free, and to start fighting the Japanese, ostensibly with him. Dissension on the present scale in China was, of course, only helpful to the Japanese.

Chou En-lai, the mediator, came out from Yenan to suggest a compromise. Instead of wanting the country to be "anti-Chiang against Japan," the communists decided that they would instead unite with the Generalissimo against Japan, as they had first envisaged. It took about three weeks for all these issues to be resolved—to the extent to which they were resolved. Then Chang Hsueh Liang surrendered; he is said to have been under house arrest since that day. The government still cordoned off the Red areas, but it was publicly agreed that both parties, Kuomintang and communist, would join in the fight against Japan, under Sun Yat-sen's Three Principles.

This drama should have made it clear to the world that war with Japan was now absolutely inevitable, given the stubborn determination of the Japanese army to seize the country. But it did not. None of these decisions was announced in a way which was as clear as hindsight would suggest; the two old internal groups continued to spar. It was one of those coups d'état which are, at the time, peculiarly baffling.

The Three Principles (National Independence, Political Democracy, and Social Well-being—the Peoples' Livelihood) were always being evoked, anyway. People did not take them very seriously, as a rule—that is, the first was evident and accepted; the second—well, that might come; and the last somehow escaped the scrutiny it should have had from most of us. Resurgent nations are always clinging to newly formulated principles—of course, they must—but the world waits to see how much of this is lip-service. Social well-being, according to Dr. Sun, was supposed to involve the sharing of land and the restraint and control of capitalism, two factors which were certainly sorely needed in the country. The ten years of Kuomintang rule had not yet resulted in any sharing of the land; capitalism was under a certain control, but as to restraint . . .

These socialistic ideas were to an extent an offshoot of the attempts of the T'ai-p'ings to even things up in China. Marx, during that long rebellion, had found their ideas of change and revolution, and their subsequent actions, extremely interesting, as a true type of peasant revolution, and today the Chinese communists honor the T'ai-p'ings as forerunners. That extraordinary and desperate rebellion, partly really inspired by noble, though little understood, Christian ideals, but more motivated by past sufferings and deprivations, left a lasting mark on the country. Their excesses, their leader's woeful self-exaltation, led them to an inevitable collapse; yet something remained, some inkling of what people sensed a just government might effect, and these hopes were interwoven with the Three Principles—which are still held in honor.

T'ai Ku Shan

IN THE WINTER of 1937 I moved to T'ai Ku Shan, on the wall, above the river at the other end of the town. Many of the embassies were here, as well as some of the old-established firms, which had long ago leased land close to, or even on, the wall, and built houses there for their employees. The Customs people lived in this area, here was the International Club—there were a number of large, pleasant gardens, and it was altogether an agreeable place to live. I had been invited to share a small bungalow belonging to the shipping firm of Butterfield and Swire, which, unused by the firm, had been rented to the American Ambassador's secretary. This little house was actually right on the wall, reached by one hundred and two stone steps, which led up from the ground below, on the city side. I maintained my firm ties with the Ku Lou Tung district, not only because of my job at the T'ao Yüan, but through having lunch every day with my friends the Thompsons. The city was enlarged for me through this move.

Josephine, with whom I shared the bungalow, was an ardent rider, a winner of races, and through her I began to find ways of returning to my sadly neglected riding. I had brought a pony up to Nanking with me, a white, rather nondescript creature with an ambling gait, whose name was Spring Wind—an inappropriate choice. He was stabled in the Italian Riding School, the best place

I could find, but I was too busy to ride him most of the time, and used to lend him to anyone who would exercise him. The school was rather far away from Mo Ts'ou Lou—the Italians were there to teach Chinese cavalrymen to ride, and naturally didn't want to be located in a busy part of the city.

The existence of such a school seemed a little bizarre to me, and, in fact, I never met anyone who taught there, or was a pupil, but still it did exist, and it took care of Spring Wind well enough. At the end, when the Japanese came, I had to abandon him, along with my saddle and all my gear; there was no time to arrange anything. I only hoped he helped someone to escape.

People used to ride outside the wall, among the hills. There was in among the lower slopes an unexpected stand of pines, a place where the wind soughed, needles lay thick on the ground, and the scent of pine was strong. In the spring wild anemones grew here, a flower I had never before seen in China—a furry flower with a pale green stalk, and petals which were dark purple, crimson, or blue. It was an unexpected place to come upon, and solitary; no one even seemed to come up here to collect fallen branches. The ponies loved it, and would canter through the aisles the pines formed, with evident elation.

The Wai Chao Pu, the Foreign Office of the Kuomintang, was then very eager to promote easy and informal relations between their people and the foreigners—in the thirties this was something you still could not take for granted. As a matter of policy, they decided to cultivate this partly through encouraging sport, and to this end laid out a golf course on the slopes of Purple Mountain, and also announced a hunt. Few of them could play golf or ride, but they recognized that these two activities were socially smart, and ought to further the growth of friendships between the two communities.

The Purple Mountain golf course was beautiful. The Foreign Office built a small club house, and installed an instructor. I used the course free—I don't know whether anyone paid. But not a great many people played there in the short time it was in existence; and there wasn't much mingling, except among old friends. Very few Chinese came, though the Minister of War, General Ho, used to go round the course, with his armed bodyguard serving as caddies, Mausers drawn. We watched him with amusement and a sense of drama, but not of companionship.

There were, I think, only two hunts. That was really too ambitious a project, given the circumstances—you cannot just announce a paper-chase out of the clear air, leave it to a few wild, competitive spirits to set the course, and expect a true chase. That can only evolve gradually, from riders who know the country and each other. Still, the attempt was a gallant one, and very hilarious. It was after Christmas early in 1937 that the first was held, as I remember, when it was bitterly cold, the hills bare and the ground hard as iron. I went out with a few friends to the meet, where the ponies had been sent on ahead.

As we neared our destination, we saw by the roadside, quite alone, a figure in admirably cut breeches, patiently waiting, to whom we offered a lift. He accepted it with relief, introducing himself as Commander Hughes, whose gunboat, the USS *Panay*, lay at anchor in the river. He had heard of the hunt and started out for it, but his arrangements had broken down somehow. He had started walking, determined to have his ride, when we came along.

In the field where the *mafoos* and ponies were assembled, there was a brown pony with a ticket tied to his bridle, on which was written, "Mr. X——'s friend." Commander Hughes was delighted to see it—he being the friend. Riding in his company much of the day, we were all kept chuckling by his quick humor and turn of phrase. An accomplished rider, accustomed to hunting in Virginia, he still found that day's sport, wild and rough as it was over unknown terrain, very demanding, very interesting.

No one seemed really to be running the hunt; we never met, or recognized, let alone knew, who was the Master; the checks were not properly observed, and nearly everyone got lost. Crowds of interested peasants, well wrapped up in padded cotton, waited at probable jumps, hoping for grief. We suspected that the person who had laid out the course (to the extent that this had been done) was a German lady, married to a man in the Asiatic Petroleum Company. She was always in the lead, a bold, in fact a reckless rider, whooping, wildly exhilarated, galloping hither and yon. It was a strange and inconclusive day; finally we gathered ourselves together and drove home.

As far as one could see, no one met anyone else, except as we had, as companions in confusion. It was international, but there were very few Chinese among the riders; it was hardly a success, imaginative though it was to have tried it. It was just a *"journée folle."*

One of the riders was a young man in the Asiatic Petroleum Company, called Cliff, whom I remember chiefly through a chance remark, a trivial gesture. I used to meet him sometimes on horseback, and sometimes at the International Club. One day when we were both lunching there, I saw him produce a large bottle of tonic and solemnly pour it over his vegetables and meat. "Food in China," he explained to me, "is not as nourishing as food in England, and as I'm very thin my doctor has told me to pour this stuff on everything I eat." I was not exactly surprised by this statement, even though it came from a young man who appeared to be bursting with health, because most of the Westerners were nervous about their health in China, but it was sufficiently preposterous to linger in my mind. How well we ate in China! The fish, fresh from the sea or the lake, the chickens, the ducks, the desserts enveloped in spun sugar, the *zakouska*, the wonderful Chinese meals!

During the war, struggling along on rations, one could hardly believe that we had ever had such an abundance of good things. And prewar England, though there was plenty of meat and good vegetables, was still murdering these, boiling its cabbages for two hours, turning its soups into library paste with large chunks of flour. The postwar skill in cookery, which came with the disappearance of cooks and the scarcity of materials, had not yet dawned.

I daresay Cliff also thought back in astonishment a few short years later to his dark bottle, when, a prisoner of the Japanese, he was working on the Burma railroad. He survived, showing he had great stamina, thin or not. What did he make of his salad days in Nanking, when he had doctored his handsome meals with a patent medicine, as he received his meager handful of rice from his cruel gaolers?

On December 1, 1937, Sapajou had a particularly brilliant cartoon in the *North China Daily News*.

Four figures are presented, all playing chess. The one in the left background, three times the size of the others, is Stalin, playing all the others simultaneously and blindfold. He leans his elbow on a table on which are piled two large volumes, one of Lenin, one of Marx.

The three other corners are occupied by the slender figures of the Nazi, who had started with the "Mediterranean Opening"; of the Black-Shirted Italian, with his tasseled cap, who is working on the "Spanish Debut"; and of a Japanese with the "Far-Eastern End-Game." Stalin is deep in thought, his legs wound round each other, one huge hand thrust into his pocket—his antagonists are naïvely delighted, gay, cheerful.

Nanking Germans

THERE WERE in Nanking then about a hundred German advisors to the Chinese army. They far outnumbered the German Embassy staff (which in those days, like all the other diplomatic establishments, was small) but we rarely saw them, as they kept very much to themselves. They were very busy training Chiang Kai-shek's officers and men, and certainly observing acutely what was going on around them. Only two made their presence felt in the international community: General von Falkenhausen, who was the Head of Mission, and Oskar von Bodin. The former and his wife were cultivated, sympathetic, and musical—everyone liked them. I was terribly sorry to learn, a few years later, that he had become the military governor of occupied Belgium.

Oskar von Bodin was a tall, thin cavalryman, a person of great charm, always jocular, and the life and soul of every party he attended. You were always glad to see Oskar. He married an Australian lady while he was in Nanking; unfortunately for them, his profession made their lives very difficult, as the Japanese War broke out soon afterward and they had to be separated most of the time. I was told that they tried at first to keep on the same side of the Japanese lines; but it became impossible, and she went to Germany to await him. In order to get her letters past the censors she had to interlard them with frequent "Heil Hitler's," and her friends realized that she was again in an almost untenable position.

Then World War II broke out, and in it Oskar was killed on the Russian front. Curiously enough, years later, after the war, when we were living in the British Zone of Germany, my husband was allotted a chauffeur who had also been a driver for von Bodin and had greatly admired him.

There was a First Secretary at the German Embassy at that time in Nanking, whom we came to know as a man of courage and principle. Herr R. was married to a very sweet girl, beautiful, quiet, and charming—an unusual type, as was her husband. You felt their presence among the other Germans.

When the Japanese War broke out, Herr R. did not conceal his outrage at the Japanese assault on the Chinese, which they persisted for some time in calling "The China Incident." He used to retaliate by calling World War I "The Great Incident." He also took great exception to his own country's treatment of the Jews, and of its policies generally. German Jews were then pouring into China, but the embassy and consulates ignored them, as they were obliged to do, if they were to keep open. Herr R. had, it seemed, some Jewish blood far back in his ancestry, and made no attempt to disguise the fact. So of course he lost his job. I used to wonder what happened to them, and worry. But when this happened so many of us were in flight, and had broken with the Germans we had known, that we lost track of many we would have liked not to have lost.

Summer, 1937

IN SPITE OF all the fearful storms raging in and outside of China my last summer there was a halcyon period (till August, when I had to run for it). In the big garden on the wall high trees were in flower, the gardenias bloomed, casting abroad their wide nimbus of sweet and heavy scent, and pheasants perched on the acacias, next the dusty pink tasseled flowers, calling, calling. The creamy, exotic blossoms, the long-tailed, brilliant birds, seemed a setting for a magical stage. The early summer mist rose up from the river, resting softly on the wall, and I would be off, running lightly down the hundred and two stairs, as light-hearted and eager as though the world were not collapsing round us, as though I had not danced till two that morning.

So many people had gone away "for the heat" that the rest of us drew together, talked more, entertained each other more. The embassy staffs went away to the north, the missionaries went to the hills or to the sea, leaving only a few stalwarts behind. After the great heat of the day—and Nanking was ferociously hot in summer—the nights seemed cool or, at any rate, cooler, and they were star-studded and beautiful.

The city, too, offered in the great heat of summer glimpses of itself which seemed not only beautiful, but as though they contained much more than outwardly was revealed, in a strange way —for instance the grey donkeys that I encountered in the narrow lanes, their panniers full to the brim with scarlet peppers . . . it was almost a setting for Ali Baba.

We were joined that summer by an unusual number of naval officers from the warships which came and went on the Yangtze, and seemed often to be at Nanking: particularly HMS *Danae*, a light cruiser, and the gunboats, the USS *Panay* and HMS *Ladybird*. The USS *Augusta* sometimes came to Nanking, also, but I don't remember her being there in that hot weather, whereas the *Danae* came frequently enough to play a role in our lives—we came to know the cheerful and lively company aboard. They were thirsty for the pleasures of the land, yet were as good hosts as guests. We dined on the ship; they made themselves at home in the International Club, where we all foregathered. Here we would dance on the roof, which was just at the height of the topmost branches of the trees, through which we saw the large low stars of summer. Scorpio, that long, easy constellation, would stretch itself far across the skies before it was time to go home, before the cicadas and the fiddlers stopped playing in unison. How fortunate we were that air conditioning hadn't touched us, else we would certainly have been sealed up in some lower room, the joys of a summer night cut off. As it was we could make the most of the balmy and fragrant air, full of delicious sounds—frogs croaking, disturbed birds making sleepy cries. Fans were arranged on the floor, creating some breeze—though hardly touching the heat. But a fan there was better than in an office, where if it cooled you it also removed all the papers from your desk.

It made a great difference to small foreign communities like this one in China suddenly to have newcomers—a whole ship's company—blow in full—eager, full of fun, looking at things in a new way, keen to understand the news of the country. The British navy was then still supreme, bringing its special aura with it. When not tarnished by snobbery this might mean a real feast of thought and interest.

The men on the river gunboats had another cast of thought. They had a limited round, mostly up and down the Yangtze or lesser streams; the vessels were low and small, their decks a matter of inches from the swift-flowing, eddying brown water; there were not many aboard, the days were long and monotonous. But a cruiser like the *Danae* was always full of life; she moved up and down the coast, and everyone aboard had plenty to do and plenty of company.

I have always had a great love of summer and for prolonged heat. I love the lush growth, the dark leaves, the flowering trees, the cicadas, the strong sun (provided I can keep out of it), and the deep shadows. The poor don't suffer so much in summer either, with their bare feet and meager clothing, and it's a relief to sense their respite.

Josephine, who had rented the T'ai Ku Shan bungalow, went north with the rest of her peers as soon as the heat began, and I had then to find someone to share the little house with me in her absence. There was a newcomer in Nanking, a girl who needed a home, not wanting to stay in the hotel. We took a chance on each other, and quickly found ourselves in sympathy.

It was as though, a strong wind blowing, but still far above the roof, I had stretched up my hand to catch, as the currents rushed by, a few precious, brightly colored hours. Friends who would last a lifetime were suddenly deposited by those winds, right there, under the gardenias, within the wall.

Jean, the newcomer, had found a job in the Ministry of Railways, where she helped to edit the English translation of a quarterly, which was, to her amusement (trained as she was to the swift, exacting pace of New York City), already long overdue. She was also charged with (theoretically) improving the English of a highly-placed official of the Ministry (in fact, of the Minister himself, Chiang Chia Ngau), whose Oxford accent made her very conscious that she herself hailed from Des Moines. Occasionally she was sent for, to give him a lesson: then he would present her with a long list of words which he had lately encountered in his reading, and did not want to take the time to look up. This constituted a lesson. Alas! Alas! "Today I knew four out of twenty," she would report to me. "Do you know what 'curiologic' means? Or 'nidulant'?"

Within the fine halls of the splendid new buildings of the Ministry, under its tilted green-tiled roofs, she found her office routine just as refreshingly different as she had hoped when she was working in New York City and saving to go to China, her cherished dream-journey. On Mondays there was always a ceremony in honor of Dr. Sun Yat-sen, which she, the only foreigner, attended respectfully, along with everyone else. Though she couldn't speak Chinese, it was clear enough. She was given two widely-separated offices, one for the morning, one for the afternoon. In the middle of each day, a cortège of coolies arrived in her morning office, picked up her typewriter, files, chair, stool, and even her handbag, and with them she was led away through distant courts to another site. She never understood why, she wasn't there long enough. To her it all seemed consonant with the Gorgeous East, which had so long held her in fee. Ah! Now here it lay, spread out before her!

We used to go out boating on the Lotus Lakes, outside the wall, the Hsüan Hu. We would take supper, and passing through the gate by the water, stand under the willows, negotiating with rival boatmen, as to which one of the square-bowed, carved, comfortable houseboats we should hire. The boatmen would pole us off, and we would start on a slow passage through lanes in the moat and lakes which had been kept free from the lotus.

We particularly liked to do this when the moon would play her part. To see the moon rising above the crenellations of a high Chinese wall is one of those marvelous experiences. Her rays shone down on the immense green leaves of the sacred flower, which were spread wide over the water, with the high, thick green stems rising among them, each supporting its generous pink lotus; the path of the moon, gliding over these intricacies, found itself in the channels of the moat. It became cool. It was perfectly quiet, except for an occasional voice, perhaps a song. No radios were unleashed in that peaceful air, there were no motorcycles to chug off regardless, wreaking havoc. We had many limitations, but at least we were without these trials.

These decorative, top-heavy wooden craft, so handsome with their good carving and gilded characters, made their way slowly on a circuit which was part of the plan of the lakes. A few other boats were plied here and there—not too many, not too few. We seldom stayed late: the gates would be shutting if we lingered long, we had far to go, and the next day we would all be hard at work. But a few hours there brought an immense refreshment. It was always hard to leave, to go back under the wall.

The country, though aspiring and hopeful, was still in the grip of its old malaise, one faction pulling against another. There were the nation-builders on the one hand, and the racketeers on the other, both Chinese and foreign, and of course the Japanese collaborators, and the communists, besides the profiteers pure and simple who were out to make money fast from anything at hand— opium or guns or oil—while, often enough, they discoursed in a lofty manner upon *Wang Tao*, the Princely Way.

If only the Japanese had stopped tormenting this country which was struggling so valiantly to revive, if only the foreign nations had exerted pressure on those islands! But instead, the big business elements of the world seemed determined to supply the Japanese with all the oil, all the scrap, all the munitions, they wanted.

Strangely, perhaps, most of the Western women seemed to be passionately pro-Chinese and anti-Japanese, raging at Jardines and Standard Oil, and the rest, while the men were relatively callous (that is, within the business communities). The merchants, cynical after many decades of disorder, after the debacle of 1927, didn't respect the Chinese—they said it was a case of a plague on both your houses, and they intended to do as their pockets dictated. The meretricious features of business are ubiquitous, and are just as likely to be expressed by a man with a cultivated voice and a taste for the arts as by a person who acts and looks the rogue he is.

Yet, beyond all this, the basic issue was then not at all clear to most people: would this country, now freeing itself from the trammels of the past, choose to work with the democracies of the West, or would it embrace the communist doctrines, and follow Russia? To most of us that question would then have been irrelevant, we felt so sure that most of the leaders were committed to the attainment of freedom for the individual, as a goal, if not a present possibility. How blind we were!

The thin drops went on falling inexorably through the water-clock. There wasn't going to be time . . . yet we hoped on. We all knew that we were living on a volcano which almost certainly would blow up; yet we continued to hope that somehow, somehow . . . it would not. Anyway, not *now*. But of course, that wasn't anything very surprising, that's the way most of the race has always staggered on. We have to hope.

Yet with all these incidents piling up, thick and fast, and on each occasion Tokyo expressing the same pious blend of indignation and sorrow, who did not wonder when the Japanese would make their ultimate, fatal strike, with deadly purpose? Which pear, from the hand of which Korean *ronin*, would be the last?

Part VI
MARCO POLO BRIDGE

The Blow Falls

So the year drew round to that July 7 when, as the Japanese were holding massive manoeuvres in North China, the Chinese forces near Lu Kou Chiao became embroiled. The balloon went up, and we all saw it then, floating high, high, in the empyrean.

When the news of Marco Polo Bridge came through on that hot July morning of 1937, we all knew that the Sino-Japanese War had begun at last. It was strange, this sense of inevitability. So many of the incidents, over the years, were so grave that they might well have provoked a major conflict—yet this clash at Lu Kou Chiao was recognized immediately as war itself—the years of provocation and docility were over.

In the next weeks it became clear that the north, where the fatal engagement had been joined, would not resist. The plains of Hopei and Chahar, the cities of Peking and Tientsin, held too many cynical, weary, corrupted (and often drug-sodden) Chinese.

For a month most of the Japanese forces stayed up in the north, or so it seemed. Up there too, remained the foreign embassies to China, still enjoying the cool airs and blue waters of Peitaiho. They observed that the different armies confronted each other in these regions, they saw no reason to bestir themselves. Then suddenly the news came that the Japanese were on their way down to the Yangtze—by the time we knew this they had almost arrived. Their warships began to steam into the Whangpoo at Shanghai.

Everything began to occur at great speed. The ambassadors rushed down to the capital like homing pigeons, with them, of course, their staffs. Sir Hughe Knatchbull-Hugesson arrived on the *Danae*, which had been sent up posthaste to fetch him.

In the general fracas this held a personal note for Jean and me. The American Ambassador came down very quickly by train; with his staff was his secretary. This meant that she would be back in the bungalow, and Jean had to pack up in a great hurry and go back to the Metropole Hotel. Our summer idyll was over. There was scarcely time to lament, too much was happening, too fast. But personal factors will intrude even in the midst of great up-heavals, and sometimes they hold within them something rather comic. Those pears, for instance—and in the case of the bunga-low, this element appeared in the form of a rat.

Josephine, a person of Spanish descent and temperament, much older than Jean and I, arrived in Nanking in an unhappy frame of mind. She loathed heat, she had had to leave her ponies behind (and racing was her passion), and she did not really care about the Chinese, the Japanese, or politics of any sort; she needed some outlet for her misery. Then she saw the rat in the pantry.

Jean and I, with three servants, even though the house was so tiny, had been light-hearted housekeepers. The wall certainly must have harbored rats for centuries, as had the city below. I hold no brief for rats, but with a great country in dissolution before our eyes, what was one rat more or less, here or there? However, Josephine knew very well that her young and irrespon-sible lodgers had wantonly enticed the creature in.

We were now approaching the middle of August. The clocks began to strike—loud, obvious clocks, no more poetic water-clocks. It was hourly clearer that the Japanese were concentrating vast forces in the center of the country, and that we ourselves were standing right in their path, that the campaign was going to be fought out exactly where we were. We were accustomed to being furious at the Japanese—now they appeared in a curiously livid light.

At breakfast on August 12, Josephine announced to me that she had arranged for a firm to come out that very morning to disin-fect the bungalow, and that we would have to be out of it for three whole days and nights . . . We were to stand on the hill and watch the city burn, I thought, while we were being de-ratted. I hurried into my room and began to pack, as fast as lightning, finding myself taking entirely unpremeditated steps, following a premonition I did not consciously sense. I had been too busy to plan for myself, the T'ao Yüan had been so demanding, with all these events in the air.

The day before Dr. Buck had told me that the Japanese intended to close the railway between Shanghai and Nanking. I was incredulous. Even though most of my life had been passed in an atmosphere of near-continuous local wars, warlord campaigns, and Japanese engagements, I still had no idea of what war, serious war, could mean, and was so ingenuous as to cry out: "But they can't do that! It doesn't belong to them!" He answered, "This is *war*. They don't care about civilians."

A few weeks earlier, while in Shanghai, I had unexpectedly bought myself a carved camphor chest, something I had long intended to do but always deferred. It had just arrived in Nanking, and stood, shining and fragrant, in my room, its wooden crate still on the verandah. I now found myself filling it with my treasures: my flute and music, books, pictures, favorite dresses. I got the servants to lift it back into its crate and hammer down the lid, but I did not even think of putting my mother's Shanghai address on it. I stood there for a few moments, looking down on the garden, lying still and lovely in the sweet early light. It was the last time, for I never went back. Perhaps the bungalow really was fumigated, I never knew—by the time the three days were up, everything had changed.

At the office everyone was occupied with packing or burning papers. It was arranged that I was to go down to Shanghai on the following day, and stay there, working on the book, *Land Utilization*, which was in the press. Someone had to look after the proofreading, and guide it through its last stages, which were being undertaken just as the whole fabric of the country was being undermined. A party was being made up: the British Consulate in Shanghai, almost overwhelmed with a rush of cables, had asked HMS *Danae* to lend them some men to help in the cipher room, and two Royal Marines were going down by train. I could go with them, and with the British Ambassador's Secretary, Walter Graham, who was going too. Two stranded American tourists were to join us—we would make six altogether.

On the evening of August 13 we went in the station, where the resourceful marines had already secured a corner of a third-class carriage on a train, which, whether it ever reached Shanghai or not, was at least going to leave Nanking. The marines, in every way the best-equipped, had neat white seamen's duffle bags; the rest of us had only what we could carry. The station was (relatively) almost deserted—probably most people thought the trains had already stopped; the atmosphere was one of silence, fear, and uncertainty. We, however, still enjoying the immunity which once belonged to noncombatants, had a cheerful send-off. My neighbor on the wall, who lived in the big T'ai Ku Shan house, was there—looking at me as I leaned out of the window, he said, "Soon lice will be walking up those white arms." We still thought this sort of remark funny. As the train pulled out, Walter, struck by a sudden thought, called back, "I say, Ivor, just tell my boy to dust my books, will you?" This request was well on a par with the pears and the rat. We hadn't grasped the situation at all yet, in spite of what we were doing.

It took us thirty hours to get down to Shanghai, and was much like thousands of such journeys which were about to take place, the world over, in that decade. There was no water, no food, no attendants, and no news. Drivers sometimes halted the locomotive amidst fields, got out, and went away, remarking to the troubled air that they would go no farther. Somehow we pressed on, in this train or another, each of which was more and more crowded. People thought Shanghai would be safe. But it was not, relatively, a bad journey, nor was it even the last train—they ran fitfully for a little longer.

The countryside had never seemed lovelier—the fields so green, the creeks mirror-still under the willows, the thatched cottages an etcher's dream, the waterwheels turning above the rice fields. Inside the carriages, by contrast, it was terribly hot and horribly dirty. We all sat patiently, watching the rout of the country people, the distracted families, the sad progress of the refugees, helping anyone we could.

Dusk fell late on the evening of the 14th, as we neared Shanghai. We did not know that already, on that day, more people had been killed in the city than had suffered the same fate in London during the whole of World War I, but we had been considerably shaken by the look of the people we saw coming away from it. Several open freight trains had passed on the other track, crowded with frantic-looking people, people of an unearthly green pallor, and with wide-staring eyes. We were astonished—were these the calm, controlled Chinese we knew? What had happened? In 1937, in spite of Spain, the answer "bombing" was not at all automatic, though it soon would be—and too, very soon the Chinese would be taking such disasters with an amazing sangfroid. But you have to adjust yourself to these situations a little first.

Finally the train stopped, not at a station, but next to some streets. The driver climbed out and went away, and as the noise of the wheels ceased, another sound, a muffled, booming, staccato medley of sound, took its place. Guns! Fire flashed above us, and we saw two planes dodging in and out of the low grey clouds. A dog fight. The battle of Shanghai had begun.

We did not recognize our surroundings or realize where we were. All the shops were shuttered, there was not a light, nor anyone about. Our fellow travelers melted away. Finally we found a telephone, the Consulate sent cars for us, and we were driven into the city. How I blessed my good fortune in having this escort—I could never have come down alone. By the next morning the marines, the Ambassador's secretary, and I were all at work at our respective jobs, going in and out of sandbagged buildings, minding the curfew, while the war went on in the sky, on the river, in the suburbs.

Invasion

THEN CAME the infamous first months of the Japanese War.

The north was silent, feeling itself powerless, persuading itself that endurance under tyranny was the lesser evil. Unable to entertain the thought of exposing Peking and its treasures to the Japanese bombers, they consoled themselves, as Sapajou showed in one of his cartoons, with the conviction that ultimately the Japanese could not win. "I'll die," said the Chinese girl to the tiger in the cartoon, "but eating me you'll die too!" She holds in her hand a bottle with the label "War Arsenic."

The Chinese teachers in the Language School, whose perfect Mandarin made clear which part of the country was their home, shrugged their shoulders when they spoke of this capitulation. They knew that in Peking, under the sunlight, things didn't look as they did south of the Yangtze. In Peking there was that domination of charm that made people soporific—even to think of the city seemed to put the situation in a different dimension, as though you could push this cruel world out of sight behind the rose-colored walls and the amber tiles, as though the sound of those Aeolian pipes above you, as the pigeons soared aloft, could drown out anything else. No one really blamed the Peking people. But other northern towns were not engilded—Tientsin soon was made intolerable by the presence of the enemy, and terror spread far and wide into the country districts.

For the Yangtze Valley there was no respite from bombing, artillery, troops, drugs, propaganda, and the misery of millions of displaced persons, war on a vast scale. Everyone, even the Westerners, could not but be embroiled. This Sino-Japanese conflict, which had so long been endemic and was now open war, was too great for anyone to ride out on the basis of privileged immunity.

The French, with their Concession, where they alone were sovereign, were able to keep the Japanese at bay; but the International Settlement was at a grave disadvantage. The Japanese had equal rights with the rest of us, so no nation could do more than reprove and exhort. Germany and Italy had no wish to do either, including the Japanese, as they did, with themselves in the Axis Powers.

Business played its usual ambivalent role—the Japanese never lacked oil, scrap, arms, or the other necessities of war. Neither the local firms nor the great international companies resisted the enormous profits offered them, with very, very few exceptions. Some individuals even personally helped the Japanese, like the Englishman who sold them his houseboat, but such cases were rare, and thought despicable.

Protests rained in upon the Japanese but, intoxicated by their first easy victories and their own hypnotic propaganda, they were naturally not to be deflected by argument. If it was pointed out to them that their planes, in defiance of agreements, were flying over the Settlement, they would blandly deny it. This would happen even if a plane were at that very moment passing above the building in which a press conference had been convened, and in which the question was being raised, where we had to shout because of the noise of the engines, and could see the Rising Sun on the wings of the interloper through the windows we sat beside. I went to some of these conferences myself. They were presided over by a representative of the Japanese army, one from the navy, another from the air force, and a consular official. The press soon realized that it was futile to expect any reasonable answers to their questions; the whole exercise was only a façade.

After the first disastrous bombs fell on the city and a state of emergency was declared, a good many Western women and children left Shanghai, evacuated with naval and consular help. The British went to Hong Kong, where they encountered so terrifying a typhoon that many of them wished themselves back in Shanghai; the Americans were sent off in a ship which happened to be bombed, right there in the Whangpoo. Not many were hurt, but it was a bad time—however, they went on to Manila in spite of it. But most of Shanghai's millions stayed, for the usual reasons of having a job to do, no place to go anyway, and no money to go with.

The population of the city, as was always true in times of trouble, rose enormously. Refugees poured into the city in greater numbers than ever before, country people who thought it must be safer in the Settlement and the Concession than where they were on the land, defenseless, as the Japanese overran the fields. In this they were probably right, but what was Shanghai to do with millions of destitutes in the midst of a war of this scale? What could be done, though, was done, little as it was compared to that all-engulfing need.

The papers used to carry notices like these:

NOTIFICATION

IT IS HEREBY NOTIFIED that I have been requested by the British Military Authorities to inform British subjects that as the result of the Japanese advance Westwards last night, the left flank of the Japanese Forces now rests on Jessfield Railway Bridge.

As the advance progresses, hostilities will probably follow the boundary of the defensive perimeter. In this event the area within the perimeter West of Edinburgh Road may be endangered by stray rifle bullets from the fighting area.

Inhabitants of the area West of Edinburgh Road are therefore advised to avoid exposing themselves unnecessarily in this Area.

It is impossible at present to forecast the degree of danger which may develop in this Area but the inhabitants are advised to make arrangements to evacuate the Area should it be necessary.

Herbert Phillips,
Consul-General

British Consulate-General,
Shanghai, October 27, 1937

NORTH CHINA DAILY NEWS

To Our Subscribers

The situation in the Western District may make it impossible for our messengers to deliver all the newspapers this morning.

Papers not delivered will be kept at this office for later delivery, or may be called for by subscribers.

THE PUBLISHER

October 28, 1937

Directly under this was another notice, probably welcome to many a young heart:

Cathedral School for Boys
(Henry Lester Endowment)
8 Columbia Road

NOTICE

No Classes will be held to-day
and until further notice.

Both the municipal authorities and philanthropic organizations worked hard, setting up camps for the refugees, trying to find enough food for them. The task was far beyond such efforts, but the attempt was valiant. Prices for food were rising, of course, as the farmers found it difficult, dangerous, even impossible, to bring any produce to the city. I worked with some charity—I can't remember which it was—which supplied soybean milk to children in the camps. I used to write articles to the press, asking for funds; we got enough to give a great many children a bowl or two a day. Sacks of beans were brought to the millers, who ground them between heavy stones; the children would come at certain hours, each with his bowl. They were glad to get it, though it wasn't at all delicious, or what they were used to. I tasted it, at a center near Rue Auguste Boppe, one day, and thought it awful.

Every nook and cranny of the Settlement was filled with refugees. People lived literally on doorsteps, with their poor bundles, their children, beside them. When I went to work I passed many such persons every day, and used to go down with something for them—a sweater, a comb, a piece of soap, some tea. But what they needed was everything that goes to make up a living and a home. The offices were opened to them: the employees would bring in their families who would sleep on the floor at night, and huddle in corners during the day. I had friends who lived downtown, on Kiukiang Road, and who would every evening go out with pots of boiled rice to distribute—but they could help so few that it almost broke their hearts. From where they were, in the Settlement or the Concession, parts of the city unfamiliar to them, these poor destitutes could watch planes flying over the suburbs where they had lived, and dropping bombs. They were aghast with misery and bewilderment. This was a phase that passed, so resilient and competent is the nature of the ordinary Chinese, but at that early stage they were still in a state of shock.

The effect of those four bombs which had fallen on the 14th of August, at the outset of the Battle of Shanghai, had been so devastating that it was as though the whole city had reeled from them. This was not to be wondered at. People who lived through them, and who observed what they did, and who were afterwards, in the course of World War II, in the Blitz of London and in active theaters of the fighting war, with the troops, have said that nothing ever seemed so bad to them as that day in Shanghai. It has even been compared with Hiroshima, in its sudden annihilating sweep. Only four bombs, dropped within a minute or so of each other, and killing at the corner of Nanking Road 729 persons, wounding 865, and then in the French Concession, at the New World Entertainment Park, moments afterward killing 1,011 and wounding 570—this was a very high toll.

Psychologically, no one was prepared for it, and there was no basis of comparison, in spite of the stories of the Spanish Civil War—of which most of the refugees had never even heard in any case. The Japanese had just started to fight in the city; the refugees were only beginning to come into the Settlement and the Concession, though in great numbers. It was a bright morning. The Nanking Road corner was crowded, as usual, especially on a Saturday noon—not only with refugees, but with cars, rickshaws, beggars, shoppers, foreigners. A good many people were up on the roofs of the buildings on the Bund, watching the Chinese planes from Lunghwa Airfield trying to hit the Japanese flagship, the *Idzumo*, anchored near the British Consulate. There were no shelters, no one thought of danger. It was the last time this happy-go-lucky attitude would ever manifest itself in the war—people didn't yet realize how terribly serious all this was—and the foreigners still felt outside danger. There were no warnings—it was just a summer's day in troubled times.

The Chinese planes, failing to hit the flagship, had been hit and slightly damaged by antiaircraft fire, which affected their marksmanship, so that it was the Chinese who inadvertently dropped these bombs on their own people and their friends. The first disaster, inside and beside the Palace Hotel and on the road, was horrifying enough—but it was compounded by no help coming for some time. The bombs had damaged all the telephone lines, and as the next disaster area was hit almost immediately, the relief squads rushed there, not knowing that Nanking Road was as badly hurt.

This event first terrified the citizens of Shanghai, then gave them an unbreakable resolve. It hardened them; they rose to an understanding of the qualities they would need, which enabled them to survive the Battle of Shanghai, determined never to surrender to their enemy.

I was very busy watching over the printing and publishing of *Land Utilization in China*, which was then occupying so many of the presses of the *North China Daily News*, and going very often to these offices, slipping in behind the strongly sandbagged entrance on the Bund. Once inside, everything went on as though we were living in normal times, British calm and Chinese stoicism combining in an atmosphere which was very reassuring in itself. Yet just on the other side of the road you could see, all down the river, one warship of the Japanese navy after another, symbolized for us by the *Idzumo*, which the Chinese tried time after time, in vain, to sink. To see these ships used to fill most of us with horror and indignation.

It was not very long before the battle for Shanghai was over—about two months. Though it ended in defeat for the Chinese and started the grand exodus to the West, yet did not seem a defeat to us; it had been such a magnificent effort that it inspired the Chinese. The end of the hostilities was almost as horrible as the beginning, as the Japanese fired the outskirts of the city, and for a whole week we watched Chapei and Hongkew burn, as well as parts of Nantao, flames and black clouds mounting to the zenith. The Concession and the Settlement remained relatively safe; the volunteers and some of the regiments guarded the boundaries, and there were always a few of our warships on the Whangpoo, exerting a restraining influence, at least keeping the Japanese from overrunning the whole area. That would come after Pearl Harbor.

Before the hostilities began there were a million and a half people in the Settlement and the Concession; when the battle was over there were four million packed into that small area. Everyone wanted to go back, if possible, to their homes and their work, and begin again. Slowly the damages began to be assessed—seventy percent of all Shanghai's industry had been destroyed; nine hundred factories, mills, workshops were wiped out; a thousand more were either seized by the Japanese or deliberately wrecked by them; and over half a million people were out of work.

Relief continued to pour into the city from abroad, but it could not meet these disasters—and, in any event, there was the problem of whether or not people wanted to try to rebuild, begin again, in situ, whether they could endure working under a Japanese military government, or even whether the Japanese would allow it.

In that first year of the war over a hundred thousand corpses were picked up on the streets of the city.

But everything was not so black, times like these in China as elsewhere giving place for their own sort of miracles, shafts of light striking through the darkness. One of the wonders of the Shanghai battle was the creation of the Jacquinot Zone, and, in fact, the very presence of Father Jacquinot himself. A Frenchman and a Jesuit, with long years of experience in China, this one-armed priest was probably the most beloved figure in the whole of Shanghai at that time. Resolute, but without rancor, he never gave an inch to the Japanese. How heartened we all were when, confronting some Japanese soldiers at the frontiers of the Concession and refusing to let them through he said to them, "There is a Nemesis which will overtake you," something no one else had yet told them to their faces. They were daunted by his character, the authority he expressed.

Constantly going to the rescue of trapped Chinese women and children, Father Jacquinot was determined to find a systematic way to protect at least a proportion of the helpless civilians caught in the hostilities, isolated in pockets of the burning and ruined town, afraid to stir from whatever temporary, precarious shelter they had found. If they ventured out they were only too often shot by the Japanese, if they stayed they died of starvation or gunfire.

The Japanese military commanders, adamant, implacable, and cruel as they were, found that they could not withstand the intense spiritual force and the nobility of character which emanated from this determined man. He made them agree, much against their will, to allow him to establish a safety zone for Chinese civilians in Nantao, something less than a square mile, stretching out from the edge of the French Concession, and with clearly defined boundaries, marked by barbed wire. For a year this zone, the Jacquinot Zone, housed some quarter of a million people. As soon as it was opened, word of it flashed like wildfire about the city, and people poured in, sheltering themselves in the empty battered houses which remained there. Father Jacquinot was himself responsible that the area would remain absolutely nonmilitary, and was consequently always at hand. Even a suggestion that a sniper might be on a roof in his Zone sent him and his scouts out at once to investigate; because of him there were no incidents.

He saw to it that there was sufficient water, and with the funds which were sent him from all quarters, he managed to feed 70,000 destitutes a pound of rice a day. The rest of his camp managed in its own way, having some money. Vendors came in from the country to sell provisions, as soon as the nature of the Zone was understood. Knowing that Father Jacquinot supervised every branch of this activity, everyone contributed who could—we knew that every dollar sent would actually be used for the poor within the Zone. The Chinese guilds and religious organizations (Buddhist, Christian, Confucian, Moslem, even Shintoist) sent funds, as did thousands of individuals, and groups like the Rotary Club. If Father Jacquinot answered for it that was enough. Yet he was no authoritarian; he possessed something of the secret of meekness.

There was another, equally obvious side to Shanghai. There was a great deal of corruption: plenty of funds and donations of food and clothing, hospital stores, sent to certain "charities" in good faith, found their way onto the black market, and the money collected dissipated like a mist, unaccounted for. Also, as far as people were concerned, there could be no compulsion except in military matters, or orders relating to the common safety, like the curfew, carrying of arms, moving about the city. Some people, Chinese and foreign, went on living luxuriously, dressing well, dining extravagantly, closing their eyes to what went on around them.

The business community was under severe stress, and, as the Japanese took over, persuaded themselves that the only rule they could follow was that of "keeping trade going," which meant collaborating with the Japanese, to some extent, appearing to be able to accept them. Some of the businessmen made fortunes out of the ruin of the country, though reluctant to admit it; others were themselves ruined. The stability they had begun to hope lay within their grasp had vanished, and they felt their backs to the wall.

A good many of the Nanking foreigners had come down to Shanghai in one way or another, and were in the city during the battle—that was already vastly preferable to being in Nanking. But a number of the professors and missionaries who lived East of the Drum Tower and other persons, also, stayed on in the capital to the bitter end, doing everything they could to help the Chinese civilians caught there. Dr. Buck's house became a sort of head-quarters for many of these men, who had only succored those defenseless, horrified persons they could reach, but were at the same time astute observers of what the Japanese were doing. By the winter most of them had left—there was no more that they could do once the city was under Japanese occupation. The whole world knew, then, of the rape of Nanking.

My housemate of T'ai Ku Shan—a time which now seemed unimaginably far back in time—came to Shanghai, but only for a few weeks, before going back to the States. The *Danae* lay at anchor for many months in the Whangpoo, her officers and men often busy on shore duties; finally she too sailed homewards. The journalists who had covered Nanking and Shanghai began to move to newer theaters of war.

Sometime that winter, when I was at my desk surrounded by proofs, the phone rang, and a voice at the other end said to me: "This is Butterfield and Swire. One of our ships has come down river, it has just managed to get through the minefields, and we find on it a large crate with your name on it. Where shall we deliver it?"

I had not thought of my camphor box, which I had packed so hastily that August morning, on my verandah on T'ai Ku Shan, for weeks—when it came to mind I mentally wrote it off, reproaching myself for thinking of such possessions when millions were perishing. Now I realized that quite unknown to me, without my ever giving it thought, my kind neighbor on the next hill of T'ai Ku Shan, the young man who headed Butterfield and Swire in Nanking, must have gone round looking at the bungalows and securing them as much as he could (Union Jacks were painted on their roofs), and seeing that box, had understood that it was my last feeble effort to pack. He had on his own initiative put it aboard one of the company vessels, and there it had been ever since, waiting till the river was safe enough to negotiate. I was overwhelmed. "What do I owe you?" I asked. "Nothing," said the voice, "there is no charge. We only want you to give us your address, so we can deliver it free, which we will be happy to do." So it is that I have my flute, my camphor box, my Chinese pictures, and my scrap books to this very day.

By the spring *Land Utilization* was finished, in three handsome volumes, and my work in Shanghai drew to a close. Before the books were bound, but when nearly everything was ready in galley proof, I had a call at my office from Father Bernard, a Jesuit working in North China. He asked me if I would give him as much of the books as was in proof, right then, as he was on the point of starting back to Tientsin, and could take them with him. The Americans and most of the other foreign nationals in that city, he told me, had been obliged to leave, and the Church was stepping into the vacuum they left, teaching in their stead in the universities.

I asked him how the Jesuits would manage to carry on, with the Japanese in such total control. "We are pro-Chinese," he answered, "but we are not anti-Japanese." A classical Jesuitical reply, but I gave him the proofs. It was to everyone's advantage to help the farmer, and neither then nor in the future did the Japanese do anything to hinder this book, which had been so long in coming out, and had aroused so much interest that even at this tragic hour it was heralded and welcomed by friend and foe alike.

As the battle went on and on, the people in the city began to feel very confined. We hadn't had much mobility outside the perimeter of the town, but what little there had been, we missed— we felt the pressure of the armies ringing us round. A few of the Europeans continued to ride along the outskirts of the Settlement, until a party was one day unexpectedly and senselessly machine-gunned by the Japanese, which put a stop to this activity. After that the ponies had to be exercised on the Race Course and in the riding schools, but, anyway, it wasn't a time for riding for pleasure when the country was in such straits. However, the young needed exercise. There was, for much of this time, a curfew, and during the day we wanted to be *active*.

The lunch period in the offices extended for two hours (we did, however, work on Saturday mornings), and it was then, during that sunny fall (for the weather was as lovely as usual) that my friend Isabel Poate and I used to play golf on the Race Course.

After a few holes we often went on down the Bubbling Well Road to have tiffin in the British Country Club. If there was time, before we caught buses back to work, we would go out into the Club gardens, and wander about. Isabel was in the British Consulate, and very busy. We were good friends, having an especial bond in music—we must have spent hundreds of hours playing together.

On November 11—Armistice Day—of that year, we went out into the gardens about noon and sat down, when to our great surprise we appeared to be hearing express trains passing high over our heads. They were shells, of course. It was an extraordinary experience for us, as neither of us had realized that if you are under a shell which is not going to touch you, its course extending in a wide arc far above, you can listen to it with perfect calm, even interest. The shells really did sound exactly like loud express trains, invisible, high above us.

Both of us, being Shanghai girls, were very used to wars of a minor sort. Once during the 1931 battle round Shanghai, while Isabel was playing duets with me in our house on Route Ghisi, Mrs. Poate telephoned from their home in Amherst Avenue, and asked my mother not to let Isabel start back till things were quieter, as "they are shelling this corner just now." When my mother passed on this message, Isabel remarked with considerable scorn, "She's just sitting there, flapping." That was a true young Shanghailander's response.

There was a good deal of dancing when the curfew was lifted in Shanghai, and Isabel and I generally went to the same parties together, and arranged foursomes with some of the young officers stationed in the town for the emergency. Like most wars, to a few of those concerned, there lay within it many happy hours for some of the people on the spot.

My sister Pocetta, meanwhile, was stuck up in North China. She had gone up during the summer, to Peitaiho, to share a bungalow on the beach with friends, and there was no way for her to get back once the battle was joined. This worked out very fortunately for her, personally, as it meant that she was able to spend many months in Peking, that being on "her side" of the line.

Dr. Buck's offices in Shanghai were large and bare—they were centrally located, and perfectly adequate for us to work in for a short time. The permanent staff there was very small: only young Gladys Wong and the equally young and cheerful office boy. Gladys had lived in Chicago; she had a voice over the telephone which brought that city to mind at once, and used to amuse us very much. She and I always got on, and during the Shanghai battle became good friends. She lived in the Settlement in the area near Jessfield Road, with her family.

On October 27 and 28 notices appeared in the press which confirmed what the Wong family had surmised; that their part of the city was coming under fire. They had in fact already decided to evacuate their flat for a few days, hoping that they would be able to return, and taking only absolute necessities and real valuables with them. (Fortunately, they were able to return.)

As Sapajou said, "The papers are getting really interesting now."

Gladys took a day off from the office to help with her family's evacuation. The next morning she greeted me with great dismay: "Oh Miss Saunders! I forgot my kewpie dolls!"

I reassured her as well as I could. But when I told Isabel about it that noon, all she said was, "How *could* she?"

Isabel and I either actually had small evacuation suitcases packed, or had decided just what we would put in—not the change of clothes and loaf of bread recommended, of course, but, in my case, my favorite Chinese pictures and essential books. Isabel had ready a pile of particularly beautifully embroidered handkerchiefs from Yates Road, and other equivalents of kewpie dolls.

As soon as the flames had died down, and the actual firing stopped, the businessmen wanted to get trade going again—and fast. To do this they had to reach some sort of modus vivendi with the Japanese, and the majority did so with few moral qualms. This entailed calling at the Japanese Consulate, discussing their affairs with Japanese officials, after which there were often parties arranged for them down in Hongkew in those restaurants which had been salvaged. It was a macabre setting for a grim sort of entertaining, which did, however, include geishas and saki, and the merchants were prepared to comply, provided they could start up again—they hoped that Shanghai was still going to be a great port, with access to a viable hinterland—otherwise most of them faced financial ruin.

One of these merchants, that winter, took me with him when he went to visit one of his factories, which lay across Soochow

Creek, on the borders of Chapei, a devastated area. His lumber yard, however, was not much damaged, and already in operation, with a number of White Russians working there—everyone wants timber after a fire. To reach it, we had to cross a bridge, guarded by a young Japanese sentry. He was very friendly, and wanted at once to take our pictures, bringing out a Kodak. I indignantly refused, and went out of range. My escort explained (falsely) that I was shy, and let himself be snapped as a souvenir indicative of Anglo-Japanese friendship. Then we went on and looked round the lumber yard. It took Pearl Harbor to show the business community how essentially degrading this sort of compromise was, and how futile.

In the spring of 1938, when Shanghai was still so largely a scene of devastation, ruin, and ashes, the German Jews began to come in in great numbers, till there were 100,000 of them in the city. They went down to Hongkew and started trying to find some way to live in this semi-European town, which had itself so few years left to run before it would be swallowed up in the coming global war. Shanghai was not, however badly hurt it had been, destroyed in the way the Japanese had ruined Nanking—it was potentially too useful to them, and they dared not (yet) touch the foreign population. They wanted to lean as much as they could on extraterritoriality as long as it lasted, as long as it made things easier for them. The Jews, then, in spite of the terrible conditions they encountered, still had some comfort to draw from the fact that there were many Westerners left, most of them (except for the Germans) sympathetic with them, and understanding something of their problems and needs. They were, in the main, resilient, trying to think out ways of survival, ways to start businesses, trying to learn something of the unknown country to which they had so unexpectedly come.

When my task in Shanghai was finished I was granted three months' leave, and went to London for it. At that time by far the quickest way to reach Europe was via Siberia—it took only sixteen days from Shanghai to London, which we thought almost incredibly fast. There was always an element of risk involved, in that the Soviets might at any time suddenly close their frontiers for indefinite periods, but for many years people did come and go, relatively without incident, on this long journey.

Via Siberia

THE FIRST STAGES of this trip were disheartening, in that they confirmed the strong grip the Japanese military had on China. I began by taking a Japanese coaster, the SS *Hoten Maru*, to Dairen, which had been under Japanese occupation for over thirty years. We left the docks on the morning of March 8, a cold grey day, the clouds heavy over the spectre of what had been the lively district of Hongkew, and as we went up the river I watched our progress with a sinking heart. The long lines of Japanese warships, the ruins ashore, the dark river, combined in a picture of utter desolation. Passing Woosung a few hours later, it seemed from the decks that this little town, too, was no more than a mass of charred black beams. The only living figure I saw was a spruce Japanese officer, mounted on a great black horse, which was stepping sideways, lifting its legs high, picking its way among the cinders.

The next day we entered Tsingtao, where a boom had been thrown across most of the mouth of the harbor. The funnels and masts of many sunken ships were sticking up out of the water, and from the land waved the flag we loathed to see, that of the Rising Sun. No one went ashore.

Dairen still retained a certain Russian tsarist imprint, with its large stone buildings, but at the same time there was no doubt that it was now a Japanese town. It seemed staggeringly Japanese to me: in the department store there were only Japanese salespeople and Japanese customers, and all they had to sell were (delightful) Japanese goods. Outside the city, at the little inn opposite the Hashigawa Golf Course, where I stayed, all the players seemed to be Japanese. It was lovely out there, amidst the low, dry, rolling hills, under a sparkling blue sky, in the marvelous air, but one might as well have been in Japan as far as the people went. They were civil enough—the "China Incident" was far away, but there was something in their bearing . . .

Driving into Dairen and round the coast, the Russian traces confronted you: there were those ruined Russian forts at Port Arthur, the mansions, the wide streets, the suggestions of imperial dreams. It all seemed part of a never-ending tale. Manchuria was so rich, so tempting! Everyone wanted it. Yet it had not satisfied the Manchus themselves, in the past—they had felt compelled to swoop down on China. So fresh from the theater of a ferocious drive for power I found all this discouraging.

However, the few foreigners I met in Dairen found their posting far from unpleasant. One day I had lunch at the British Consulate, where the Consul, a young man, seemed anything but depressed, deploring only the great number of callers he had, many of whom appeared at extraordinary hours, even very early in the morning. "My idea of hell," he said, "is to come down in the morning and meet twenty strangers at breakfast."

There was at that time a marvelous train, the *Asia*, which ran two or three times a week up to Mukden and Harbin, and which was spoken of as the best, the most modern, the most comfortable train in all the world. It was a show piece—an indication of what the Japanese could provide. As far as I could see, their estimation of the *Asia* was perfectly correct: I have never met its equal. It seemed to glide like a swan as it sped through that rich countryside, on, on, past the wide fields, and its lines had just that note of elegance, even chic, which only the Japanese can give their machinery.

I knew well, and I had been reading reports for many years on the subject to substantiate all I heard, that this train was in truth only part of a grand illusion—that only the railway zone and a few of the larger towns of Manchuria (Manchukuo, as the Japanese insisted on calling it) were really controlled by their captors —that bandits and guerrillas were everywhere, and when the *kaoliang* was high in the fall all travel was unsafe. (*Kaoliang* is very tall and thick, an ideal shelter for bandits, their hiding place for centuries.) But as we traveled on, it seemed hard to accept this. The silent, flat fields, which as the day advanced became covered with snow, looked so orderly, the Japanese everywhere appeared so self-assured.

The one incongruous note offered by the *Asia*, with its velvet curtains and deep-cushioned seats, its utter cleanliness, was the fact that all the passengers were at once divested of their shoes, and put into shabby straw slippers, many sizes too large. This added to our ease, but not our appearance. It was the custom in trains in Japan, so naturally it had to be done here, part of the Japanese Empire; it added a quixotic note, accentuating the luxuriance of the rest of our setting.

About noon we came into Mukden. On the platform waited the two persons with whom I was to make the rest of the journey. They too came from Shanghai, but had started north earlier than I; there was snow on their fur hats, and they were stamping their feet—it was much colder already.

Their proud, imperial bearing did them no good at all, when it came to their feet. In a minute they too were pushed into straw slippers, and looking extremely foolish as they padded down the aisle. You can be six feet tall and have on well-cut English suits, but the slippers will make a mockery of you nevertheless.

We all went down to the end of the carriage, which was like a glorious bay window, sat on the floor on the thick carpet, and played chess for the rest of the day. During these hours we were given many pages of complicated forms to fill out, telling the Japanese almost every detail of our lives, past, present, and future, with which we made such sport as we could. Late that night we came into Harbin, and put up at the Grand Hotel, a hostelry which had seen much better days.

The next day we embarked on a Chinese Eastern Railway train, a poor affair compared with the *Asia*, and went due west, in the company of thousands of crack Japanese troops, formidable fighting men who made themselves very unpleasant, as they passed the hours in drinking whisky and became very drunk indeed. No matter how much fighting was going on in the south, Japan did not dare leave this frontier unguarded, the classic, timeless situation in these parts.

Among the sheaves of forms which continued to be handed out that day there was one particularly provocative question: "From where arriving, where are you?" This was asked in the neighborhood of Tsitsihar, a name familiar to us owing to the perennial skirmishes along the Amur, but now seeming to indicate nothing but snow-covered wastes.

By morning we had reached the small frontier town of Manchouli on the Siberian border, where we were to change trains once more, boarding the Trans-Siberian at last. Here we were obliged to go through Customs, and the porters, charging us in rubles at an arbitrary rate, were so expensive that we carried our bags ourselves. The Russian train was drawn up, waiting for us—a small handful of passengers—its shabby coaches distinguished by their chimneys, promise of warm cars and boiling samovars.

Before we left Manchouli there was time to go and drink tea at the inn, a typical square wooden building of the town, not far from the station. It was more a home than an inn—there were lace curtains at the double windows, stiff velvet-covered sofas of the Victorian era, big oil paintings, and a rubber tree, an incongruous sight next to a snowy window. Water was already boiling in the samovar, and our glasses were filled for us by the lady of the house—a tall, slender, elegant Russian. We spoke together for a few moments, and when we rose to go she shook hands with each of us, saying, "I hope we shall soon meet again." Nothing could have more strongly illuminated the loneliness she must have felt in that remote town. She must have come to know, a little, many of the travelers who frequently crossed on the Trans-Siberian, but even so, there was a poignancy about this farewell . . .

A few days later, when we were already in Russia, Hitler marched into Austria. Soon afterward the frontiers were closed, and it was impossible to get a visa, and I had to return to China by the slow Suez route. I regretted not being able to call on the lady in Manchouli once more; I wonder how the coming war affected her.

I returned to China in June, having sailed from Genoa, then full of evidences of Mussolini's grandiloquent rule, but lovely nevertheless. When the ship called at Hong Kong, I found there a telegram from Dr. Buck, asking me to come straight up to Hankow, by the railway from Canton. By the time I opened this message, Hankow was patently hanging in the balance, and in four more days had fallen to the Japanese. Meanwhile I had reached Shanghai, and was repacking my bags. Dr. Buck and the rest of his office went on to Szechwan; he wired me to go back to Hong

Kong and work there, where he had some time before set up a skeleton office, so in a few days I was again at sea.

Hong Kong, that summer of 1938, was still psychologically remote from the mainland, still very much a provincial British colony, but even there some spent eddies of the turmoil across the water were beginning to be felt. The battle at T'ai Erh-ch'uang, which had taken place in April, though a victory for the Chinese, had had to be followed by the evacuation of Hsuchow, an important rail junction—the Japanese, stung by this reverse, had retaliated in strength with the "Tung Shan Operation." The Chinese currency was weakening, and people were beginning to become accustomed to the fact that the Japanese, temporarily at any rate, were extraordinarily successful. How could they ever be dislodged? What would ever end this war? Perhaps it would go on for thirty years, a hundred years . . .

I stayed in Hong Kong till the 10th of October (the Double Tenth, China's great day), living out at beautiful Repulse Bay, swimming in that wonderful phosphorescent water, seeing the fishermen put out at night, hanging their lights low and beating the waves to attract the fish. It was for me an idyllic season, the eye of the storm. By the time Dr. Buck sent for me I had become engaged to a young man who, as a boy, had discussed theology with the White Russians of the Min Yüan in Tientsin.

Yünnan

THIS TIME I was asked to go to Yünnan. Chungking, where Dr. Buck was working, was so crowded that it was almost impossible to stay there at all, but Kunming (the capital of Yünnan) was much easier in this respect. I was delighted—I had always wanted to see this great province "south of the clouds," as its name implies. As I had to take with me a horrible amount of office material —files and a large typewriter, besides other impedimenta—I was to go by ship and train.

Chungking lies under the clouds most of the time, low on the river, but Yünnan, six thousand feet in the air, dry and clear, sparkles with sunshine. It is the only part of China proper which escapes great heat in summer; its climate is equable though it lies so far south—just above the forests of what we used to call Tonkin, on the Burmese border. Remote, quite different from the rest of China, it was almost like another country; in a state which was so varied and diverse this province made up one of the most dissimilar components, and the Yünnanese were themselves well aware of this. They did not feel that it should be taken for granted that they were automatically a constituent part of the nation—at this hour they were loath to see the refugees from the coast pour in, and they did not want to honor the Nationalists' currency, censorship, or control. They would have liked to stand apart, though their own local government was far from satisfactory, run as it was by Lung Yün, a governor of the old warlord breed.

They were a mixed population, of Chinese, and also many tribal hill people who are akin to the Kachins and Shans of Burma, people like the Lolos and the Miaos. They spoke, however, a beautiful pure Mandarin, due to the lengthy presence of a Manchu garrison, which used to be stationed at Tali, a town reputedly reminiscent of Switzerland.

The whole region is a mass of mountains, very beautiful, and sheltering in its forests almost fabulous creatures, like the russet, silver-tipped flying fox, and the mild, lumbering pandas. It had been under strong French influence for decades—it was the French who had built the railway which ran from Hanoi up to Kunming, and on which I would travel.

I went down to Haiphong from Hong Kong on a small coaster, which held only half a dozen passengers, and from there overland to Hanoi, then a beautiful city, very French in appearance and manner, everything transposed into the Oriental mode. The avenues were wide and straight, shaded with wide flowering trees, and from the shops and the cafés, whose tables were set on the sidewalks, came the music of the Paris boulevards. It was hot and sultry, people moved slowly and gracefully, and the Annamite girls were beautiful and lissome.

All the way from Haiphong I had watched peasant women at work in the fields. They wore immensely wide basket hats, with a conical crown, the brim encircled with a deep blue fringe, giving them a great deal of protection from the sun. They seemed to me even while absorbed in their hard, back-breaking toil, more feminine than their counterparts in the north, the Chinese women who labored in the rice fields. If these humble persons were unhappy under the French rule, if they were even truly aware of it, it was not apparent to the observer. I saw no sullen looks in my brief passage. If people are burning with resentment it is generally evident, even to the passerby, in a few days.

Hanoi's main hotel was small, provincial, and amusing, full of people who were passing through from the China coast, heading inland. I met there an old friend of my family, Evans Carlson, and went with him for a cold drink at one of the sidewalk cafés.

We had known him ever since he first came to China as a young marine, and lost his heart to the country. Later he returned as an attaché to Peking, where he studied the language, and was driven almost to despair by the problems that faced the nation. By the time I saw him in Hanoi he was having grave political differences

with his corps which ultimately led to his resignation—his admiration of the communist headquarters in Yenan was doing him
no good at all in official circles. He was convinced that the whole
world would soon be at war, and that the West was not facing
up to the inevitable, not preparing for what lay ahead. Evans' life
had been both hard and sad, and his lined face showed it, but he
was very cheerful company, always ready to laugh, and immensely interested in what was happening round him. He was
coming out of China then, I can't remember where he was going
—only that I never saw him again.

The train for Yünnan ran about three times a week, as I remember. I left on a hot night; we could see nothing from the windows,
but could sense that we were passing through jungle. I lay in my
bunk and wondered about Indo-China—I had seen almost nothing
of it, yet it had produced a profound impression upon me, which I
could not define. It would be almost thirty years before I could
read Edward Schafer's *The Vermilion Bird*, and learn of Annam
as it was under the T'ang, exotic and haunting, a place both of
charm and sorrow. When after this long span of years I was sent a
copy to review, I recognized at once in it the very feeling I had
had in those few days so long ago and far away.

In the morning I left the train, and had a French breakfast at a
railway inn, before entering the white Michelin which went up
the mountains to Kunming. There were only a few passengers
making the ascent, and the journey was not long enough for us to
make each other's acquaintance; besides, the scenery was so overwhelming that I was completely absorbed in it. The narrow road-
bed hung above the Red River, the Rive Rouge, thick and turbulent, making its descent through a deep gorge. It really was red,
too. In the course of that day we passed through an enormous
number of tunnels, all cut by Greek stonecutters who had been
brought here specifically for this purpose by the French.

Rising from the plain the whole aspect of the world around us
changed rapidly—after the hot jungles, the tangled vegetation, the
banana trees, we came into a thinner, clearer air, while our vision
was limited to two scenes—the cliffsides which gave our light
white vehicle just enough room to pass, and the turgid river so far
below, cutting its way through the ravines. We stopped for
déjeuner à la fourchette at another railway inn, and, as the afternoon wore on, came to the tin headquarters, the town of
Mengtzu. Here two passengers, an American couple, got off. He

had a post at the mines, I learned afterward. His wife was wearing a smart straw hat with flowers, very charming, very American, very unlike Mengtzu. As she left the train she remarked to a neighbor, with whom she had had some conversation, that as long as their *Saturday Evening Post* arrived regularly she would be all right. Little did she imagine what Mengtzu was like.

This sad town was known in China, and at such places as the League of Nations, not only for its tin mines, but for the terrible conditions which existed in them. Great efforts were being made, in certain quarters, to have these reformed, but they had come to nothing. The owners were reluctant to allow any supervision of their property, naturally enough in the circumstances.

The mines at Mengtzu were very ancient, the veins very small. According to report, every year agents would tour the province, buying up young children to work there—boys of nine or so, who could crawl into the seams. This was bad enough, but worse still was the fact that their lungs soon became affected and they began to cough. I have heard people say that their coughing filled the valley as though it had been the waves of the sea. Everyone who learned of this (except for those in authority) was so horrified that there was a great deal of agitation to have this exploitation stopped. The mine owners were, however, both extremely prosperous and entirely ruthless; they cared nothing for the expostulations of Geneva or any place else. It was an early Industrial Revolution situation.

However, the publicity which had begun to bring the conditions at Mengtzu to the attention of the world was distasteful to the owners, and it was perhaps in order to appear to comply with the demand for reform that they had gone to the length of hiring an American mining engineer to come out—the man who happened to be on the train that very day. In the alarms and prior claims of the Japanese War, conditions at the mines had been somewhat pushed to the background, unfortunately—there was already a slackening of interest.

The train then proceeded the rest of the way up to Kunming, leaving the gorge of the Rive Rouge behind, and coming out on a wide plateau as the evening approached. Kunming possessed a small, unpretentious station—the remarkable thing was, I suppose, that it had one at all—that we could have come by train, on this magnificent journey.

The hotel where I had reserved a room was only a few yards

away—the Hôtel du Commerce, formerly managed by Russians, now in Chinese hands. Its chief disadvantage then lay in its situation, because if the Japanese came to raid they would probably drop a few bombs on the station, and hit the hotel at the same time. But the other hostelry patronized by foreigners, the Hôtel du Lac, was near the arsenal, so there did not seem much to choose between them.

Yünnan is a very large province, shaped a little like a starfish, and an anomaly in that, though of the south, yet, lying so high above the jungles of the plain, it seems much more in tune with a northern region. It is cut by great rivers and possesses large, beautiful lakes. Being so mountainous, so remote, it was for many centuries independent, or semiautonomous, with links rather to the south and west than to China; it was finally brought into the country by the Mongols in the time of Kublai Khan. Many of his officials were Moslems, and so many people of his faith settled here that it became a Moslem center. The Mings, driving out the Mongols, by 1382 found the time and means to conquer this territory, and ever since it has been a more or less reluctant province of the Middle Kingdom. Probably now it has come more into line with the others, under the present rigorous government.

A salient characteristic of Yünnan, and one which has greatly influenced its development, is the fact that it has been ideally suited to the growing of the opium poppy. It used to be known as an opium province, and in the twenties it was estimated that ninety percent of the men and sixty percent of the women smoked the drug regularly. So many people were sodden with dreams and sleep that there was something stupefied about the area. The poppy is still grown there today, in immense quantities, but as locally it may not be smoked, the nature of the Yünnanese dreams must have changed very much.

However, at first sight the city of Kunming seemed lively enough. It was extremely attractive—that it was soporific was not immediately apparent. It was walled, the black-tiled houses were low, the narrow streets cobbled, many surmounted with *pailous* which were as bright and inconsequential as any in Peking, though not quite as large, and the shop fronts were painted with scenes of birds and flowers, some of these very artistically done. Traffic was almost entirely that of the pony, the rickshaw, sedan chair, and cart. There were a great many cavalcades of mountain ponies galloping through the streets, each led by a riderless but astute animal, most of them carrying cargoes of salt. If you met them while you yourself were sitting in a rickshaw their place seemed tremendous, and they made a formidable din, with their bells ringing, their hoofs striking against the cobbles. Each bore two or three huge lumps of brown salt, looking for all the world like stones, and which must have been very heavy. The ponies were tricked out with tassels and red pompons, but their coats were rough and they were thin. A troop might consist of a dozen of them, charging along with this valuable commodity, enlivening every place they passed.

It was all very medieval. The houses as a rule depended for their water on wells—conditions were still as they had been in the old days. Modernity had only now really come in an insistent way to Kunming, and now it was so late, too late to change gradually and easily. That calm which came from remoteness was shattered forever.

The foreigners in the hotels were dreadfully frustrated, except for the few, who, like me, thought it wonderful to be in Yünnan. There were a fair number of businessmen from the coast, awaiting the lorries which should have arrived long ago from Changsha, or Kweilin, or Canton, with the office equipment and freight they needed in order to start up again. There were pilots who had been uprooted from Hangchow, where they had been teaching young Chinese recruits to fly, and other pilots in the employ of Air France, Eurasia, and other lines. There were young men from England, who had been sent out by a cable company. They all felt a prey to almost total uncertainty.

It wasn't very comfortable to go on living indefinitely in the old, hybrid Hôtel du Commerce, but was it worthwhile renting a house and settling down? It would have to be a Chinese house. I liked that idea, but was reluctant to be dependent on an antique city well, even if it were in my own courtyard—and, I thought, if I made the colossal effort to set up a home, probably then quarters would be found for me in Chungking or Chengtu. Meanwhile Dr. Buck kept sending me sheaves of notes to send on to Washington. He had just been to Lanchow, and then to Yenan, where he looked on the communist base with the cool and perceptive eye of an experienced agriculturalist, as well as a man who knew the country and its ways from the ground up.

There were young men from the British American Tobacco Company, many of whom had been here before, and who would come into the dining room laughing uproariously, calling out, "Hello, George, I saw one of your lorries go over the cliff in Kweichow last Friday. You can write it off." There were the oil men, and the consular people—but they had their niches, they were not wanderers like so many of us. We were all mad to get our mail, to have instructions, to find out what was happening. The post office was, however, one of our great bottlenecks.

The postmaster was English, but he had become so disheartened by events that he had fallen ill, and no one seemed really to be in charge of his stricken establishment. The post office was a little building, near the railway station, hence also conveniently near the Hôtel du Commerce. Its floors were piled higher than one's head with immense heaps of mail. Incoming? Outgoing? Stationary, we concluded. The office was not equipped to deal with the enormous post in so many languages which now flooded in every day by air, train, and pony (the old route, which took a month from Chungking). There was also the vexing question of censorship, Yünnan claiming its rights, Nanking insisting it had superior powers.

I used to wait on the little space in front of the building, lingering while recent deliveries were being sorted, in the hope that something might be for me, and looking at the small collections of curios which vendors spread out on the ground to tempt the newcomers. One day I bought here a bronze mirror, which its owner told me solemnly was two thousand years old. It cost $500 Yünnan currency, about two U.S. dollars, and it was no tourist article —Yünnan didn't have tourists. There was so much that was old, lost, and buried within and without the walls that one looked on pieces like this with respect and some hope.

Outside the city, on the plain, there were acres of ruins, with the traces of many temples of Indo-Chinese inspiration. The statues and steles which were to be seen, broken, vandalized, and eroded, still gave strong evidence of their heritage, that medley of the styles which made the old Buddhistic temples so extraordinarily interesting—Gandharan, Greek, Roman, Indian, Chinese.

People would tell you about the governor, Lung Yün, and his exploits—how he had once held his enemies at bay at just this point in the city, manning a machine gun himself, his wife beside him. True or not, he was clearly not going to be too easy to woo into the Kuomintang camp. The Yünnanese were like him in their wish to be independent, to guard their own individuality. The

Lolos marked their houses by nailing a pair of ram's horns, painted red, over the front door; the Miaos were also very distinct as a people. One thing that had united them, not very long ago, was their intense desire that the communists, on their Long March, should not go through the city of Kunming. They had no illusions as to what would happen to it, and in the end, they managed to persuade them to go round it, to everyone's relief.

The whole city was very conscious of style, charming in its dress, aware of the niceties of ceremonious behavior. It was something of a shock to find so elaborate a place, so far away, so untouched by most of the modern world, in so highly developed a condition. Even with the debilitating effect of opium lying heavily upon most of the people, they had still accomplished a great deal. They presented an appearance very like, I imagined, that of the old Treaty Ports, some decades ago.

You saw countrywomen here in old-fashioned long tunics, beautifully embroidered and stitched in traditional patterns, with a deep yoke, frog buttons, wide sleeves. You saw Annamite ladies, mounting their ponies, their black robes lined with brilliant silk— kingfisher blue or rose. They rode astride, and as they threw the right leg across the pony this flash of color made an unforgettable picture. They would trot off, attended by grooms, pictures of the past.

The opium issue [with its baffling consequences] was constantly borne in upon us. The shops did not open till three in the afternoon—ostensibly this was because of possible air raids, as it was believed that if the Japanese did not come before three they would not come at all on a given day, as they would not be able to get back out of the mountains if they came later. That was the official story. But we began to suspect that the real business of the day never did begin till three; by that time the smokers were able to drag themselves up and go about their affairs. The blunting of the mind of much of the populace was noticeable in a hundred ways. For instance, when I asked my boy to fill my hot-water bottle after dinner to warm the bed, I would come in at ten or eleven to find that he had left it on the night table where it had become stone cold. There was a lacuna in their thinking, sad to see in a people naturally so intelligent.

A few weeks after our particular trainload had come up from Indo-China, the American couple who had got off at Mengtzu arrived in Kunming in considerable despair. They told the people at the Consulate they could not put up with the conditions they found there, and that if nothing could be done they would have to return forthwith to America.

They had been woefully unprepared. Though they were met by Chinese officials, who were civil to them, though the job was well paid and promised to be both interesting and useful, they had not understood at all what it involved. People who knew anything about China would have known in advance that housing in Mengtzu would not mean what it did in the West, and would have realized that any contract drawn up in respect to the tin mines was bound to have tremendous political overtones. But of all this Mr. and Mrs. X were ignorant.

They had been escorted, by some Chinese mine officials, to a temple where a courtyard and a few rooms had been prepared for them in the Chinese manner, and servants engaged. Everything was sufficiently clean and acceptable, had they been accustomed to Eastern conditions—but to these newcomers, rooms without sanitation or running water, where there was no recognizable kitchen, no electric light, no telephone, were impossible. Mrs. X did not know how to avail herself of her willing *amah*'s help—she couldn't talk to her, she didn't seem capable of mime. The change in her way of life was too great for her, her nature did not allow her to adapt, to find ways to manage. She might perhaps have made an acceptable pioneer in the Far West of long ago, starting from scratch, but here, in an old, sophisticated civilization which had completely different standards of comfort, she was totally at a loss.

Mr. X was whisked away, and shown the region where it was proposed that a new mine might be located. This was agreeable to him—as he said, "I never expected, and have never seen, palm trees underground." He began surveying and prospecting. Soon enough he found his site, and told the Chinese where he recommended that the shaft be sunk. During this period he had had no opportunity given him to see the layout at Mengtzu, or to look at any of the mines already there. Every day when he finished his work he returned to the temple and his disconsolate wife.

They were then having their meals supplied by the temple kitchen. Mrs. X found their food most unsuitable, and wanted to cook herself, but felt unable to manage with a few scattered braziers. She felt unable to cope with buying their supplies from the market; she was afraid of the water; she found no milk, no butter. So she made no progress at all.

The Chinese who employed her husband were aware of her distress, and arranged to have her meet the ladies of the small French community. Someone invited her to tea, and she found herself in a home, with half a dozen French matrons sitting round a table. But they could not converse—neither had the other's tongue. The French had clearly worked out a way of life which was tolerable to them, she admitted, but she had no idea how they had managed it. She might have been on Mars.

The *amah* was kind to her, becoming almost a friend—if only they could have spoken! They went for walks together to pass the time. To the Chinese woman, Mrs. X must have appeared the most fortunate of mortals, with all this obvious wealth, a background of comfort, and a kind and solicitous husband. But she was a mystery. Why was she always in tears? No one got anywhere.

The mining company, having studied Mr. X's proposal, or so they said, told him that the next step (which the bewildered miner thought funny but assumed was only some strange Chinese formality) would be to call in the local geomancer, who would work out whether the *feng-shui*, the influences of wind and water, were favorable. This was done, and the geomancer reported that Mr. X had chosen an impossible site; it would have to be moved from here to there, made to face in another direction, etc., etc. Mr. X in his turn now became beside himself.

The couple concluded that the job was impossible, and as a last resort, and in a state of rage, alarm, and confusion, rushed up to Kunming. They thought that somehow, perhaps, the Consul might straighten things out for them. If not they would simply turn around and go straight back to the States. They had not, apparently, suspected that their presence there was simply a gesture, a false front, intended to reassure the tin mine critics that something was being done to improve the area. Nothing, obviously, could be done for them in Kunming, except in the way of advice. They were urged to be patient, to start learning Chinese and French, to adapt themselves, to try and see their way through the maze. They were told that lots of us had lived in temples, that we even enjoyed doing so. We boiled the water, we found Chinese food delicious, and cooking on charcoal braziers was a simple thing. No one likes advice; not many follow it. As for the location of the mine, that was a serious issue, but the Consul had no control over the tin companies. At least the situation was explained to them; that was about all they could expect from Kunming, where a lot of people were having a lot of difficulties. But they had expected more.

Soon afterward I left Kunming, and I never heard the end of this story. Nowadays it could hardly occur. The Peace Corps would find those temple quarters luxurious; people are, generally, in these matters, less demanding, less naïve. But it was real enough then to these poor innocents.

Cities of the South

SOUTHERN TOWNS have so different an outlook, a flavor, an ambiance, from the cities of the north. Peking, Tientsin, Jehol, Mukden, can't be considered in the same light at all as, say, Swatow, Macao, Canton, Hanoi, even British Hong Kong. The luxurious, the yielding south, the south of bright flowers and brilliant birds, with its mellow softness where winter need not be feared, had, even in spite of wars and harsh modernity, cast some spell over them all.

In Hong Kong there was little of this because it was so new, so much a colony, but even there the poinsettias and hibiscus grew wild on the hills, and kingfishers flashed over the streams of the New Territories. The beautiful harbor, the Peak, sparkling with lights, and the beaches, phosphorous illuminating their dark waters with a foam now diamond, now as green as emerald, partook of the magic. The ferries which run constantly across the blue-green waters between the island and the mainland give to the happy passengers a few minutes of pure pleasure, offering views of the junks and sampans, the Peak, the flights of stone steps which mount the hillside in lieu of streets. On the ferry the heat falls away, there is a light sea breeze, the air is soft and sweet.

The winter after I was married, when I was living in Hong Kong, I was constantly making this crossing, always with delight. The Rajputs were there at that time, one of the regiments stationed in Hong Kong—they too seemed very often to need to pass between Kowloon and Victoria, the main settlement of the island. They were splendidly handsome, their aquiline features set off by their intricate turbans, one gauzed end of which stood up like a plume, the other hanging down, framing their melancholy, romantic faces.

Canton was by then in the process of turning into a modern city, the old landmarks being torn down. There were only a few of the ancient, narrow lanes left; these were distinguished by their elaborate tilework, which was highly colored, wide, and extravagant, a great contrast to the pure, plain tiling of Peking. Shameen, then still the area of the foreign consulates, was a charming quarter. Separated by a creek from the city proper, it still looked like the old prints—when I saw it first, it seemed to me that I was revisiting it. The big houses with their deep verandahs stood in wide gardens, beautifully kept—there was an air of civility and calm about it, and of companionship. You felt that there would be always an opportunity there for good conversation.

In the past Shameen had had many difficulties, and was often a mark for Chinese hostility. Canton itself was long characterized by its strong, rebellious temperament, its revolutionary ardor. In the hills outside it are monuments to the martyrs of the Revolution. Your Cantonese is quick to anger, easily roused by agitators, and the underprivileged of the city—almost the entire population —were, in the twenties, strongly infiltrated by persons who had no difficulty in persuading them of the iniquities of any system which left them so poor. These passionate workers, especially the dockers, were willing to strike, month after month, tying up the port, in spite of what it cost them. Economically this region had for centuries been out of equilibrium—it was because of intolerable conditions that so many emigrants left Kwangtung as indentured laborers. Things were nearly as bad for them abroad for a long time, but they endured, and their ties with the families they left behind them were so strong that there was probably more personal knowledge of the West, among the poor here in this area, than in any other part of China.

There wasn't much of the luscious south about Canton—except latterly on Shameen—its history had been too savage, too full of intrigue and hatred, of disappointed hopes.

Swatow was only a small port, but it really did epitomize in many ways this southern charm, with its flowers, its slow tempo, its heavy air. The jagged mountains encircling the bay made a dramatic background for the little town, which, like Shameen, seemed when I saw it to be like one of the old prints of the coast.

Macao lies to the west of Hong Kong, across the water. If you wanted to see it before the war, you took a slow boat, running between the islands. You could leave in the afternoon and arrive the next morning, or you could leave early and spend the whole day on this beautiful journey. Never was water of so heavenly a blue, so much the soul of aquamarine, so pearly, never did islands seem so like the Fortunate Isles, the Isles of the Blest, as those which grace the archipelago. At last Macao would appear in the distance, a Mediterranean town, with red-tiled roofs, white walls, flowering trees, and, dominating it, set on a hill, the façade of the burnt-out cathedral of São Paulo, with its high, blackened cross.

São Paulo was built in the sixteenth century by Japanese Christians, refugees, fleeing from the persecutions of Hideyoshi, who was determined to stamp out the faith in Japan. What a refuge they must have found in this Portuguese outpost, where they were not only allowed to worship, but even to build this great monument, unique on the whole coast. In 1835 it was destroyed by a great fire—its roof fell in, and its rococo splendors were burned up. It was never rebuilt—perhaps it was recognized at the time that it was more startling, more impressive, in its ruined state than it was before. One would not have it altered. The blue sky is visible through the huge open windows, the wide, high flight of steps leading up to it remains, and the whole façade seems indicative of a moral and spiritual prestige in that decayed and profligate town. The cross stands out strongly.

It was the sight of this cross, visible far out to sea, which inspired Sir John Bowring, the governor of Hong Kong, to write the hymn which begins:

> In the cross of Christ I glory
> Towering o'er the wrecks of time.

All about Macao are low blue hills and glimpses of the sea; within it are many great trees and flowering bushes. Bougainvillea in all its soft yet brilliant tones waves from the gardens, over the arches. Though from the sea, as you neared the harbor, you felt you were coming into a southern European port, once you were ashore you realized that, in fact, it was because the white walls were so much more visible that you had thought theirs was the characteristic color—on the contrary, many of the buildings were of a variety of bright colors—as far as this went the local taste was gay, even garish. Against the bold rocks of the hills these shades were lively and interesting, in spite of the general air of being down-at-heel.

The name comes from A-ma-ngao, after the goddess of the harbor, A-ma, who must have noticed with surprise that her preserve became edged with Portuguese forts, a Praya Grande, and was made a Jesuit center.

Macao was by far the oldest of the foreign settlements along the coast, the Portuguese having arrived in these parts in the sixteenth century, during their great era of discovery and expansion. The Chinese were not pleased to see them, but somehow or other, wily and astute, conferring favors, enduring rebuffs, they hung on. In 1680 they appointed their first governor, in which year also a bishopric was created. Not till the nineteenth century was the place formally recognized as a Portuguese possession, by which time they held three islands. Here they built their villas with courtyards and openwork iron grills, like those they had at home; the governor and the bishop had their palaces. Flights of steps led up the narrow hills, the Praya Grande led round the waterfront, and there were many wells with elaborate copings. At one time Camoëns lived here, and the grotto, where he is supposed to have worked on the *Lusiads*, is one of the sights of the town.

The British found Macao a great convenience in their early efforts to get a foothold in China. When it became impossible for a man to stay in Canton, he could go to Macao, and live there in safety till conditions became easier. Wives were often left in the Portuguese settlement while their husbands went on up the Pearl River: for a long time the Chinese refused to allow any white women to live in Canton. The Protestant cemetery of Macao is a witness to the presence of many of these men, of whom the most remarkable was the great Robert Morrison. In those years of danger and constant difficulties, when he was translating the Chinese dictionary into English and the Bible into Chinese, he came sometimes to Macao, seeking refuge from his enemies. Here, too, lies the artist Chinnery, whose graceful paintings are now so popular.

But on the whole Macao itself earned little praise, in spite of its beautiful setting amidst those blue hills and pale waters, even though it was a haven for men of such eminence as Morrison, and of important political figures, among whom was Sun Yat-sen. It became a center for every sort of illicit trade, for gambling, vice, and dubious characters. The population was dispirited, run-down, and undistinguished. People in Hong Kong simply associated it with *fan tan* and questionable weekends, which was a great pity, as that meant that many never bothered to go and look at it, never made that lovely journey towards it, or saw the cross of São Paulo, standing out across the water.

Then there was Hanoi, an epitome of the southern city.

The Chinese took possession of Annam (the "Pacified South") during the Han, and held it for a thousand years—till the T'ang dynasty ran out. Later they, or rather the Mongols, captured it once more, but had only a short tenure. In all this time they neither liked the region nor were liked.

The Chinese officials who were posted south as administrators felt their appointments as a disgrace. They considered themselves exiled from civilization, from the capital and court, from the company of their friends. At that time travel was not thought to be a pleasure, and this hot, exotic area, with its too-bright flowers, too-brilliant birds, too-potent scents, its strange peoples, did not beguile their austere tastes. At last, however, even these Confucians began to lose their hearts to the sheer beauty of the place and its warm airs. They sensed, finally, the meaning of the image of the Vermilion Bird, the symbol of the region.

It was a place essential for trade between China and the islands of Borneo and Indonesia. The shipping, dependent on the trade winds and the monsoon, went also on to India and Ceylon, even to Arabia. The merchants dealt in ivory, sandalwood, pearls, fruits, spices, animals, slaves. Ambassadors, Buddhist monks and pilgrims, travelers, and traders came and went. It was a far cry from this highly colored, fanciful region, with its heat and mysteries, its handsome, negligent people, to the distant cities of central China.

By the time these exotic elements began to be savored, the T'ang fell, and it was too late for the mandarins to learn to enjoy this southern world. In any event, their innate conservatism militated against any flexibility on their part, and too, the south, with its insects, snakes, fevers, its storms and sultry heat, presented formidable problems to them in the way of everyday living. To

331

the Chinese of that time there was no very clear-cut line between Annam itself and Kwangtung-Kwangsi—all these they considered "Nam-Viet."

Long afterward the colonial pattern in the region followed lines familiar to the West: first the Dutch came, then the Portuguese—seamen, traders, adventurers. Then the missions began to arrive. It was not till the nineteenth century that the French started strongly to establish themselves—they had something less than a century of dominance.

Through all these centuries, from the Han conquests forward, the Vietnamese had a stronger or a weaker yearning for independence; their tragic history is one of dissension between the various parts of the country, and struggles against aggressors, of many failures and few successes.

Beginnings, Endings

EARLY IN 1939 I was back in Shanghai, getting ready to be married, buying embroidered linens at the Avenue Dubail Convent, and going down once more to Hongkew to order shoes from Mikawa, who had started up again, just as though nothing had happened. He had managed to save his lasts; he would have been helped to do that.

Shanghai seemed quite changed. It was as though muted; its old ebullience was gone. The Japanese had assumed control of the whole area except for the actual Settlement and the Concession, which, their confident and dominating manner made evident, they expected soon to take over in one way or another.

The German Jews were still flocking in. Dressed, even in summer's heat, in their heavy European woolens, they were trying to exist by peddling the treasures they had managed to bring with them, walking up and down the streets, ringing bells. As they had not been allowed to bring money out, they were laden with goods like fragile porcelain coffee cups, Bohemian glass, old silver, embroidery. But who wanted things like these in Shanghai? Only a few of us—I started my housekeeping with German porcelain. They wanted to start shops; a man we came to know was trying to import felt from Austria for hats, which seemed a good idea, but it was difficult to raise any capital. Munich had sobered everyone and the autumn of 1939 was casting long shadows ahead.

Scarcely a German resident in Shanghai would even allow their boy to answer the door if one of these poor persons stood outside. Either they were Hitlerites, or they were afraid of reprisals. There were a few heroic exceptions, who suffered the consequences—the Nazi net was flung wide over the world, ready to catch everyone it could.

Then World War II began, an event felt as deeply and cruelly on the China coast as anywhere else. How we admired the few Poles in our midst in those first heroic days of resistance!

Everything, once more, seemed changed. Even my own small plans had to be altered. My fiancé was English, and being of military age now could not leave Hong Kong to come up to Shanghai for our wedding. No military personnel were granted any leave from the Colony. Also, we did not want to wait till the winter, as we had expected. So in October, a month after war broke out, I found myself again sailing down the coast, this time with a high, three-tiered wedding cake among my possessions. There was still time—a very little time—to think of such fripperies. The ship being infested with ants, I became anxious lest the cake would not survive the journey and appealed to the captain. He responded at once, having the box slung from ropes in the chart room, and posting a sailor to watch it, night and day.

A few more lines, and this chronicle is finished. A year and a half later we were fortunate in being able to leave Hong Kong for India, so we missed the effect of Pearl Harbor on Hong Kong. By the time the war was over and the Japanese defeated, all this old life had gone with them. The threads could never be picked up again, it was the end of an era.

The Strange Tree

In the midst of the courtyard stands a strange tree
Whose verdant leaves rise from a rich sap.
I have pulled down a branch, and broken off its splendor
That I may send it to you, who engross my thought.
Its fragrance scents my robe, makes my sleeves sweet.
But the road is so long—how can it reach you?
How can I send it unharmed?
Yet—let it persuade you,
How grave is our separation.

A Han poem

Index